IMAGES
of America

African Americans of Giles County

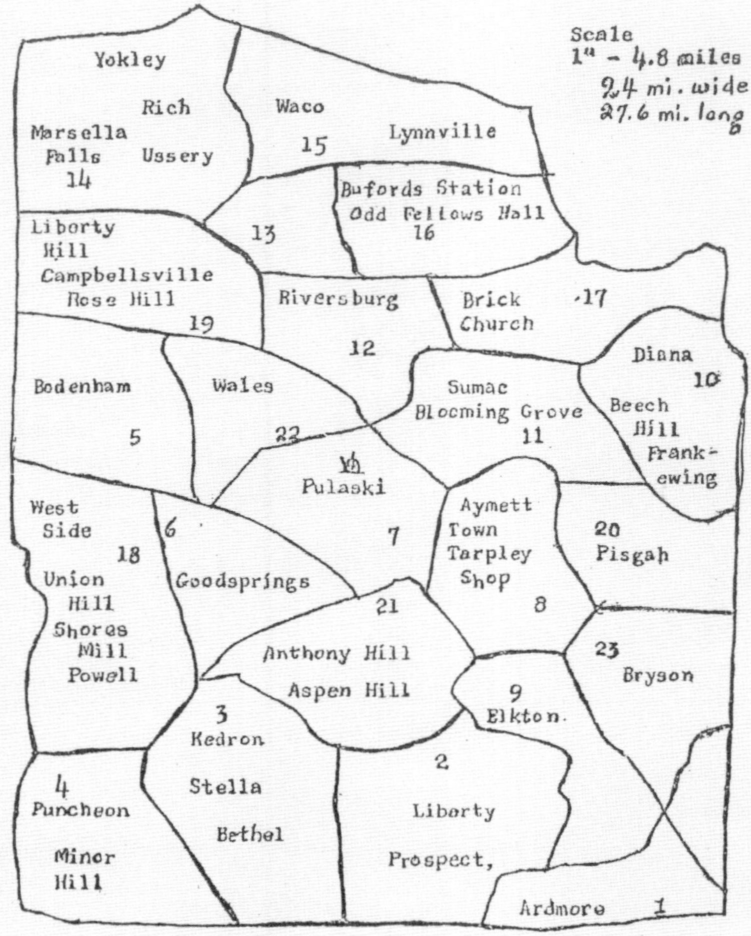

CIVIL DISTRICTS OF GILES COUNTY

Giles County is made up of 23 communities, as seen on this map. African Americans once freed from slavery took up residence in all of these communities. Some set up residences close to their ex-slave-owning families, and others moved to different locations within the county. Some areas within Giles had more blacks than others, and some locations had pockets of all-black communities, such as the African Holler of Riversburg and Dixontown in Elkton. The African American story is woven throughout Giles County's history. (Courtesy of the Giles County Old Records Department.)

On the Cover: Members of the Gardner family are seen posing for a picture on the farmstead. Pictured from left to right are Eva, Emma, and Mae Sue Stevenson; Ellen, Joe Thomas, and Mary Gardner; Georgia Stevenson; and Matt and Henrietta (Ritta) Gardner. Matt and Ritta are first- and second-generation uncle and aunt to the Stevensons and the parents and grandparents to the Gardners. Their daughter Mary Gardner married George Gardner, not related to this Gardner family. (Courtesy of Matt Gardner Homestead Museum.)

IMAGES
of America

AFRICAN AMERICANS OF GILES COUNTY

Carla J. Jones and Tonya M. Hull
Foreword by Carroll Van West

ARCADIA
PUBLISHING

ISBN 978-0-7385-6689-4

Published by Arcadia Publishing
Charleston SC, Chicago IL, Portsmouth NH, San Francisco CA

Printed in the United States of America

Library of Congress Control Number: 2009934980

For all general information contact Arcadia Publishing at:
Telephone 843-853-2070
Fax 843-853-0044
E-mail sales@arcadiapublishing.com
For customer service and orders:
Toll-Free 1-888-313-2665

Visit us on the Internet at www.arcadiapublishing.com

This book is dedicated to Matt Gardner and the many other African American ancestors of Giles County, Tennessee. It is dedicated to their descendants and all their generations to come. To all African Americans, for our endurance in the past, our thriving future, and for our history, heritage, and the unique culture that we as a people possess. Lastly, it is dedicated to the community of Giles County.

Contents

ACKNOWLEDGMENTS

We would like to acknowledge and thank all of the families who contributed pictures, the Giles County Bicentennial Committee, the *Pulaski Citizen*, and the *Giles Free Press*. We thank the members of the Giles County community and Giles County Old Records Department for information. We would also like to thank Carroll Van West of Middle Tennessee State University Center for Historic Preservation for his foreword. A special thank you to historian Antoinette Van Zelm of Middle Tennessee State University Center for Historic Preservation's Tennessee Civil War National Heritage Area and George Newman of the Giles County Historical Society; without their help and support, this book would not be possible. In addition, we would be remiss if we did not thank Thaddeus Holt (deceased June 6, 2006), who provided priceless historical information over the years. Lastly we thank the Matt Gardner Homestead Museum of Elkton Giles County for its many wonderful historical pictures; unless otherwise noted, all images are from the Matt Gardner Homestead Museum.

FOREWORD

Few places among Tennessee counties rival the significance of Giles County in African American history. As an antebellum stronghold of slavery, the county had many large plantations, where enslaved peoples learned to transform ancient traditions and customs into the new landscape of North America. These determined individuals created their own informal communities, established religious institutions, and carried out, typically in secret, the arduous job of educating their children.

The Civil War brought the opportunity of emancipation and freedom. African American men joined the U.S. Colored Troops and fought for their freedom. Many more used the Underground Railroad to grasp freedom in a war-torn land. They not only transformed their lives and those of their families but also contributed to the community's expansion and growth. In the Elkton area, Matt Gardner established a farm, ministry, store, and a school and became a rock for his neighbors for decades. In Pulaski, Gabriel Moses McKissack taught carpentry and construction skills to his son, Moses McKissack II, who helped to establish the state's first professional African American architectural firm.

This book touches upon those stories, and many others, by recording and exploring everyday life through photographs and documents. African Americans built their neighborhoods and their communities working as barbers, doctors, teachers, housewives, farmers, blacksmiths, domestics, merchants, ministers, and undertakers, to name just a few of the professions. These people take center stage in a story of African American citizens who faced many challenges and racial oppression, but who took these trials and built lasting families and a way of life to be celebrated today.

Introduction

Giles County, like so many others counties in the state of Tennessee, has limited resources for African American history, heritage, and genealogy research. It is well known that official documented records were not kept on most African Americans before the first slave census of 1850. Because most African Americans of the time either could not or were not allowed to read or write, their descendants have had to piece together their beginnings from European history or oral history that was told down through generations. Unfortunately, oral history sometimes can get distorted. If fortunate, enslaved ancestors may be found listed by first name on some property inventory—in a will or a bill of sale from one slave owner to another. If really lucky, personal documented information in that one-and-only family Bible may be found. Lastly, whether tragic, informative, or remarkable, Giles County's families' pasts may be recorded in some early county newspapers.

Because of all of the above, it is very hard to give an accurate account of the first African American settlers of Giles County. In the best estimate, after hours researching census records, it appears a majority of whites in Giles owned at least one or two slaves, and after freedom came for Tennessee slaves during and after the Civil War, most of them had formed friendships and ties that they did not want to break, and in many cases, they settled in the same communities next door or down the street from their enslaved owners and people with whom they were familiar. Some of their reasons for settling near their former owners range from family connections to work opportunities as paid day laborers. In many cases, former slave owners gave or sold land for a small fee to their former slaves so the freed African Americans could build churches and houses and farm their own land. Some white residents possibly led and guided their newly freed black neighbors, and in other cases, the white residents protected their black neighbors to some degree and helped them to become self-sufficient.

On the other hand, some blacks of early Giles County just left; they left Giles as well as the South to try and escape the past and the dismal economic conditions and violent threats of the postwar society. Many never looked back. They did this in a couple of ways, including migrating north up U.S. Highway 31 or by identifying themselves as American Indians and moving west, all in hopes of a better life. Both hopeful resolutions to their situation disconnected and fractured the black families of Giles.

For the black families who stayed in Giles to make a go of life without uprooting their family, and to finish what they had already started in slavery, which was to be law-abiding, hard-working citizens determined to make a better life and coexist as equals with the rest of the Giles County community, we applaud them! For all the black families listed on the Giles County 1870 census are Giles County's first black settlers in a free society.

The making of this book has multiple purposes. One is to highlight the early African American accomplishments in Giles. Another is to enlighten all about Giles County's early African American history and heritage. Lastly, we hope the book will show that Giles County history is Tennessee history and that Tennessee history is the history of the South and all is American history. Most importantly, we hope to let the world know that we, the descendants of the African American settlers of Giles, are proud of them for their successes and accomplishments.

One

Early Entrepreneurs and Farming

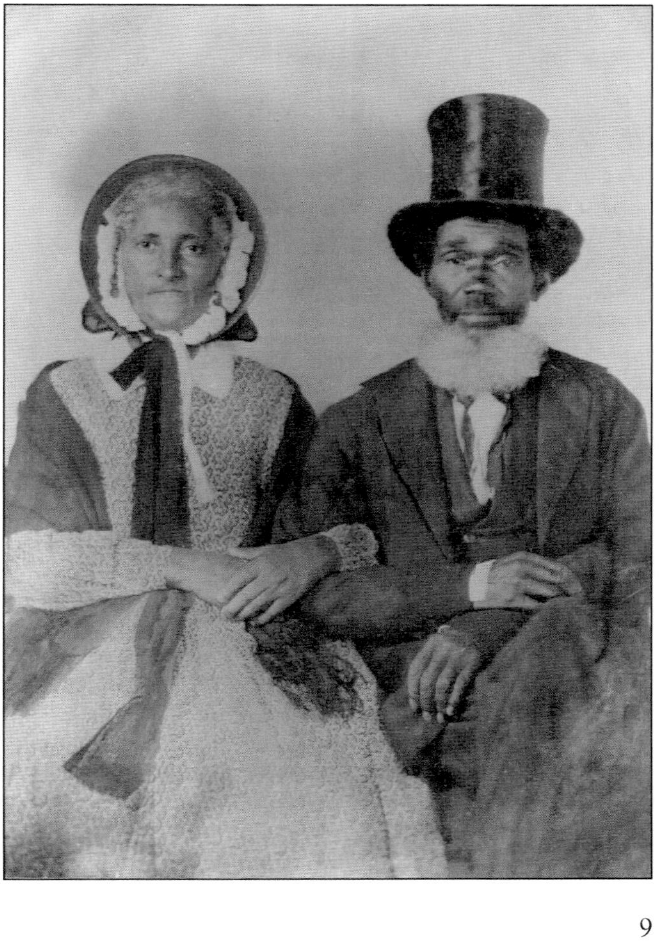

Moses McKissack came to America as a slave, being sold to a plantation owner in North Carolina. He married a Cherokee Indian named Mirian and had 14 children. Around 1850, he brought his family to Nashville to work as carpenters. They worked on the construction of the Maxwell House Hotel. At the deaths of Moses and Mirian in 1865, three of their sons—Gabriel, Oscar, and Thomas—headed to Pulaski. Gabriel had six sons, all of whom learned carpentry and design from their father. (Courtesy of Anne [McKissack] Brown.)

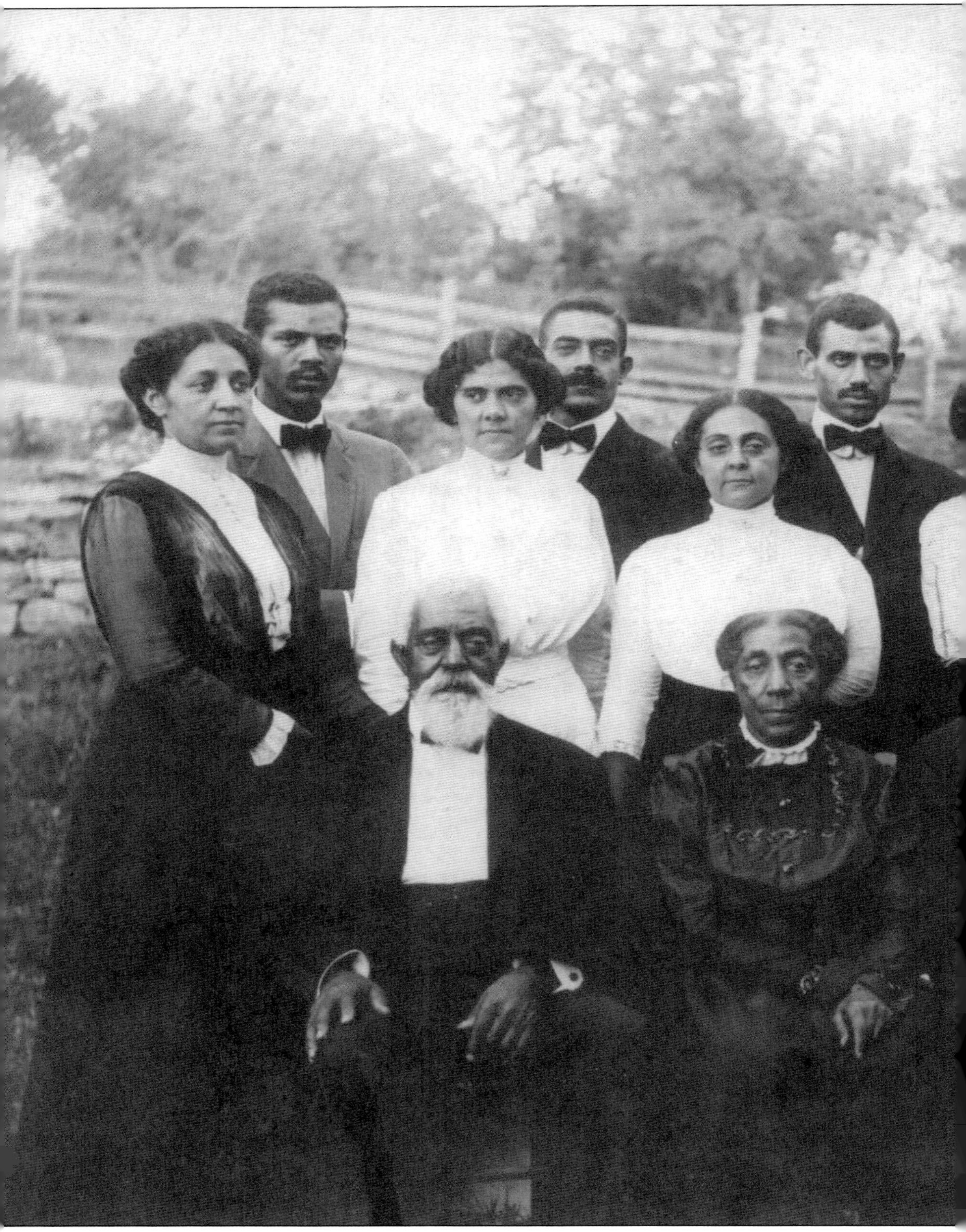

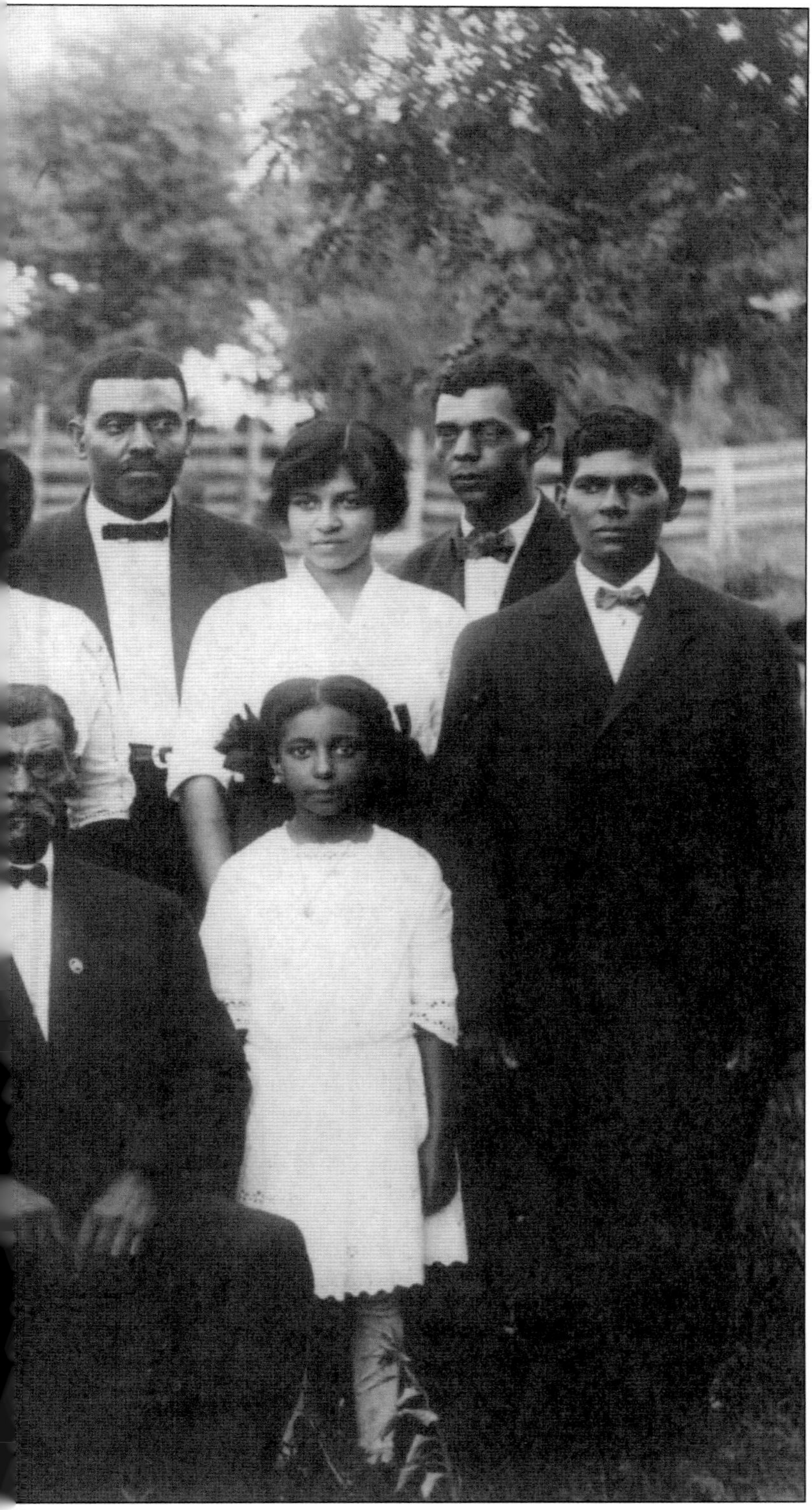

Pictured here after funeral services of Gabriel's wife, Dolly Ann, are, from left to right, (first row) Gabriel; Annie (McKissack) Gray; her husband, Henry Gray; and Anne Deberry; (second row) Amanda (McKissack) Deberry, Mary Frances (McKissack) Utley, Annie (McKissack) Maxwell, Lizzie (Black) McKissack, and Pearl (McKissack) Johnson; (third row) Calvin, William, Abraham, Moses III, Arthur, and Thomas McKissack, sons of Gabriel. (Courtesy of Anne [McKissack] Brown.)

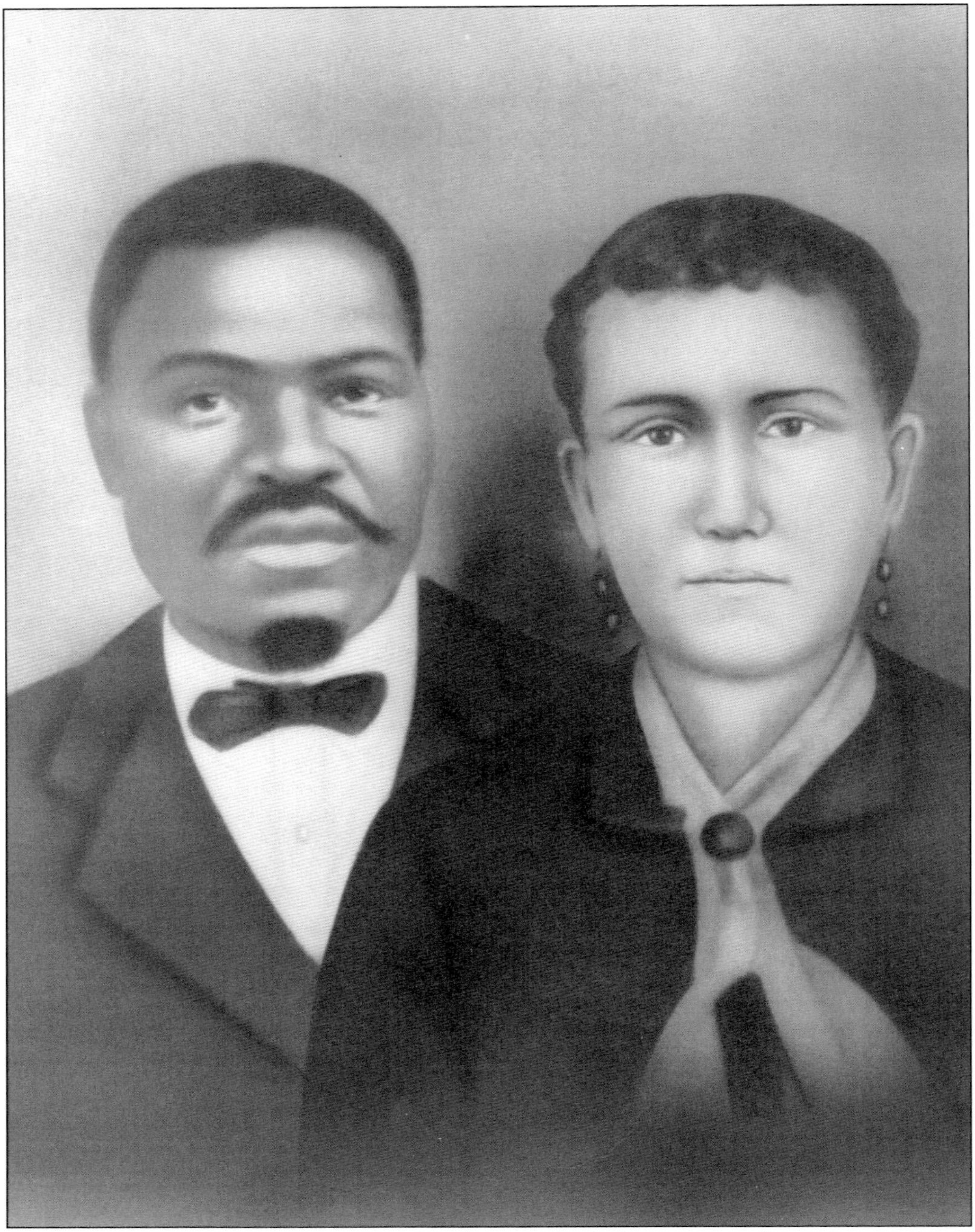

Minor and Betty (Anthony) Carter lived in the city of Pulaski. Minor was born about 1847 and Betty about 1853, and they were married January 31, 1877. Minor worked as a drayman who hauled water. A drayman was a driver of a dray, a low flatbed wagon pulled by mules for transporting goods. Betty was a housewife and cared for their children, Anthony, George, William, Bedford, Lincoln, and Mary Lou. (Courtesy of Agnes Bridgeforth.)

Jones Smith was born in 1850, married Mattie McKinney, and settled in Giles County. Jones and Mattie's children were George Washington (b. December 1869), Lizzie (b. August 1873), Alexander (b. 1874), Lula (b. 1875), Mamie (b. November 1879), Lily (b. March 1884), Charley (b. 1888), Alice (b. February 14, 1890), and Mattie "Pinkie" (b. March 1892). Jones's wife died giving birth to Mattie "Pinkie." Jones, a stonemason by trade, owned a home and 10 acres of farmland on Abernathy Hill where the family tended crops, commercial honeybees, chickens, and livestock. The affluent family also owned a surrey (a late-19th-century horse-drawn four-wheeled carriage with two or four seats, used for short pleasure trips) and two horses. See an example of his stonework on page 15. (Courtesy of descendants of Mamie Woodson, Alice Kline, and Mattie "Pinkie" Lane, children of Jones and Mattie Smith.)

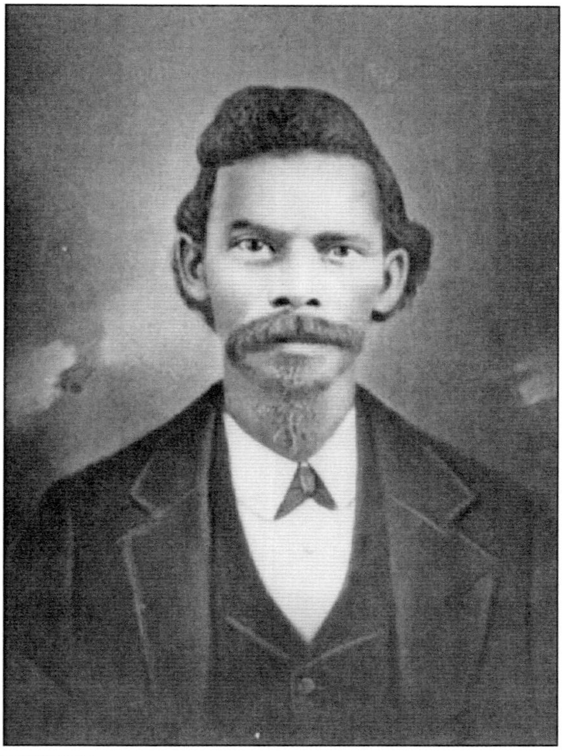

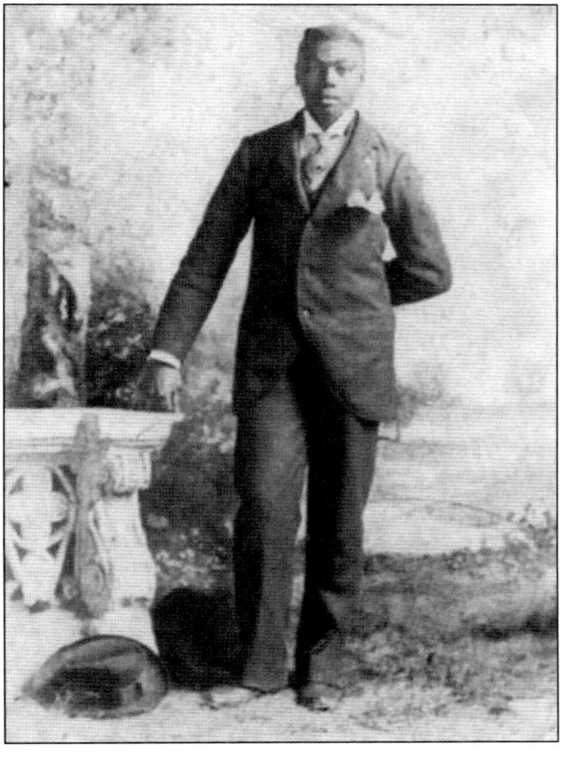

Dr. William Alberta Lewis, one of a few 19th-century African American doctors in Giles County, was raised in the Wales community. He graduated from Pulaski High School then taught school in Elkton before entering Fisk University. He was valedictorian and president of his graduating class in 1902. Dr. Lewis went on to Meharry Medical College and graduated in 1907. He later returned to the Giles community and became an outstanding citizen with many accolades to his credit. Dr. Lewis practiced for 64 years and delivered over 2,200 babies. (Courtesy of the Giles County Bicentennial Committee.)

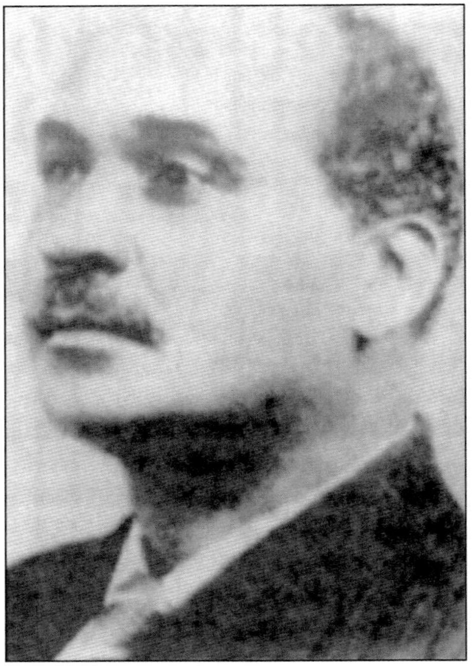

Dr. Robert Fulton Boyd was born a slave on the Solon E. Rose plantation in July 1857. His parents are believed to be Ransom and Lucy Boyd, and his sibling were Francis, Wesley, Jennie, Cornelius, Edward, Elizabeth, William, and Dee. Boyd moved from Giles to Nashville and worked under some of the most famous doctors and surgeons of his time. Boyd received his medical degree in 1882, a dentistry degree in 1887, and later a pharmacy degree. He founded the Peoples Savings Bank and Trust (now Citizen Bank in Nashville) and the American Association of Colored Physicians and Surgeons (now the National Medical Association). Boyd has numerous accomplishments and accolades to his credit. (Courtesy of the Giles County Bicentennial Committee.)

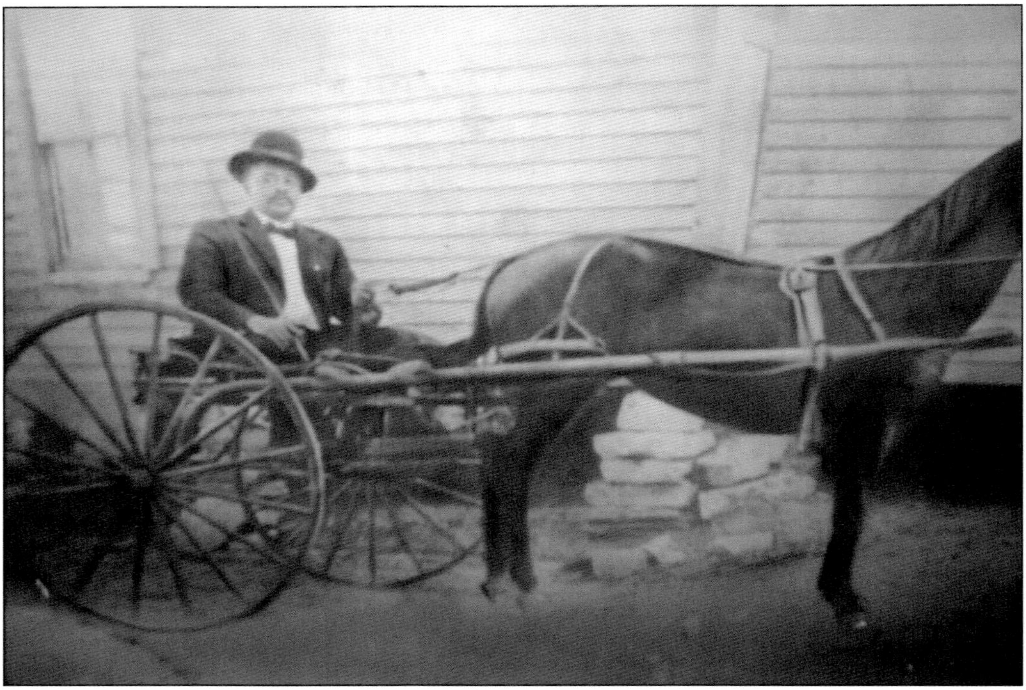

Sim Bledsoe, pictured in this *c.* 1900–1920 photograph, was born about 1878 and was one of Elkton's first black businessmen. Sim owed a barbershop in the town of Elkton. He cut white people's hair at the shop in town and black people's hair at his house. In addition to barbering, Sim also bred and raised horses. Sim's wife was Minnie, and their children were Thomas, Huelon, Titus, Lucille, Dassie, Curlie, and Izeola. (Courtesy of Izeola Morris.)

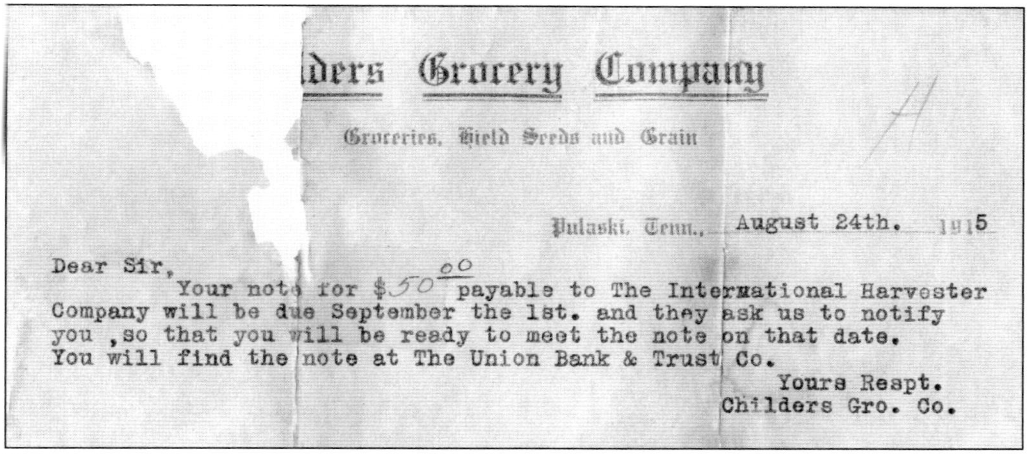

...lders Grocery Company

Groceries, Field Seeds and Grain

Pulaski, Tenn., August 24th. 1915

Dear Sir,

Your note for $50.00 payable to The International Harvester Company will be due September the 1st. and they ask us to notify you, so that you will be ready to meet the note on that date. You will find the note at The Union Bank & Trust Co.

Yours Respt.
Childers Gro. Co.

The sender of this 1915 letter from the Childers Grocery Company in Pulaski was probably acting as an agent for International Harvester. It is notifying a Giles County resident of payment due on a note, possibly for a planter purchased a year before this date. It states that the note is to be paid at the Union Bank and Trust Company in Pulaski.

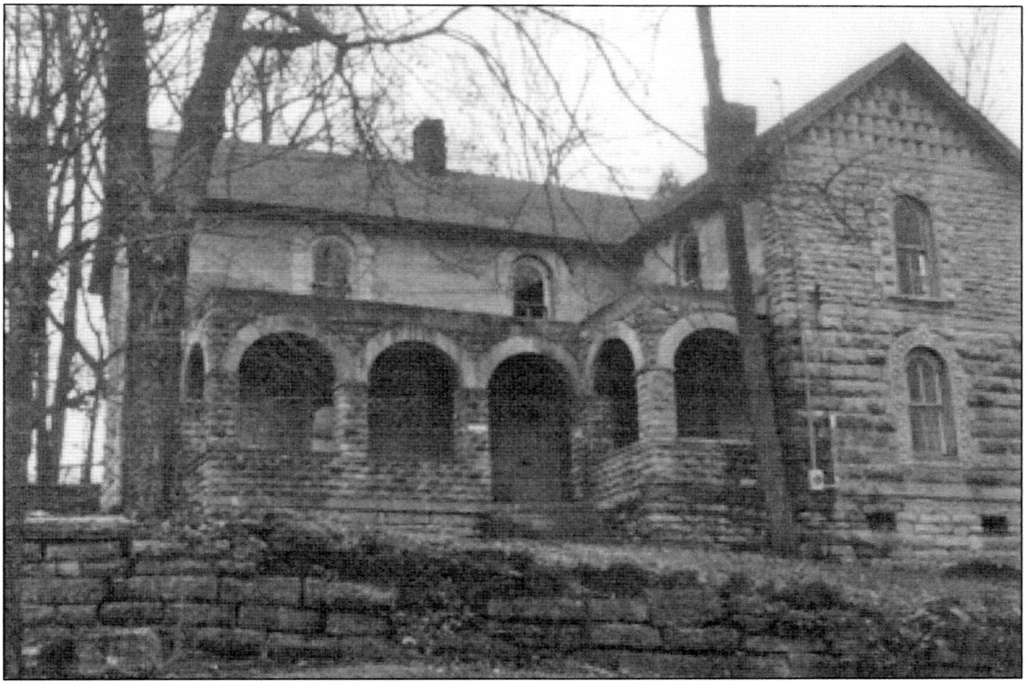

This rock house has unique and masterful stonework. The house was built by Jones Smith beginning in the 1870s. Smith passed his skills to his sons, and many of their buildings still stand today. A fine example of his handcrafted and -polished stone windows was featured at the Tennessee Centennial Exposition in Nashville in 1897. On Saturday, January 28, 1905, a wall that Smith was hired to take down at Martin College collapsed, killing him instantly. The February 2, 1905, *Pulaski Citizen* obituary noted that "Jones Smith, col [colored], a well known stone mason and contractor . . . was one of the best known and most prominent stone work contractors in the county." (Courtesy of descendants of Mamie Woodson, Alice Kline, and Mattie "Pinkie" Lane, children of Jones and Mattie Smith.)

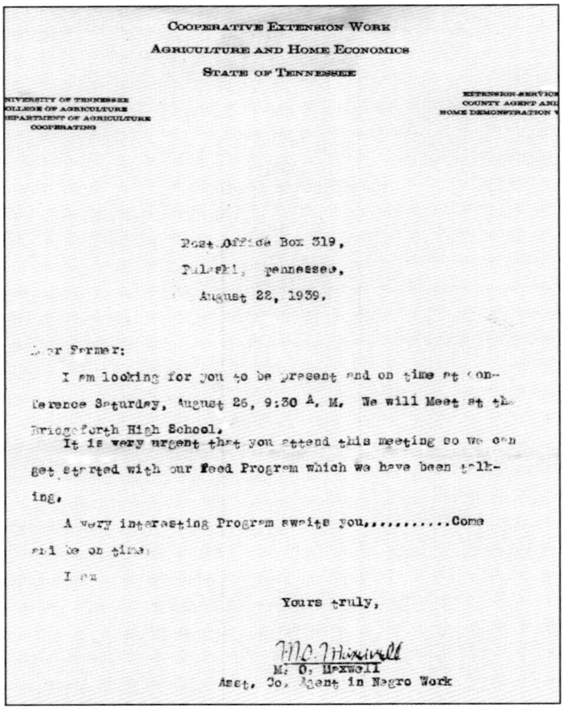

COOPERATIVE EXTENSION WORK
AGRICULTURE AND HOME ECONOMICS
STATE OF TENNESSEE

NIVERSITY OF TENNESSEE
OLLEGE OF AGRICULTURE
EPARTMENT OF AGRICULTURE
COOPERATING

EXTENSION SERVIC
COUNTY AGENT AN
HOME DEMONSTRATION

Post Office Box 319,
Pulaski, Tennessee,
August 22, 1939.

Dear Farmer:

I am looking for you to be present and on time at Conference Saturday, August 26, 9:30 A. M. We will Meet at the Bridgeforth High School.

It is very urgent that you attend this meeting so we can get started with our Feed Program which we have been talking.

A very interesting Program awaits you..........Come and be on time.

I am

Yours truly,

M. O. Maxwell
M. O. Maxwell
Asst. Co. Agent in Negro Work

This 1939 request went out to black farmers in Giles County informing them about a food program; it is signed by M. O. Maxwell, an agent in the Negro Work program. The World War II program was begun in 1940 as a response to the Depression by Gov. Prentice Cooper. The Tennessee Home Food Supply Program encouraged farmers to participate in growing 75 percent of their own food instead of spending money to purchase food through an open market.

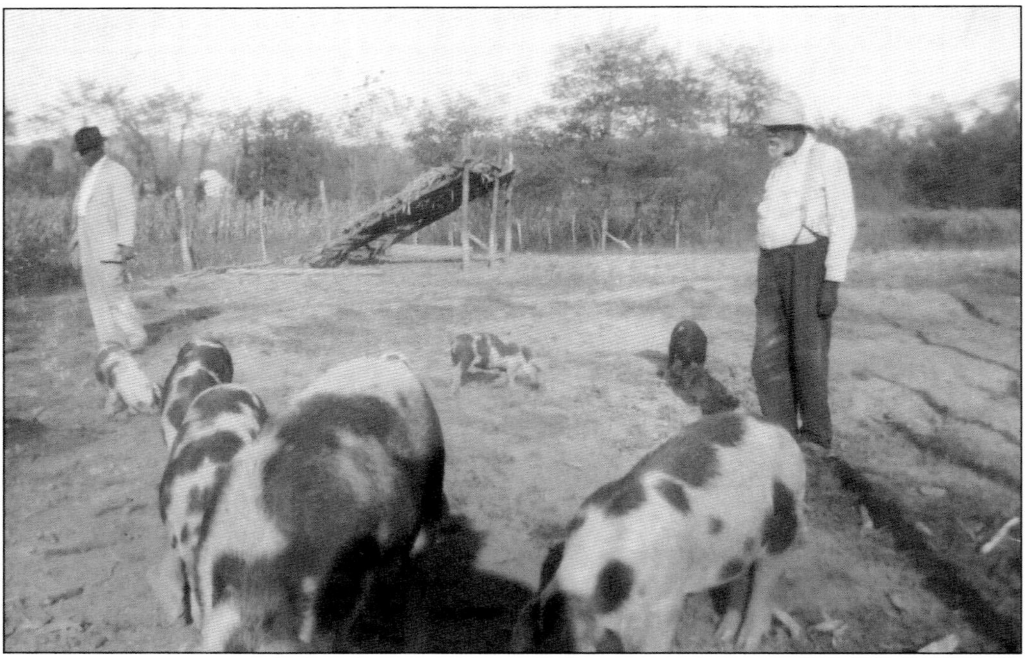

Matt Gardner (right) was one of a small number of African Americans to sustain a large farming operation after the Civil War. On his farmstead, Matt erected outbuildings for his farm products and livestock but most importantly for the local black community. Among the outbuildings were a sorghum gin and a storehouse that he operated to sell foodstuffs to neighbors for cash, exchange, or credit.

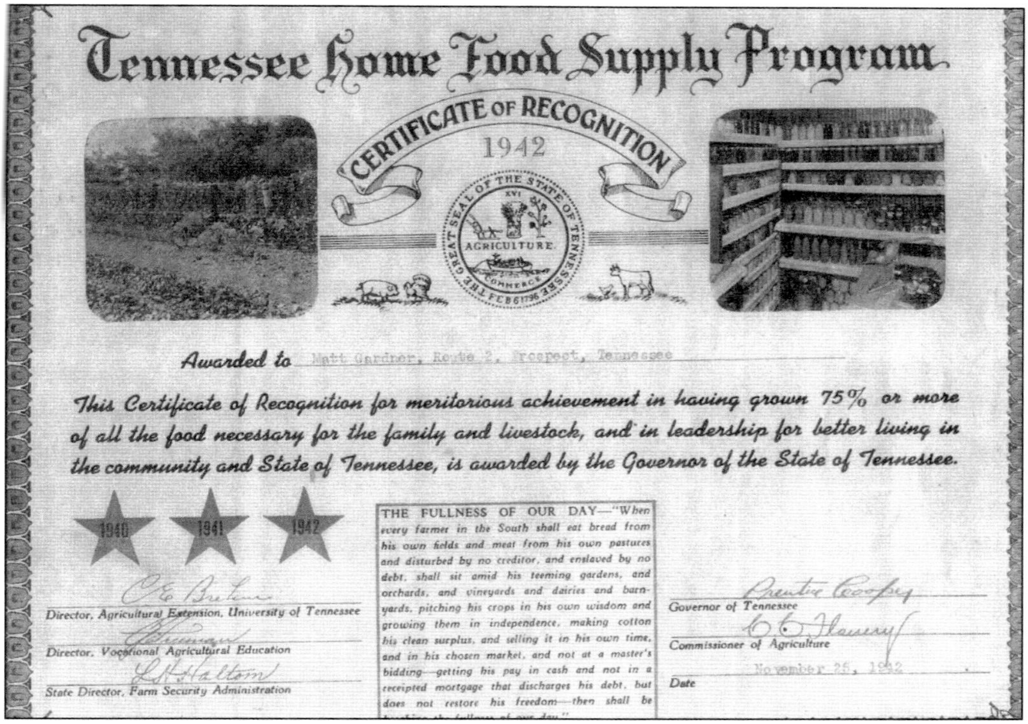

Tennessee Home Food Supply Program

CERTIFICATE OF RECOGNITION

1942

Awarded to Matt Gardner, Route 2, Prospect, Tennessee

This Certificate of Recognition for meritorious achievement in having grown 75% or more of all the food necessary for the family and livestock, and in leadership for better living in the community and State of Tennessee, is awarded by the Governor of the State of Tennessee.

THE FULLNESS OF OUR DAY—"*When every farmer in the South shall eat bread from his own fields and meat from his own pastures and disturbed by no creditor, and enslaved by no debt, shall sit amid his teeming gardens, and orchards, and vineyards and dairies and barnyards, pitching his crops in his own wisdom and growing them in independence, making cotton his clean surplus, and selling it in his own time, and in his chosen market, and not at a master's bidding—getting his pay in cash and not in a receipted mortgage that discharges his debt, but does not restore his freedom—then shall be*

Director, Agricultural Extension, University of Tennessee

Director, Vocational Agricultural Education

State Director, Farm Security Administration

Governor of Tennessee

Commissioner of Agriculture

November 25, 1942

Date

This certificate of recognition from the Tennessee Home Food Supply Program was awarded to Matt Gardner. The recognition is for meritorious achievement in having grown 75 percent or more of all the food necessary for the family and livestock and for his leadership for better living in the community. It is signed by Gov. Prentice Cooper on November 25, 1942.

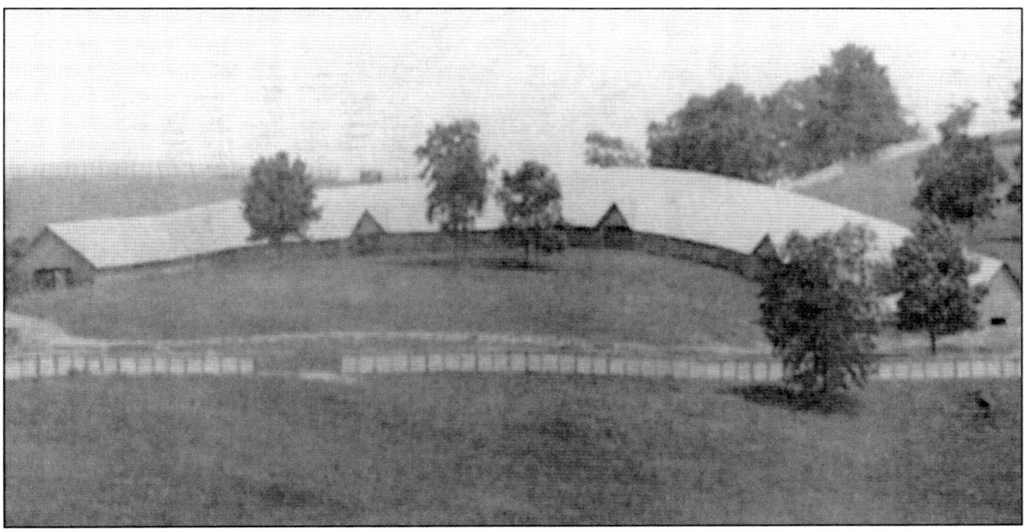

The Milky Way Farm in Giles was founded and built by Franklin C. Mars, maker of the Milky Way candy bar. Between 1931 and 1933, African Americans were employed as day laborers in the construction of the farm. During the Great Depression, the farm employed many African American men as hired farm laborers, allowing them the means necessary to feed and clothe their families through the Depression. (Courtesy of the Giles County Bicentennial Committee.)

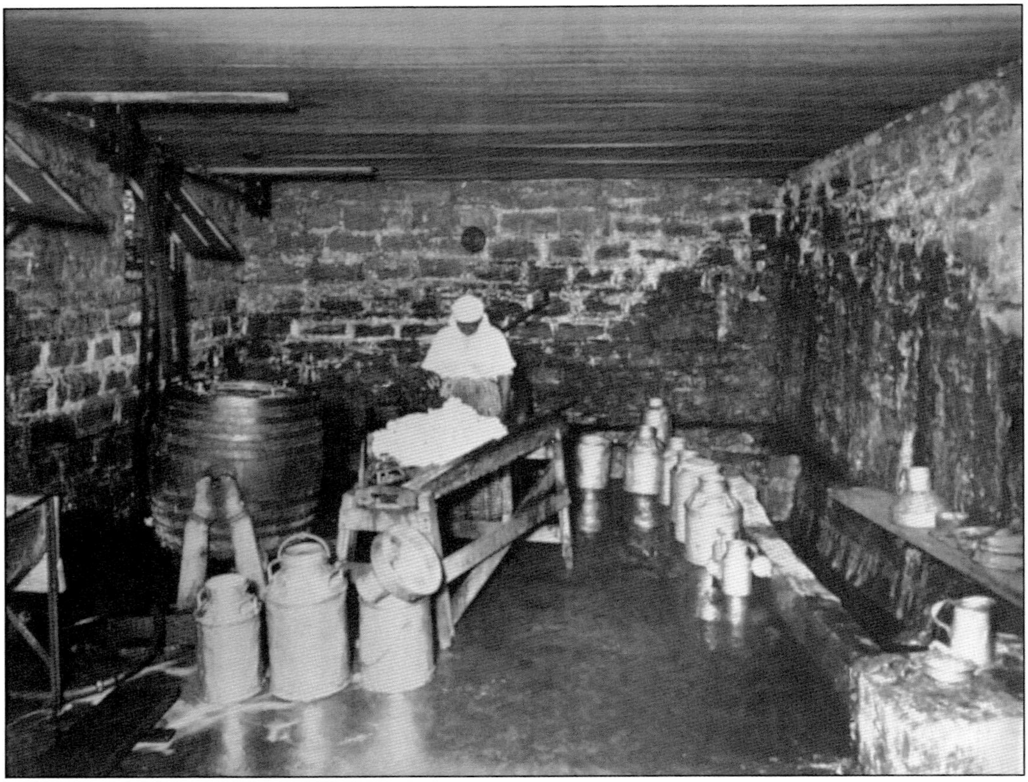

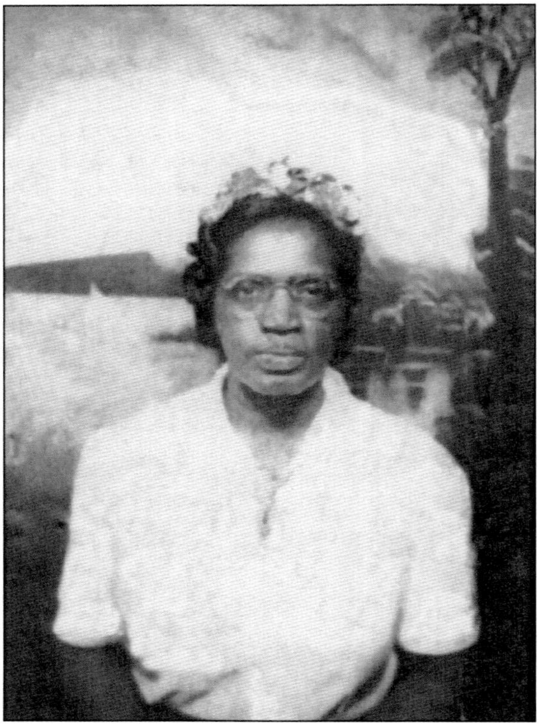

The Cresentview Dairy Farm in Giles employed African Americans, including women, to work in agriculture and farming at its dairy as well as at its many other outbuilding across the dairy farm. This picture shows a woman working in the dairy on the farm. (Courtesy of the Tennessee State Library and Archives.)

Ethel Bailey Bridgeforth Vance was born on February 29, 1892, to Louise Gardner and Empsy Bailey. Ethel grew up and was educated in the Elkton community. While growing up, she had the chore of ironing a number of big white sheets, only to discover this chore was for the Ku Klux Klan organization. She later married Philmore Vance and moved to Logan, West Virginia. Ethel passed away in September 1985 at the age of 93. (Courtesy of Michiko Bailey.)

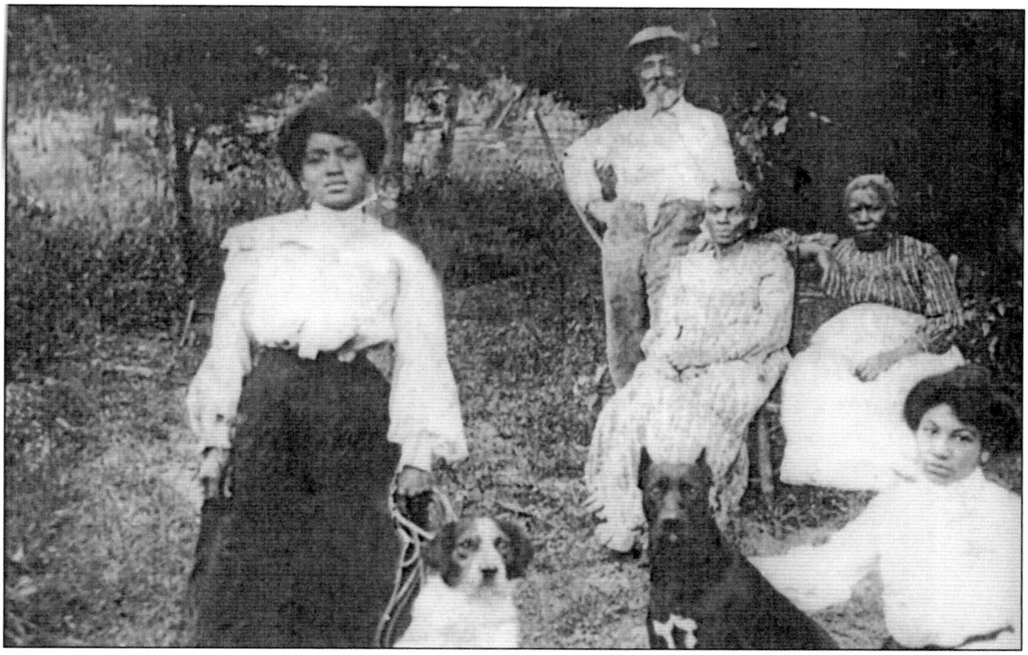

This *c.* 1880 picture is of Phillip Rhodes standing in the background with his wife, Jennie (Flournoy) Rhodes, seated in front of Phil; friend Mariah Martin is seated next to Jennie. In the foreground are their twins, Minnie (left) and Sally (right), and the family dogs. Not pictured are the couple's other 10 children: twins Bateman and Margaret, Benny, Lucy, Carl, Mariah, Samuel, Judy, Phillip, and Pamp. Phil was a farmer and a lawn-and-garden caretaker by day. (Courtesy of Richard Crenshaw.)

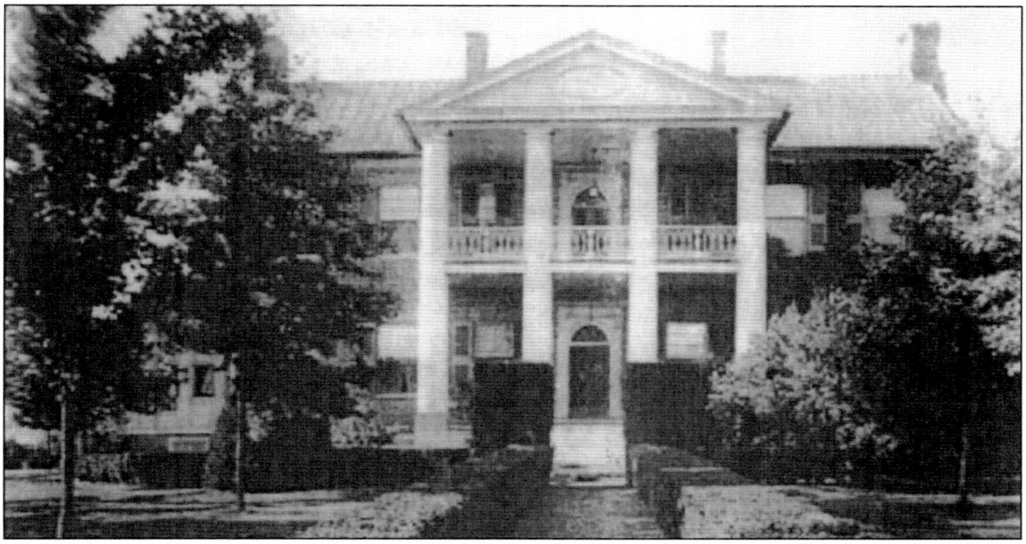

Clinton Place, located in Pulaski on Annie Wade Road, was known for its distinctive charm because of its elaborate gardens. The landscape measured 408 feet by 240 feet, half of which was filled with formal gardens with walks bordered by dwarf boxwoods. There were three hedges of tree boxwoods 16 feet high, crepe myrtles 25 feet tall, and giant magnolias. There were pines, cedars, laurels, and a cucumber tree, all cut, groomed, and maintained daily by ex-slave Phil Rhodes until some time after the Civil War. (Courtesy of Richard Crenshaw.)

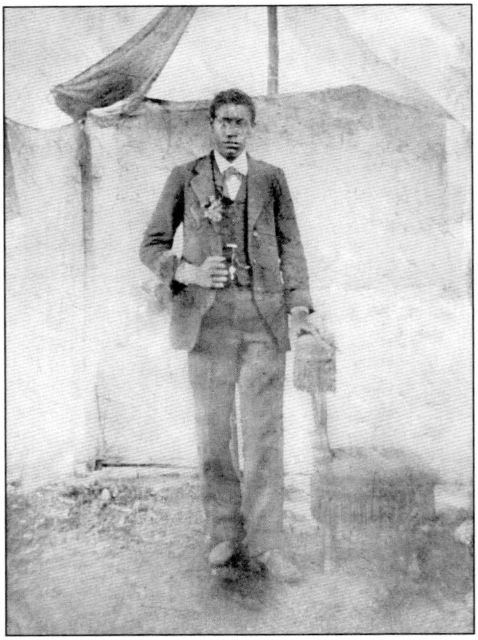

Many looked to traveling photographers to have the opportunity to put on their Sunday best and have their pictures taken. Photographers would set up tents in the communities, fairs, or carnivals where individuals would come to have their pictures taken, as seen in this tintype. A couple of different props would be available to add to the picture, such as chairs or ornate stands. Tintypes were often made by unskilled traveling photographers.

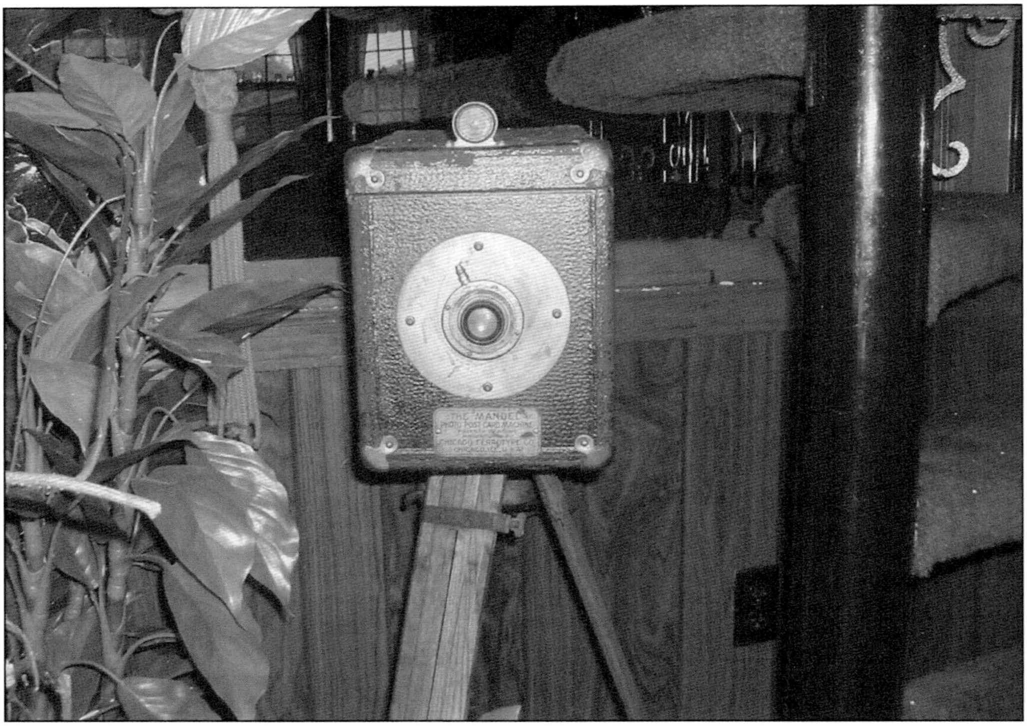

Tintypes were popular, as they made photography available to the working class, not just the well-to-do. Later studio-style cameras and personal box cameras were developed, as shown above, which allow individuals to go into a studio or purchase their own cameras to capture and preserve family history and memories on their own. Giles's first black traveling photographer was Willie Daly. (Courtesy of Anne Brown.)

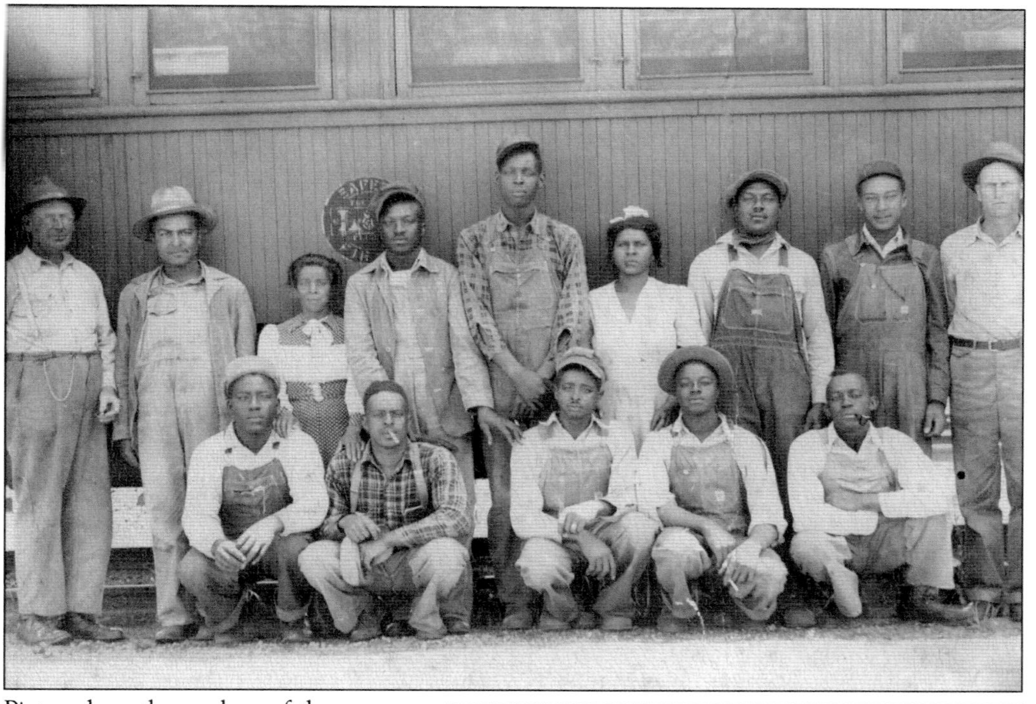

Pictured are the workers of the railroad work train that ran between Nashville, Tennessee, and Decatur, Alabama. The work train was part of the Louisville and Nashville rail system that was originally the Nashville and Decatur Railroad. The women on the work train had the responsibility of taking care of the laundry and cooking.

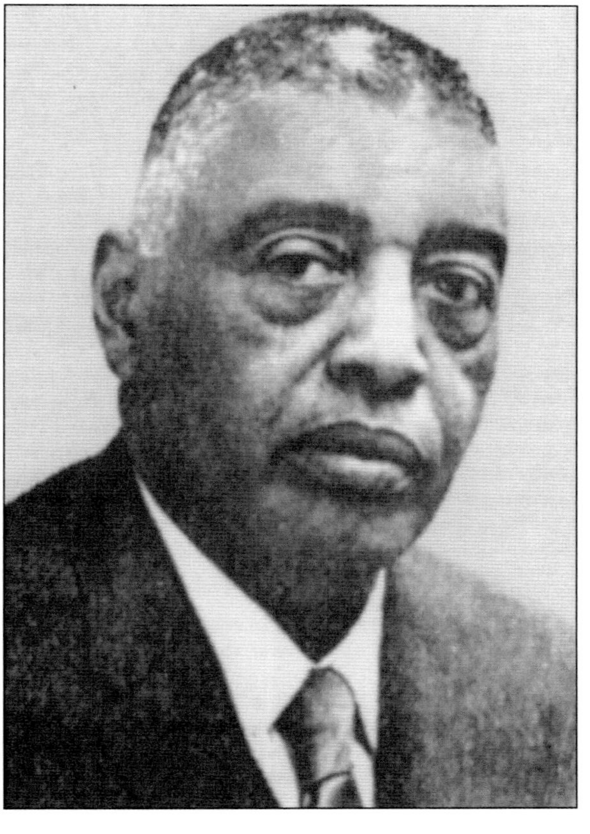

In 1944, Dr. David Marshall Spotwood (born in 1907) started his practice in Pulaski, and he continued until his death in 1970. During his years of medical practice in Pulaski, he served one term as president of the Giles County Medical Society. He was vice president of the Giles County Tuberculosis Association and served on the board of directors of the Giles County Mental Health Association. Prominent in the education field, he became the first African American to serve on the Tennessee Board of Education. (Courtesy of the Giles County Bicentennial Committee.)

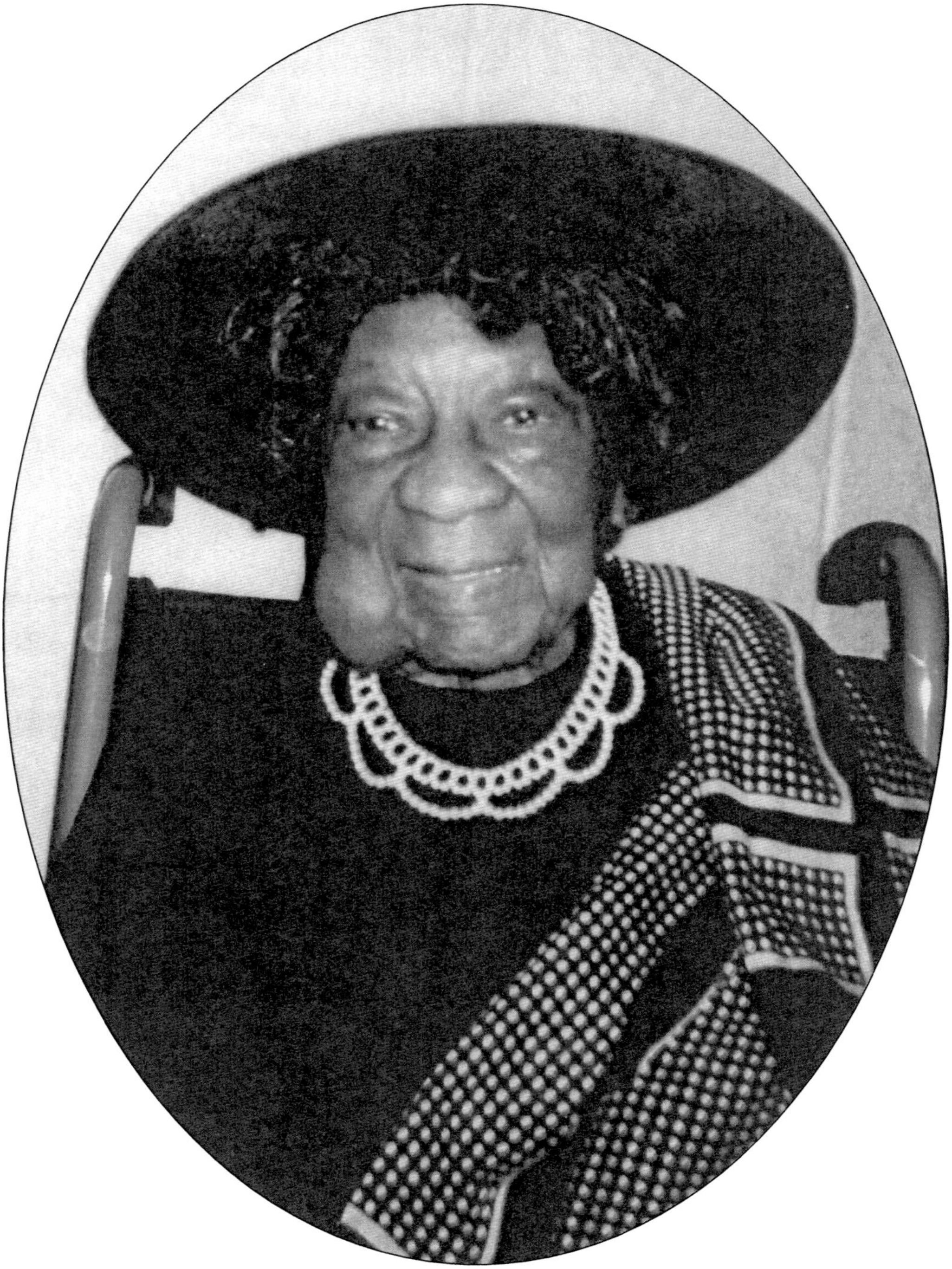

Rosa Nell (Bridgeforth) Driver was born on May 12, 1901, in Elkton to Rev. Samuel and Henrietta (Reedus) Bridgeforth. Rosa was the 20th of 23 children. As a young woman, she married Harry Gardner, and the couple had two sons, Robert and Henry Evans. In 1942, she married Rogers Driver Sr. The couple owned the Blue Berry Hill Club in Elkton.

Two

A Mind is a Terrible Thing to Waste

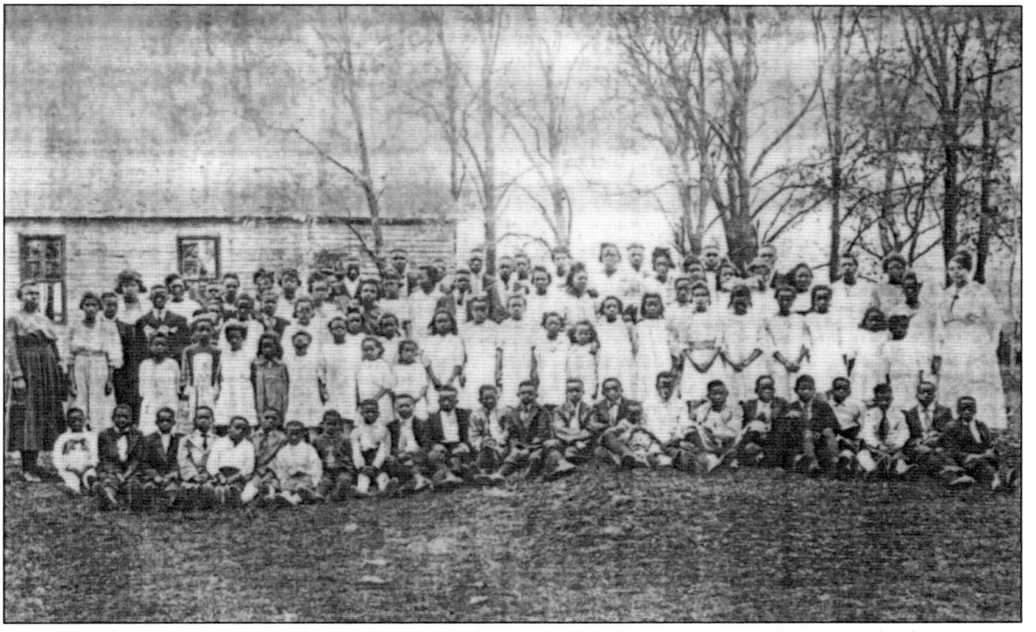

Matt Gardner financed and helped to build the first school for blacks in Elkton in the late 1800s. He also provided room and board at his home, as well as pay, for the teachers who taught at the school. This early-1900s picture of the Elkton Colored School includes teachers Ada Mae Doughty (left) and Inez Pullins. Some of the students in the picture are Madeline Gardner, Iwilla Eddings, Bubba Huston, Tom Gardner, Ellen Cooper, Ella Mary Eddings, Tub Bledsoe, Shellie Gardner, Alberta Eddings, Yancy Swinea, Josephine Gardner, Thaddeus Holt, Anna Lee Eddings, Mary Margaret Garrison, and Robert Louis Sherrill.

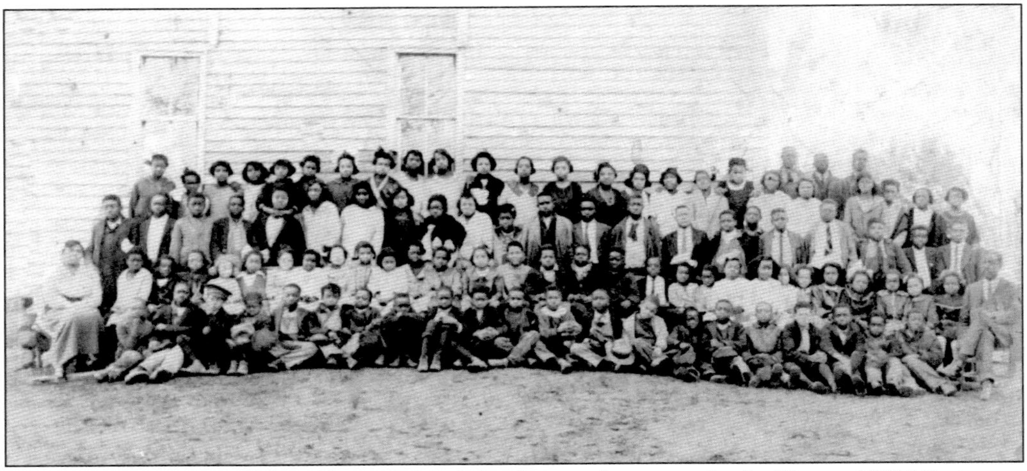

This c. 1924 picture of the Elkton Color School was taken outside the Union Hill Missionary Baptist Church after the school burned around 1926. Pictured are teachers Ida Mae Doughty (left) and Sam Bridgeforth (right). The students are, from left to right, (first row) 2 unidentified, Quabon Swinea, Glen Grisby, Clinton White Oakley Bridgeforth, and 15 unidentified students; (second row) 8 unidentified, Sweetie Bledsoe, unidentified, Lura Mae Bridgeforth, Will Ross Gardner, Mannie Ross Dunn, Pittsfield Swinea, unidentified, Vandaliear Brown, Sam Beatty, Thaddeus Holt, 5 unidentified, Ellen Cooper, and 5 unidentified; (third row) Bubba Huston, Charlie Gardner, 3 unidentified, Ella Mary Eddings, Lou Beatty, unidentified, Fannie Mae Short, Iwilla Eddings, 2 unidentified, Gaston Gardner, 4 unidentified, Tom Bledsoe, and 4 unidentified; (fourth row) Versie Anderson, 5 unidentified, Alberta Eddings, unidentified, Rachel McLin, Anna Lee Eddings, unidentified, and Georgia Lee Beatty. All other students are unidentified.

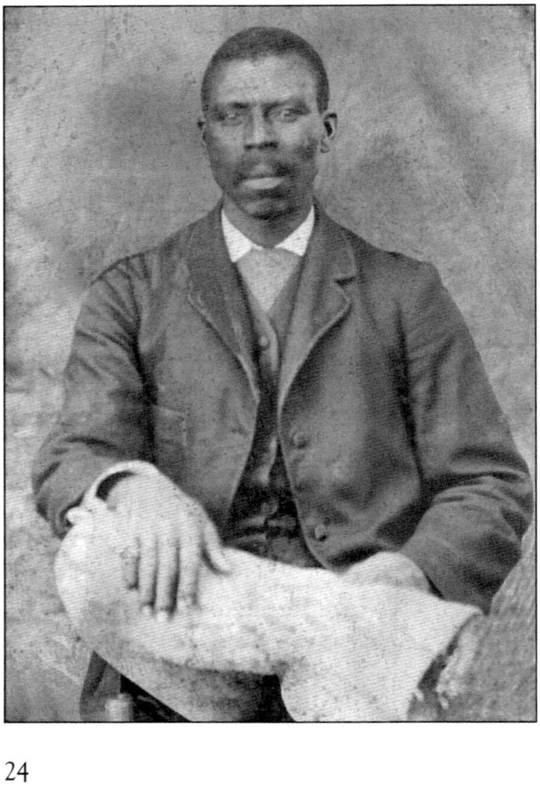

This early tintype is of A. Thomas Hill, who is believed to have taught at the first colored school in Elkton from the mid-1880s until the mid-1890s. After teaching in Elkton for many years, he became the first principal of the colored public school in Pulaski and was part of the first-known faculty of Pulaski High School.

Austin Baugh, known as Professor Baugh, lived in Elkton at one time. It is believed that his father was also named Austin and his mother was named Leana. The 1880 census shows Austin's siblings were named Alabama, Virgie, and James. Baugh was a teacher in about the 1890s at the first colored school in Elkton.

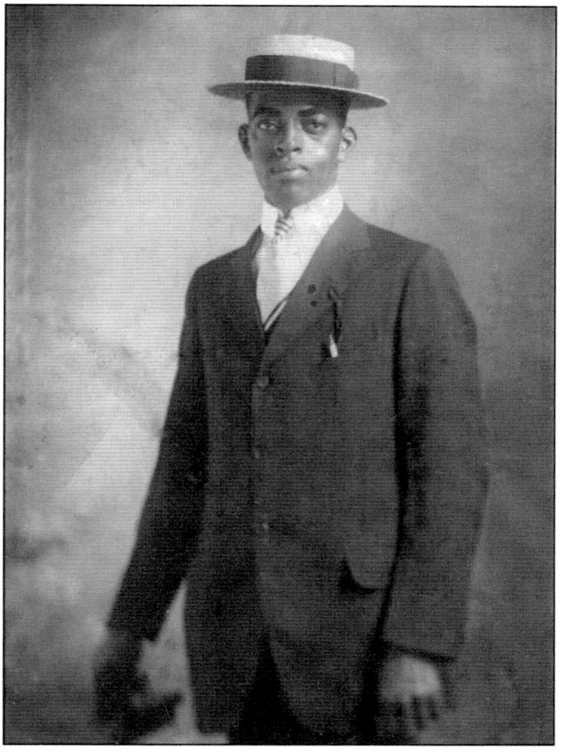

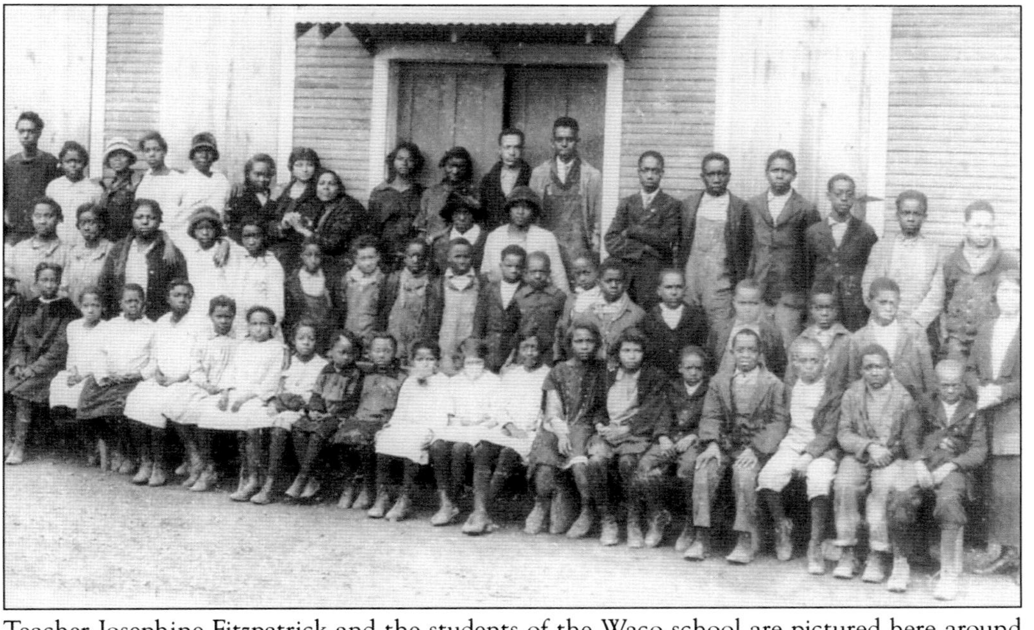

Teacher Josephine Fitzpatrick and the students of the Waco school are pictured here around 1920–1921. One of the largest schools for black children was Waco Elementary. The school was built in 1921 and had a sanitation system for drinking water but no stove for heat. School records show that in the first year, there were 49 boys and 63 girls enrolled at the school and that their ages ranged from 6 to 19. (Courtesy of Giles County Library Genealogy Department.)

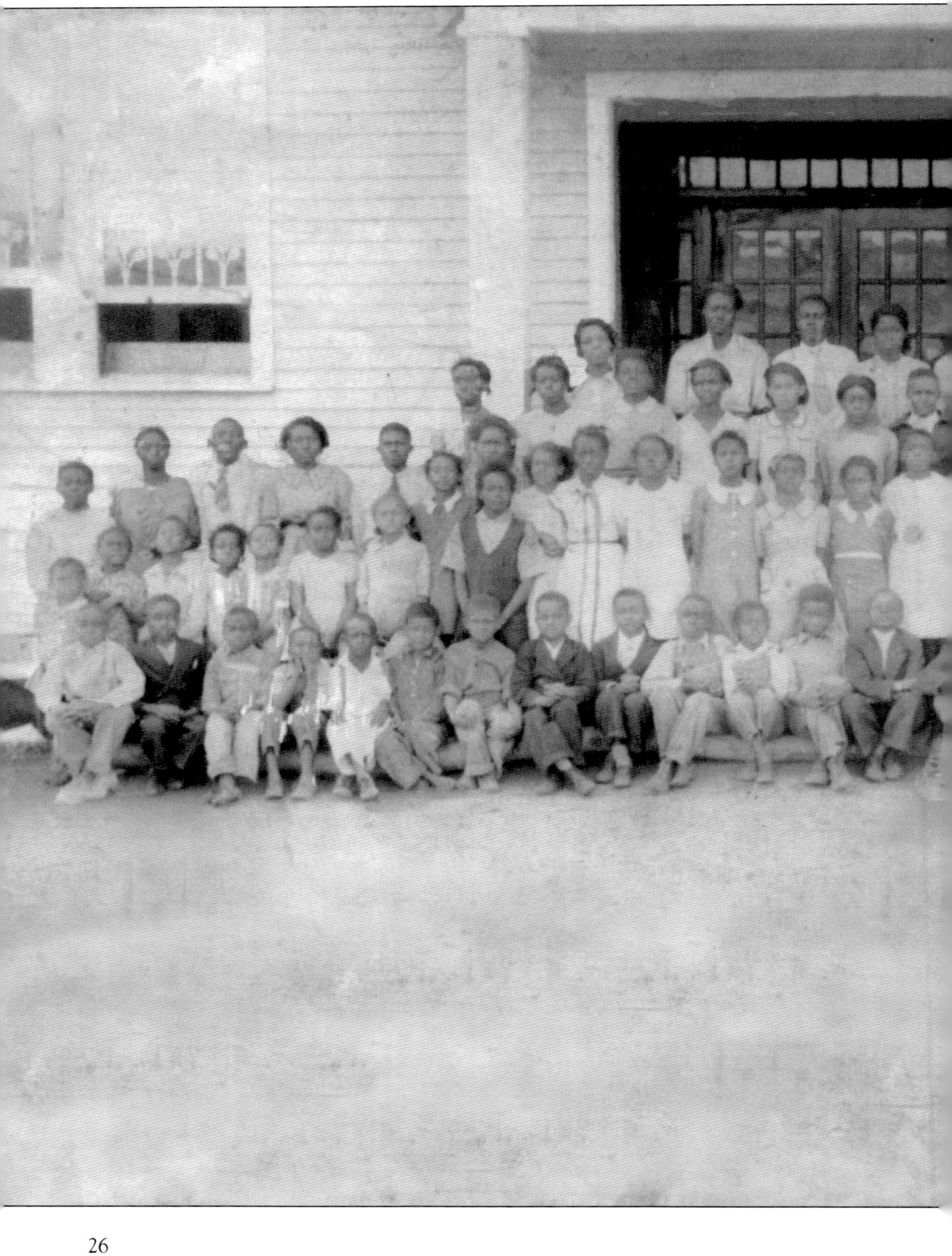

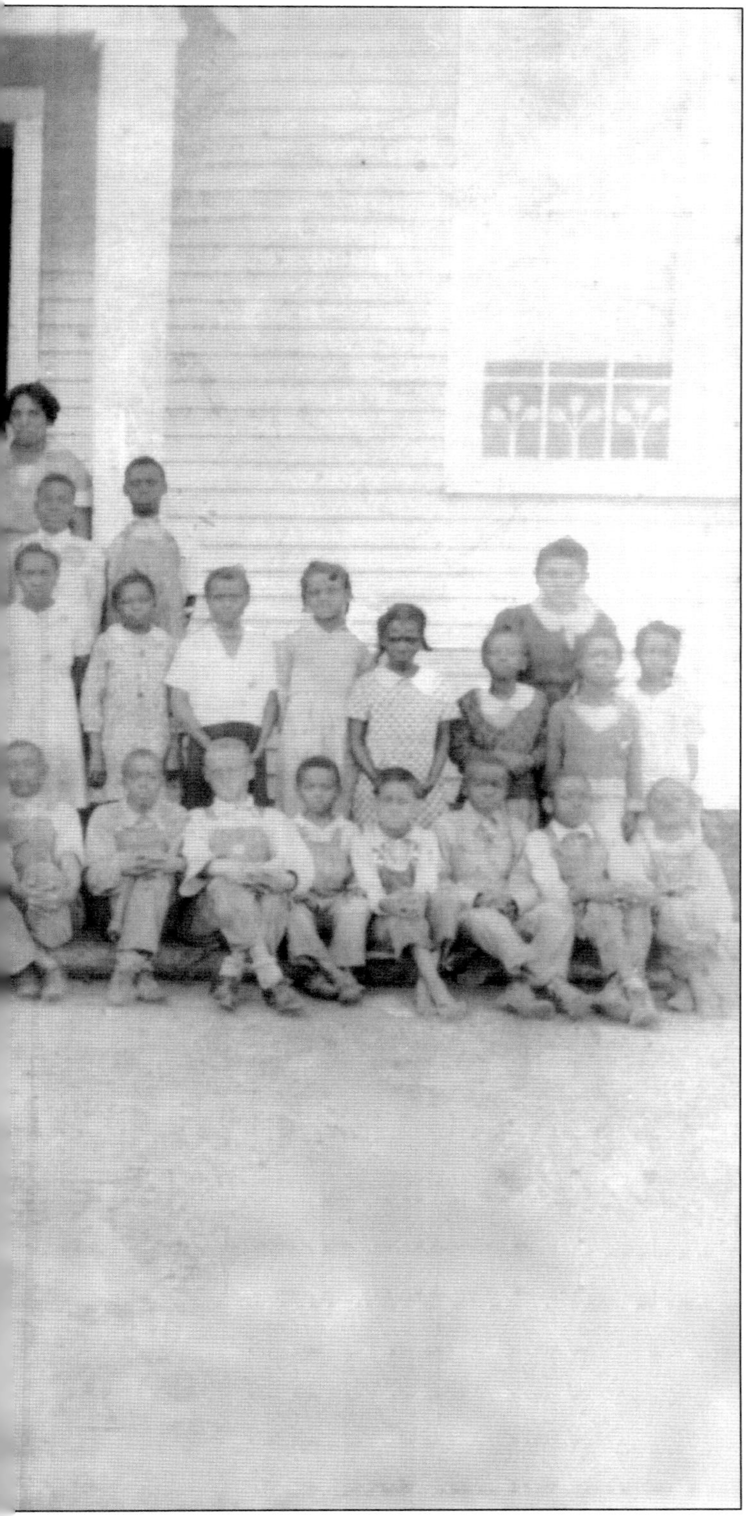

The Holts Elementary School class of 1937–1938 is pictured here. Shown from left to right are (first row) Cleophus Driver, Mcafee Upshaw, Richard L. Johnson, Clyde Anderson, Pete Sloss, Bob Swinea, Sidney Gardner, Wendell Ballentine Roy Driver, William C. Benson, Thomas Driver, Will Owens, Thomas T. Sloss, Flournoy Gardner, Ridgeway Driver, John Harris, Joe T. Gardner, Edward L. Hardin, Howell Swinea, Efron Johnson, Willie R. Gardner, and David L. White; (second row) Belle Driver, Mattie Mason, Louise (Scruggs) Bridgeforth, Mattie S. Lee, Edith Driver, Constance Anderson, Dorothy J. Gardner, Gladys Driver, and Mabel Holt; (third row) ? Floyd, Cornelius Moody, Robert C. Johnson, Marie Johnson, Rogers Driver Jr., Millie Sloss, Mattie S. Bledsoe, Myra Sherrell, Juanita Gardner, Marie Driver, Millie Driver, Elizabeth Driver, Elnora Anderson, Adell Gardner, Laura L. Benson, Roberta Benson, Charity E. Brown, Elizabeth Gardner, Phobia Owens, Irene Mason, Alice M. Sloss, Odell Sloss, and teacher Lou Alice Jones; (fourth row) Nell Row, Cora L. Sloss, Fannie L. Anderson, Flora Owens, May Swinea, Mary J. Hall, Bud Reedus, George H., Driver, David Holt, and Johnny M. Anderson; (fifth row) teacher Lenora Ballentine, Eurdora Eddings, Sterling Eddings, Stella M. Hardin, Tyre Johnson, and teacher Jenny C. Dailey. (Courtesy of Bob Swinea.)

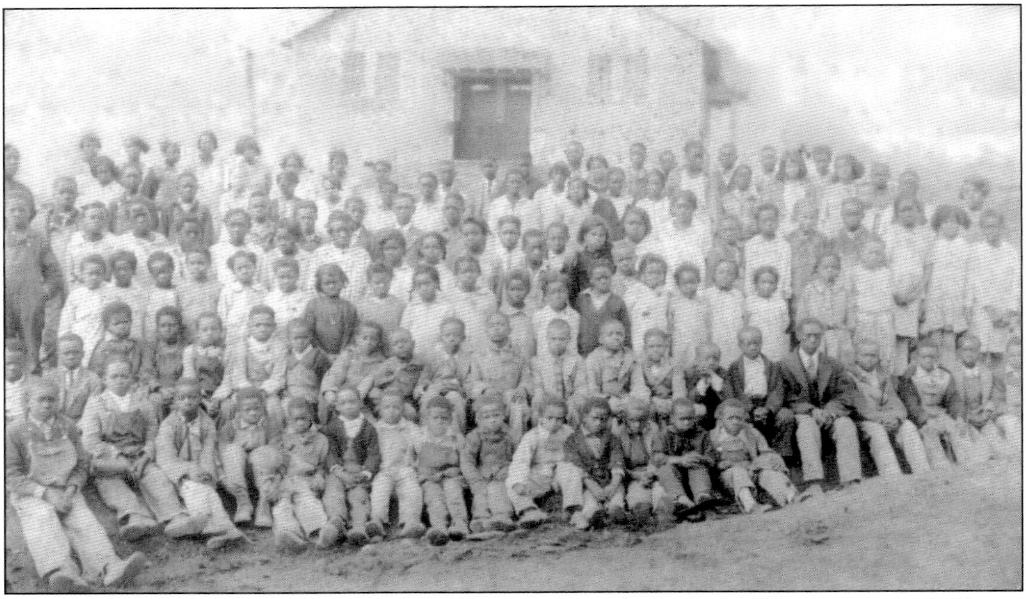

Pictured is the Elkton Colored School in 1930–1931 with teachers Alice Coleman (left) and Jennie (Doughty) Daly. Students are, from left to right, (first row) Frank Martin Coleman, John Howard Sherrill, James Ross Brown, 2 unidentified, John Ed Rowe, and 8 unidentified; (second row) Robert Gardner, Sproll Driver, Jack Gardner, 2 unidentified, John Louis Sherrill, unidentified, Martin "Cunt" Gardner, unidentified, John "Shag" Gardner, 2 unidentified, Atha Garrison, Rogers Driver, Henry Evans Gardner, Howard Bledsoe, John Black, unidentified, Sam Driver, and 2 unidentified; (third row) 4 unidentified, Effie Lee Driver, 14 unidentified; (fourth row) Raymond Gardner Jr. at left. In the other rows, the rest are unidentified but include Mattie Reedus and John L. Johnson, Eleanor Rowe, Ellen Cooper, Richard "Son" Bledsoe, Tennie Driver, and Sam Harney Sloss.

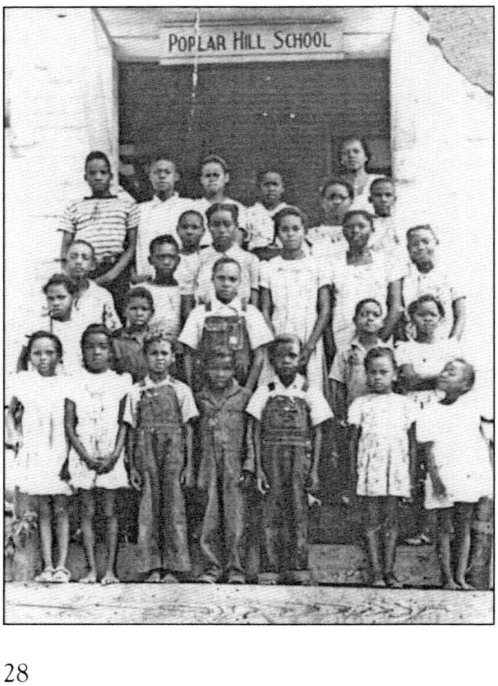

This is a 1941 picture of the Rosenwald Poplar Hill Colored School. The school was built in 1929 on property purchased by the local citizens and the county. Some of the teachers were Lillian Mitchell, Mattie Gilbert, B. H. Morrell, John Brown, Mamie P. Harris, Kathryn Driver, and Aline Coleman. Pictured from left to right on the top row are George Brown, Willie Lee Wheeler, Mary Ella (Wheeler) Benson, two unidentified, and Mack Brown. The only other identifiable child is Jerry Wheeler, second from right in the third row. (Courtesy of William L. Brown Sr.)

Brother and sister Richard Jr. and Louis Harwell are all dressed and ready for a day at school. Both were born in the Aspen Hill community. They are the children of Richard and Mary (Foust) Harwell. Richard was born on September 20, 1910, and attended school up to the sixth grade. Louis was born on November 7, 1914. She later married O. C. Gardner of Elkton, and together they had two girls, Joann Gardner and Phillistine (Gardner) Moody. (Courtesy of Joann Gardner.)

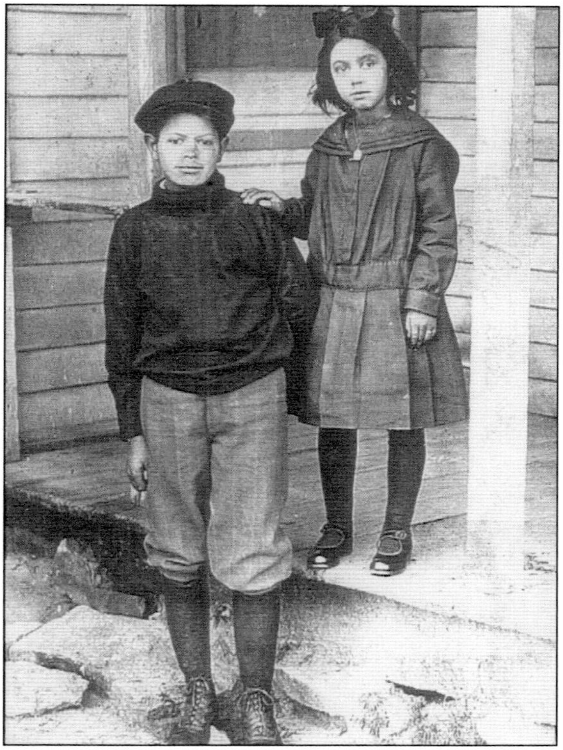

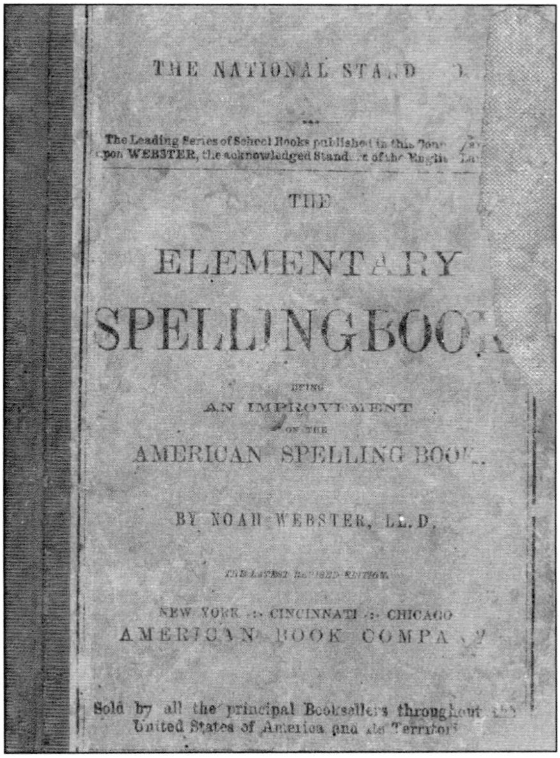

This c. 1880 elementary spelling book by Noah Webster, LL.D., was also used in the colored school at Elkton during the mid- to late-1880s. According to students who attended the school, the children had all the same books that the white schools had. The students commonly referred to the book as the "blue speller." Students also stated they had a book called the "red reader." They also used the *Everyday Arithmetic* book. Written by John B. Gifford, it states that it is "a practical mental arithmetic." The cost to purchase it was 24¢, and it could be exchanged for 12¢. The contents ranged from the normal problem-solving questions to algebra, ratios, and measurements. The advanced book even includes how to calculate interest rates, some book keeping and accounting, and tax information.

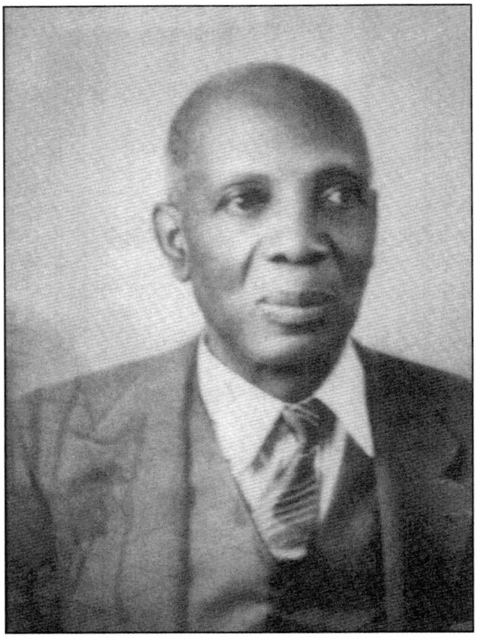

James Thomas Bridgeforth was a pioneer in establishing county schools for black children and was a prime mover in organizing Broadview School, where he was principal. When the county built a new high school for black students, he retired, and the new school was named in his honor. Professor Bridgeforth also taught summer school classes at his alma mater, Tennessee A&I State College, and was a minister in the AME church. (Courtesy of Agnes Bridgeforth.)

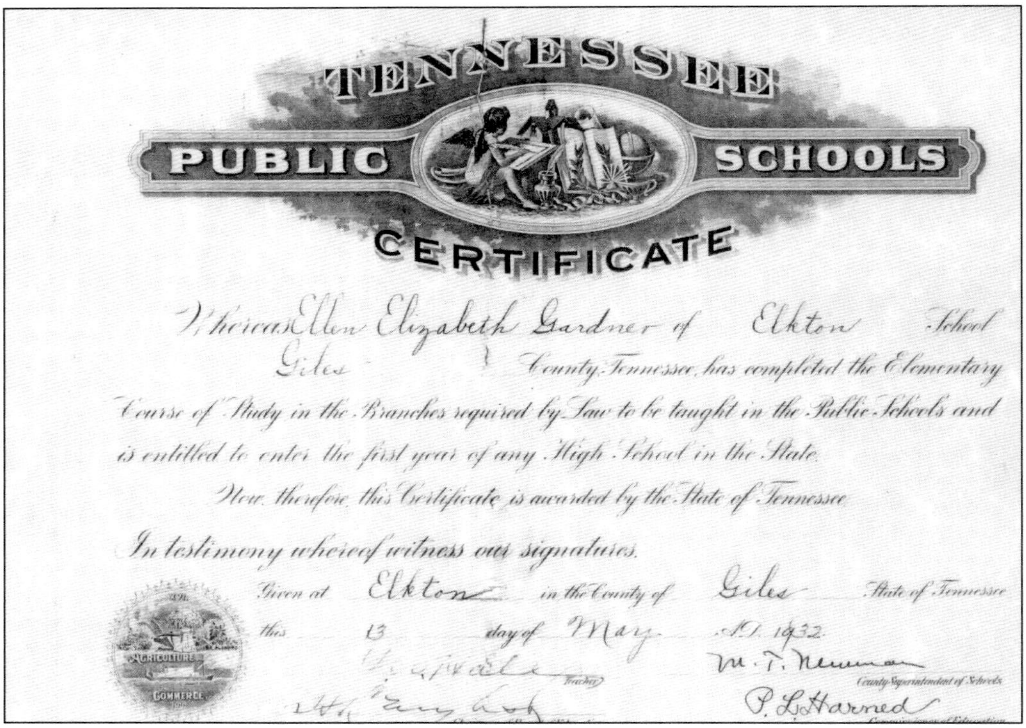

TENNESSEE

PUBLIC SCHOOLS

CERTIFICATE

Whereas Ellen Elizabeth Gardner of Elkton School Giles County, Tennessee, has completed the Elementary Course of Study in the Branches required by Law to be taught in the Public Schools and is entitled to enter the first year of any High School in the State.

Now, therefore, this Certificate is awarded by the State of Tennessee

In testimony whereof witness our signatures.

Given at Elkton in the County of Giles State of Tennessee this 13 day of May A.D. 1932

Teacher

M. T. Newman, County Superintendent of Schools

P. L. Harned

This Tennessee Public Schools certificate was awarded to Ellen Gardner in 1932 for graduating from Elkton's first public colored school. The certificate is for completion of elementary courses needed to enter any high school in Tennessee and is signed by then-principal George Hall. Elkton's first public colored school opened in January 1930 and was funded by the Rosenwald School Program and the Elkton community.

Three

Places of Praise and Worship

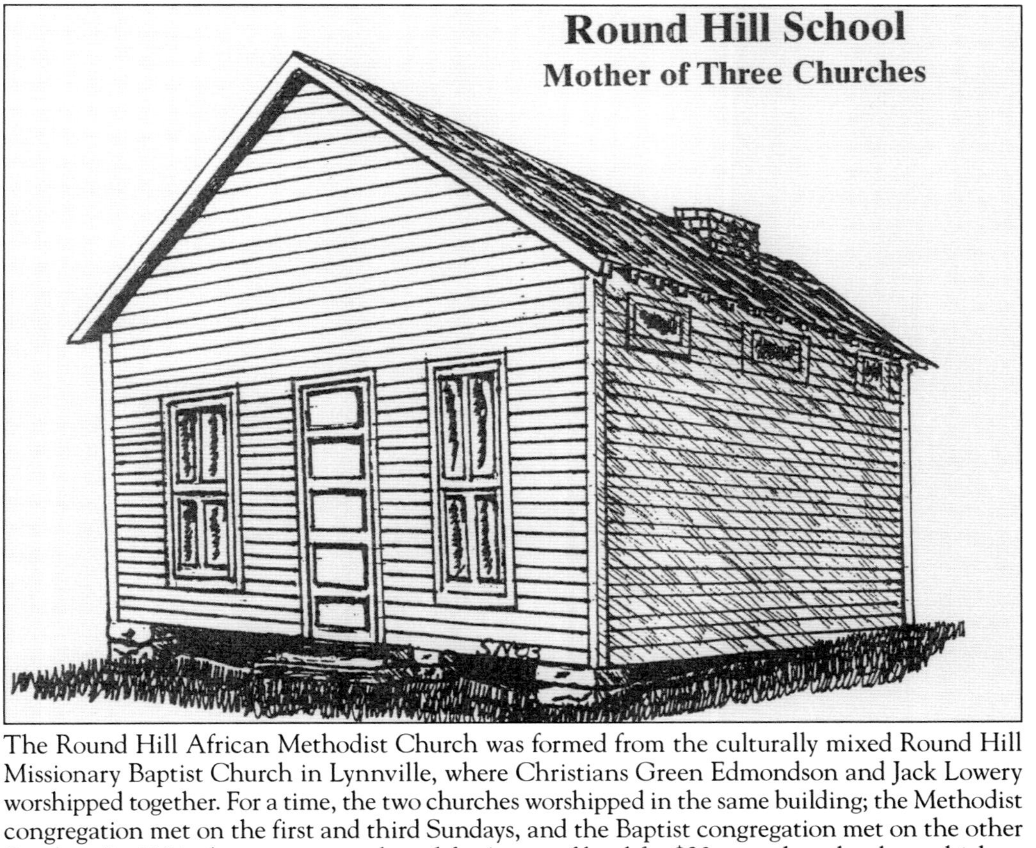

The Round Hill African Methodist Church was formed from the culturally mixed Round Hill Missionary Baptist Church in Lynnville, where Christians Green Edmondson and Jack Lowery worshipped together. For a time, the two churches worshipped in the same building; the Methodist congregation met on the first and third Sundays, and the Baptist congregation met on the other Sundays. In 1884, the trustees purchased for 1 acre of land for $30 near the school on which to build a church. (Courtesy of George and Sherry Newman.)

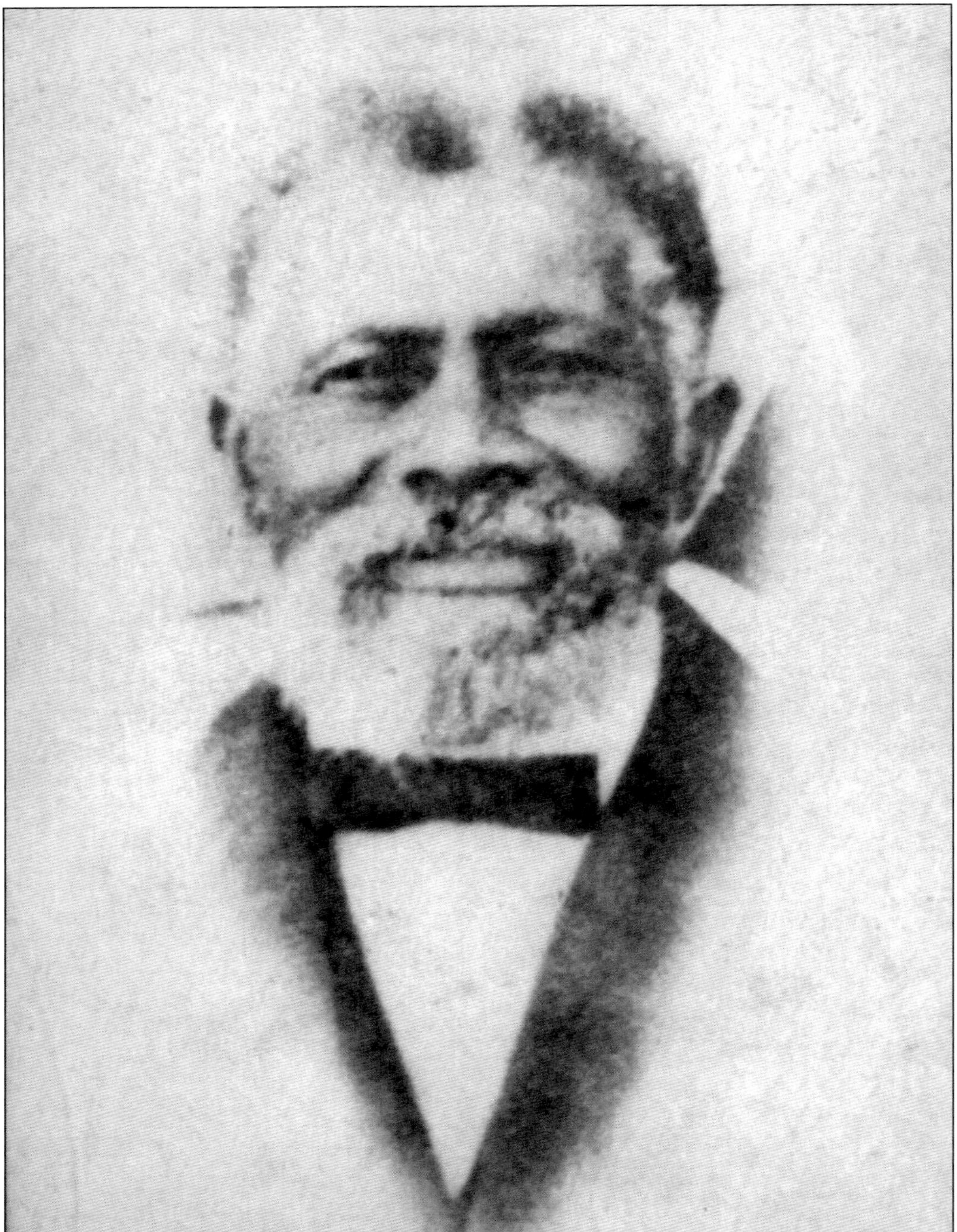

In 1902, Matt Gardner, a minister in Elkton, purchased a 15-acre gravel island in the middle of the Elk River to do baptisms for his congregation and other church congregations in the community. Matt traveled around Giles County, Tennessee, and Limestone County, Alabama, alternating Sundays preaching the word of God at different churches. He was the pastor of St. Rebecca Primitive Baptist in Conway and in 1911 became the pastor of the New Hope Primitive Baptist Church of Elkton. He was here until his death.

About 1870, a group of men met on the farm of Bland Brown in the Popular Hill community. They came together to discuss the need for a church. The group of ex-slaves selected Brown as their leader because he could read, write, and keep records. Bland spoke to his former owner Mr. Reed, a rich, generous landowner. Reed gave 2 acres of land, which he deeded to all the colored people of district 2 of Giles. In 1873, the members began to build Brown's Chapel African Methodist Episcopal Church. In 1910, Booker T. Washington spoke at the church. (Courtesy of George and Sherry Newman.)

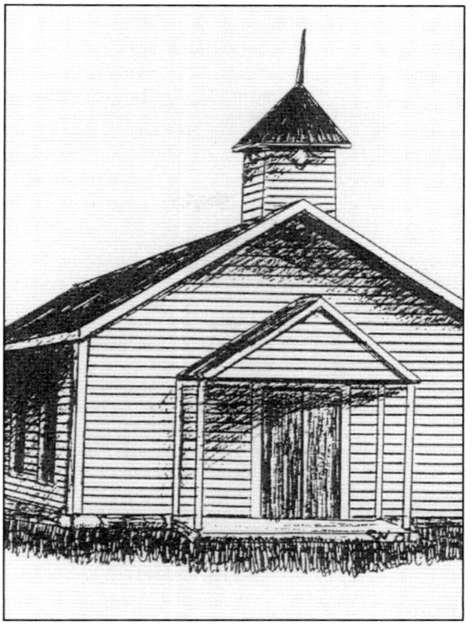

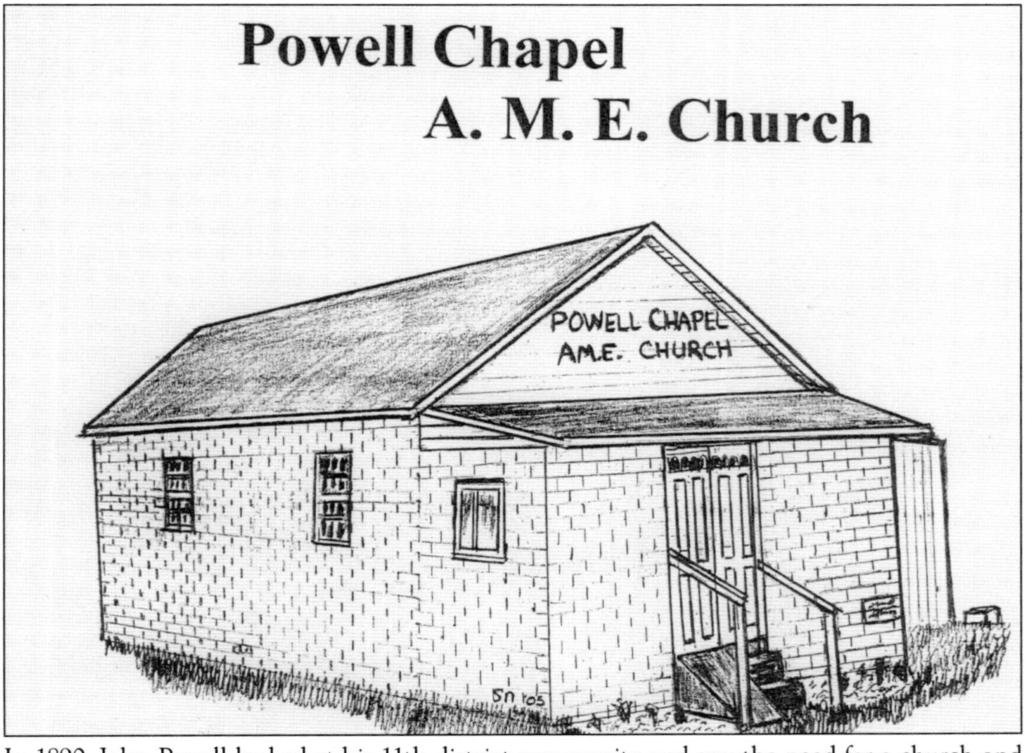

In 1890, John Powell looked at his 11th district community and saw the need for a church and school for blacks. On March 8, 1890, Powell gave a field of land to be used for both a school and church. In honor of the gift he had given, the church was named Powell Chapel African Methodist Episcopal Church. Reverend Ridley was the pastor for the first 12 years. (Courtesy of George and Sherry Newman.)

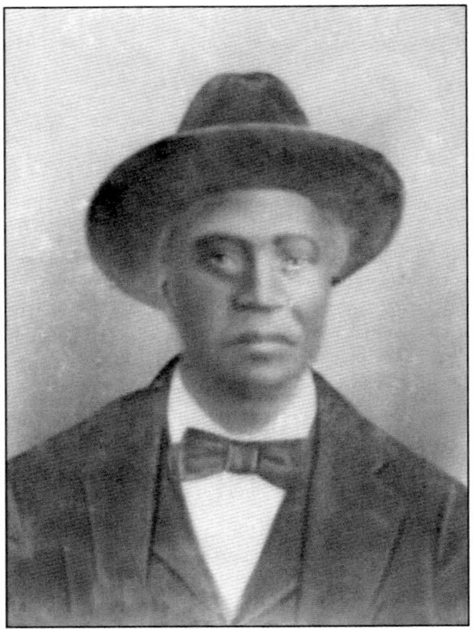

Sam Bridgeforth was born in Limestone County, Alabama, on November 13, 1846, to Miles Houston and Polly Baugh. Sam moved to Elkton at an early age and married Millie Gardner on February 27, 1868. To their marriage came 13 children: Martin, Asa, Hezekiah, William, David, Teao, Lula, Rachael, Marthey, Viola, Robert, Mitt, and Miles, who died in infancy. After Millie passed away, Sam married Henrietta Reedus on July 23, 1891, and to this union came 10 children: Della, Martha Jane, Rosa Nell, Naomi, Ellamentri, Robert, Henry, Ruth, and two children who died in infancy. (Courtesy of Lula Bridgeforth.)

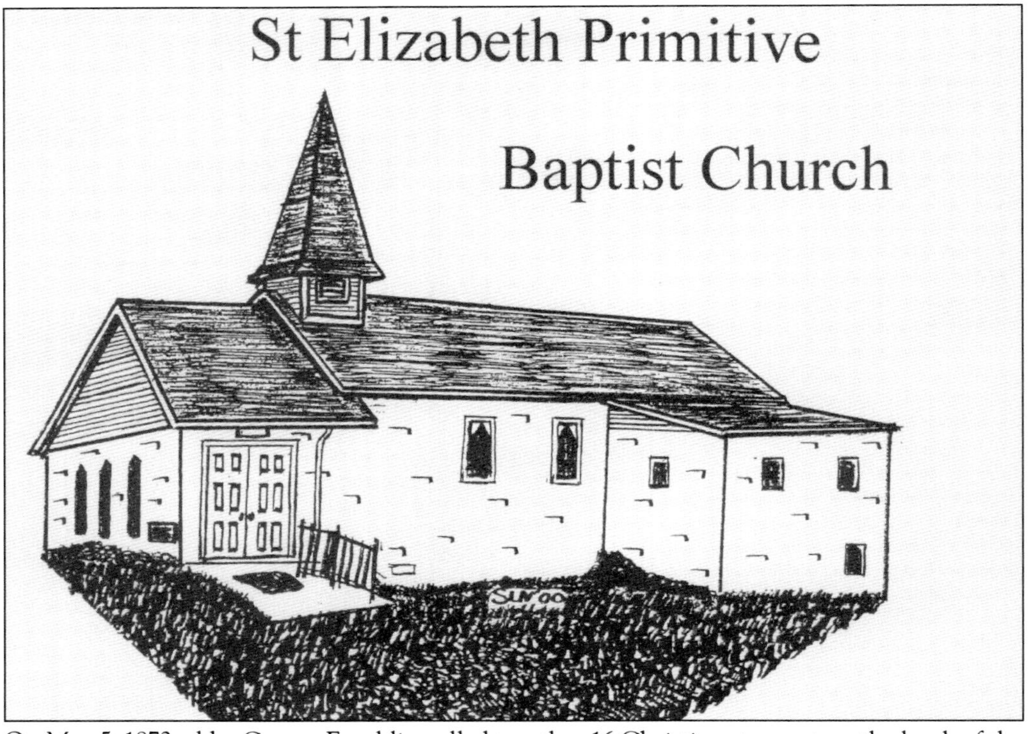

On May 5, 1873, elder George Franklin called together 16 Christians to meet on the bank of the Elk River in Elkton and organize the St. Elizabeth Primitive Baptist Church. The seven deacons of the early church were Spencer Sloss, Arthur King, George Gardner, Burly McLinn, Jim Simmons, Lott Grisby, and Tom Gardner. Other elders and pastors of the early church included Moses Matthews, Howell P. Swinea, Samuel Bridgeforth, and Raymond Gardner. Gardner served from 1914 until death in 1963. Gardner and his wife, Beulah, donated the land for the current church edifice. (Courtesy of George and Sherry Newman.)

This is a picture of St. Elizabeth Primitive Baptist Church's ledger containing the church members and their offerings for Sunday night's church anniversary on December 14, 1943. Most offerings ranged from 25¢ to 50¢, and it appears that between the offering and dues for this anniversary, a grand total of about $10.12 was collected.

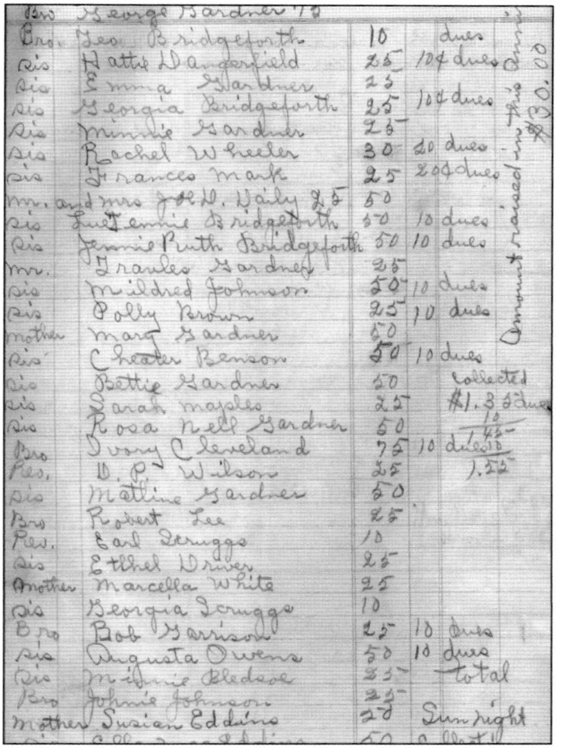

Bro	George Gardner	12	
Bro.	Geo Bridgeforth	10	dues
Sis	Hattie Dangerfield	25	10¢ dues
Sis	Emma Gardner	25	
Sis	Georgia Bridgeforth	25	10¢ dues
Sis	Minnie Gardner	25	
Sis	Rachel Wheeler	30	10 dues
Sis	Frances Mark	25	20¢ dues
Mr. and Mrs	John D. Daily 25	50	
Sis	Lue Jennie Bridgeforth	50	10 dues
Sis	Jennie Ruth Bridgeforth	50	10 dues
Mr.	Francis Gardner	25	
Sis	Mildred Johnson	50	10 dues
Sis	Polly Brown	25	10 dues
Mother	Mary Gardner	50	
Sis	Chester Benson	50	10 dues
Sis	Bettie Gardner	50	collected
Sis	Sarah Maples	25	$1.35 dues
Sis	Rosa Nell Gardner	50	
Bro	Ivory Cleveland	75	10 dues
Rev.	D. P. Wilson	25	
Sis	Mattline Gardner	50	
Bro	Robert Lee	25	
Rev.	Earl Scruggs	10	
Sis	Ethel Driver	25	
Mother	Marcella White	25	
Sis	Georgia Scruggs	10	
Bro	Bob Garrison	25	10 dues
Sis	Augusta Owens	50	10 dues
Sis	Minnie Bledsoe	25	total
Bro	Johnie Johnson	25	
Mother	Susian Eddins	50	Sun night

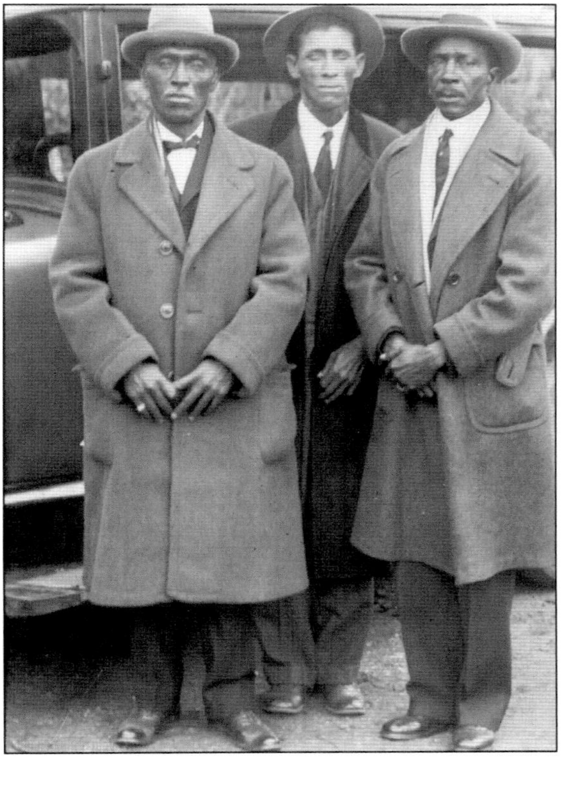

Pictured are, from left to right, Revs. Harvey Butler, Raymond Gardner, and Sam Walter—all men of the gospel. Whether Missionary Baptist or Primitive Baptist ministers, all fellowshipped together from time to time. Some were pastor of more than one church at a time, and others rotated each Sunday in a month to a different church in and around Giles County.

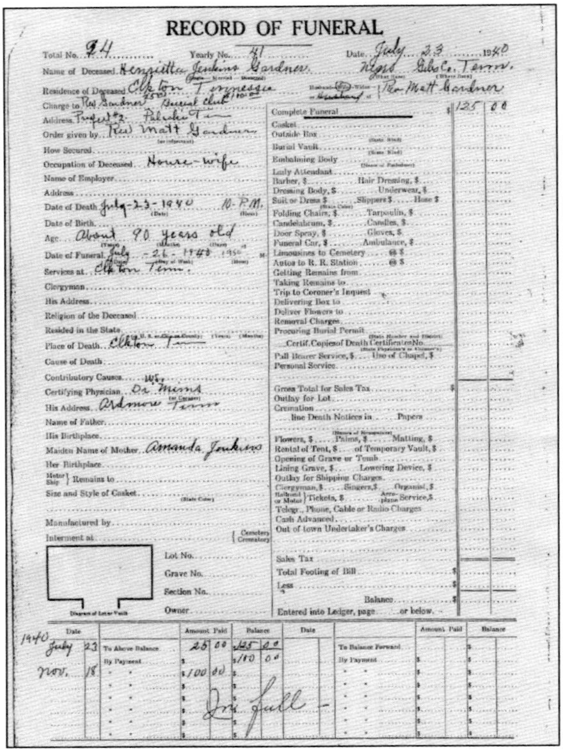

RECORD OF FUNERAL

Total No. 94 Yearly No. 41 Date July 23 1940

Name of Deceased Henrietta Jenkins Gardner Negro Giles Co. Tenn.

Residence of Deceased Elkton Tennessee Husband or Wife of Rev Matt Gardner

Charge to Rev Gardner $25.00 Burial club $100.00

Address Project #2 Pulaski Tenn

Order given by Rev Matt Gardner

How Secured

Occupation of Deceased House-wife

Name of Employer

Address

Date of Death July-23-1940 10-P.M.

Date of Birth

Age About 90 years old

Date of Funeral July -26- 1940 1950

Services at Elkton Tenn.

Clergyman

His Address

Religion of the Deceased

Resided in the State

Place of Death Elkton Tenn

Cause of Death

Contributory Causes

Certifying Physician Dr Mims

His Address Ardmore Tenn

Name of Father

His Birthplace

Maiden Name of Mother Amanda Jenkins

Her Birthplace

Motor/Ship Remains to

Size and Style of Casket

Manufactured by

Interment at (Cemetery/Crematory)

Lot No. Grave No. Section No. Owner

Diagram of Lot or Vault

Complete Funeral $125.00

Casket; Outside Box; Burial Vault; Embalming Body; Lady Attendant; Barber, $ Hair Dressing, $; Dressing Body, $ Underwear, $; Suit or Dress $ Slippers $ Hose $; Folding Chairs, $ Tarpaulin, $; Candelabrum, $ Candles, $; Door Spray, $ Gloves, $; Funeral Car, $ Ambulance, $; Limousines to Cemetery @ $; Autos to R. R. Station @ $; Getting Remains from; Taking Remains to; Trip to Coroner's Inquest; Delivering Box to; Deliver Flowers to; Removal Charges; Procuring Burial Permit; Certif. Copies of Death Certificates No.; Pall Bearer Service, $ Use of Chapel, $; Personal Service

Gross Total for Sales Tax $; Outlay for Lot; Cremation; line Death Notices in Papers; Flowers, $ Palms, $ Matting, $; Rental of Tent, $ of Temporary Vault, $; Opening of Grave or Tomb; Lining Grave, $ Lowering Device, $; Outlay for Shipping Charges; Clergyman, $ Singers, $ Organist, $; Railroad or Motor Tickets, $ Aeroplane Service, $; Telegr., Phone, Cable or Radio Charges; Cash Advanced; Out of town Undertaker's Charges

Sales Tax; Total Footing of Bill $; Less $; Balance $; Entered into Ledger, page or below.

Date			Amount Paid	Balance
1940 July	23	To Above Balance	25.00	125.00
		By Payment		100.00
Nov.	18		100.00	

In full

Pictured is a 1940 funeral record from Queen Anne's Funeral Home in Pulaski. The record shows that this person is the 41st individual the funeral home has prepared for burial in that year. Records also show that Dr. Wright Sylvester Mims of Ardmore, Tennessee, was the attending physician and the total cost of the funeral was $125, of which the burial club paid $100. Myrtle (Wilson) Nelson went to the houses of burial club members every month to collect 35¢ for their participation in the club. Some time later, the name was changed to the burial association. (Courtesy of Anne Brown.)

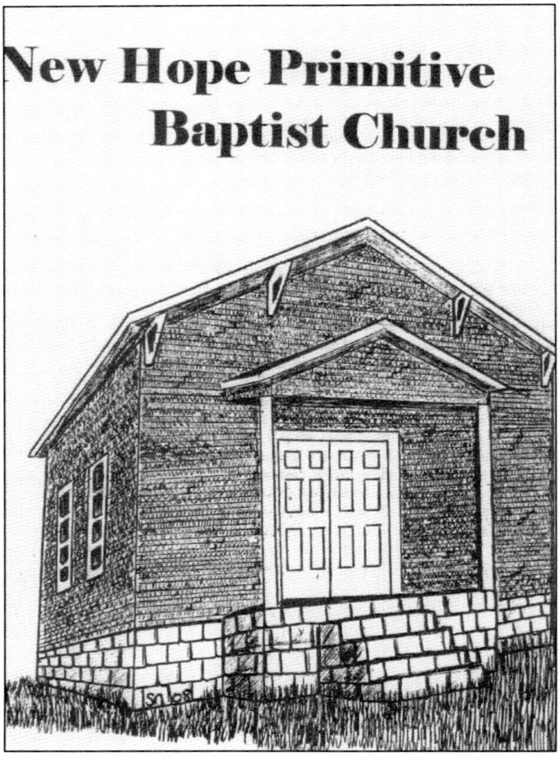

New Hope Primitive Baptist Church in the Conway community is one of oldest African American churches in Giles County. Cousins Wiley and Cal Gardner and Ralph Holt organized the church in 1870. Minnie Vasser, a white woman, gave the members the land to build the church on. The church had a floating pastor for many years, then came Pastor William Green and Joe McKlin, who was an assistant pastor for 63 years. The first permanent local pastor of the church was Rev. Matt Gardner. (Courtesy of Roosevelt Whitfield.)

Even though it has no membership today, New Hope Primitive Baptist Church still stands and looks as it did 139 years ago. The church has a total of 25 pews. Pictures of their most memorable pastors, Matt and Raymond Gardner, still hang on the wall after many years. There was no running water, so there was no baptism pool; this was a river baptism church. (Courtesy of Roosevelt Whitfield.)

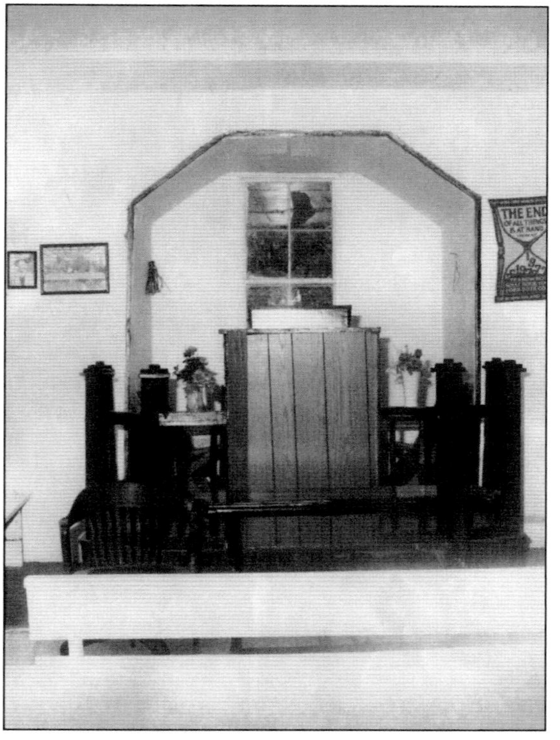

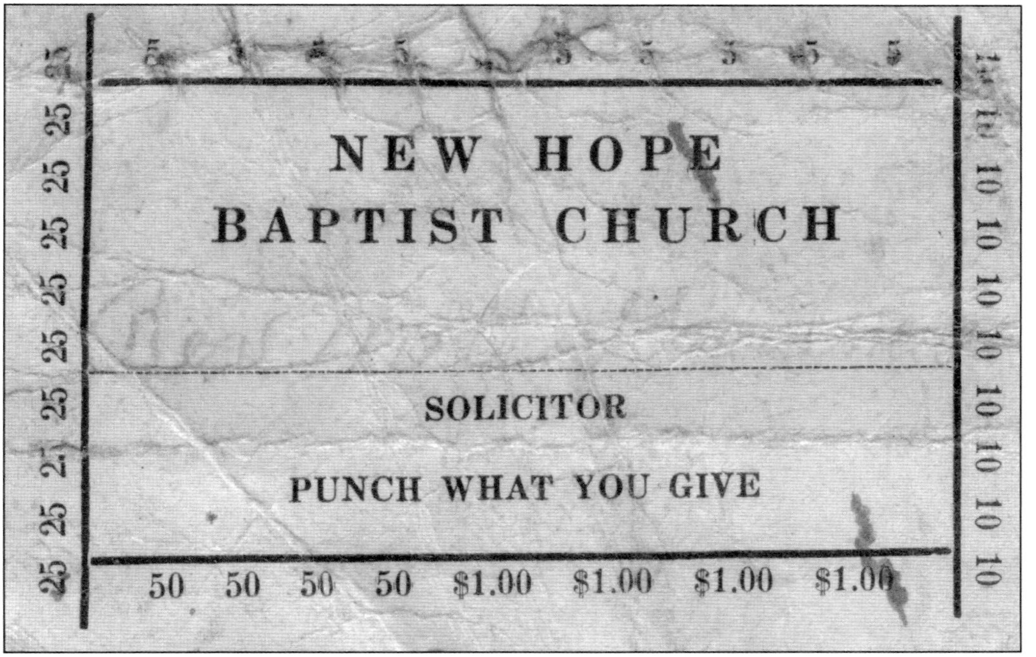

This picture shows how New Hope Primitive Baptist Church and others kept a record of their members' contributions of tithes and offerings—by having them write their name on the back of a punch card and punch out the amount of money that they were giving. The card would go in the basket along with the money. The solicitor would be the pastor of the church.

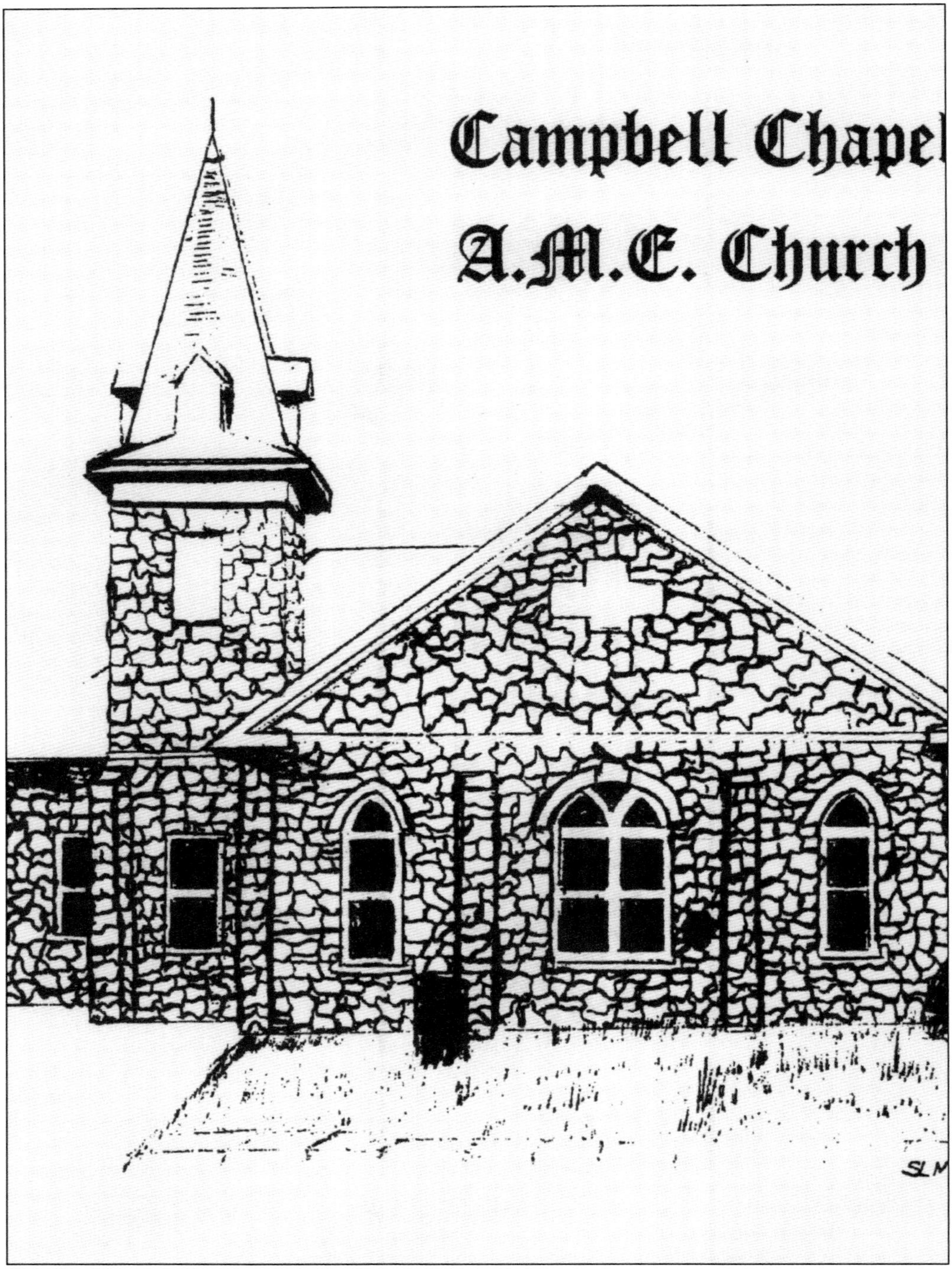

Campbell Chapel African Methodist Episcopal Church was organized in southeast Pulaski in 1873 in what was known as "Methodist Bottom." The church was actually built on the corner of Flower and South Rhodes Streets. The church was named after one of its two founders, Reverend Campbell and A. Thomas Hill. The church is now on the National Registry of Historical Places. (Courtesy of George and Sherry Newman.)

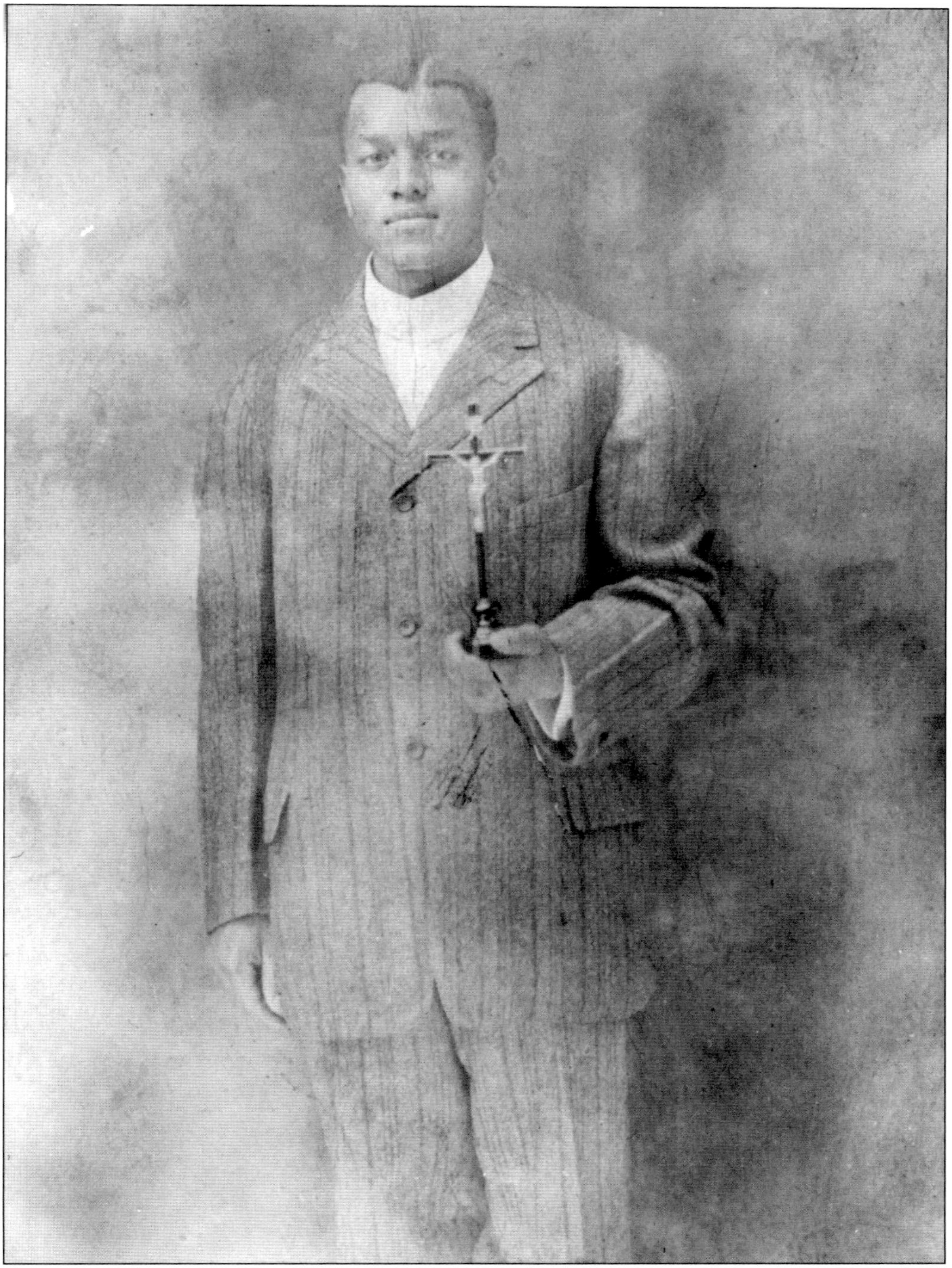

James Alex Davis, a minister, is seen in a very nice clergy shirt and pin-striped suit and holding a crucifix. He was born in 1859 in Pulaski. He was the son of Robert and Sarah Davis, and his siblings were Alice, John, James, and William. On December 13, 1876, he married Isabella (Pruitt Lewis), and the couple had four children. James died in 1947 in Indianapolis, Indiana. (Courtesy of Philena Morgan.)

Phoenix Chapel A. M. E. Church

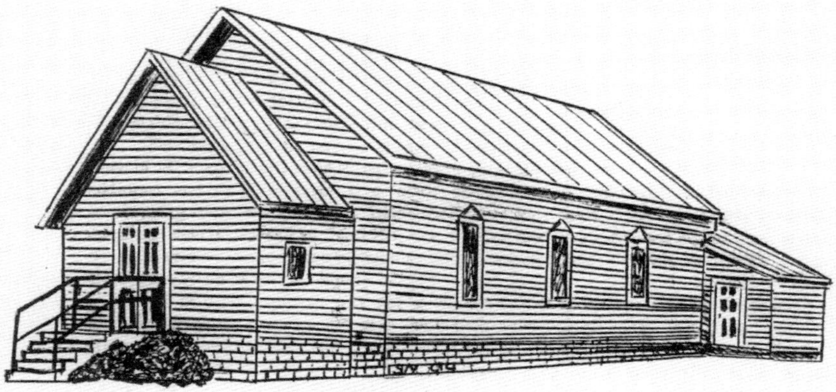

In the mid-1800s, there was movement to build black churches, schools, and lodges in rural areas of Giles. It was during this time that Phoenix Chapel African Methodist Church was built on a hill north of the Prospect community's depot. The land to build the church was purchased from Dr. Joseph Gray Mason. In 1917, the first church was declared unsafe, and the congregation had to move to another building; in 1928 that edifice burned down. In 1930, a new church was built. Pastors of the church include Rev. D. G. Rose. (Courtesy of George and Sherry Newman.)

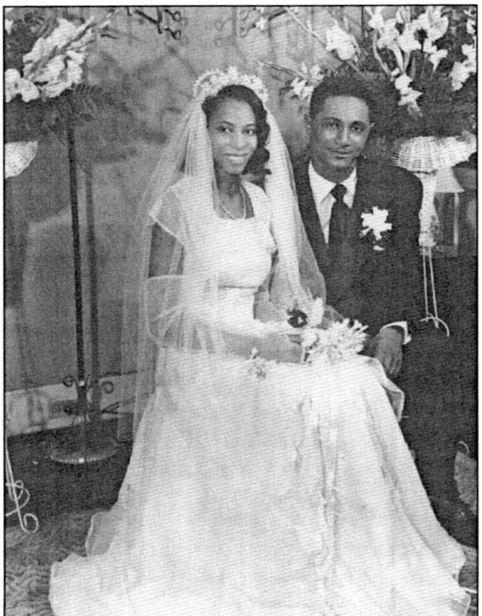

Weddings, held in churches today, were in early years commonly held in the bride's home, as seen in this wedding picture of Martin Luther Gardner Sr. and Mildred Louise Johnson. Martin was born on February 22, 1919, to Raymond and Frances Gardner. He was raised and educated in the community of Elkton. Martin later moved to Louisville, Kentucky, and served in U.S. Navy. On May 17, 1949, he married Mildred, and to their marriage came three sons: Martin Luther Jr., Thomas Livelle, and Nathaniel Albert. (Courtesy of Martin Gardner Jr.)

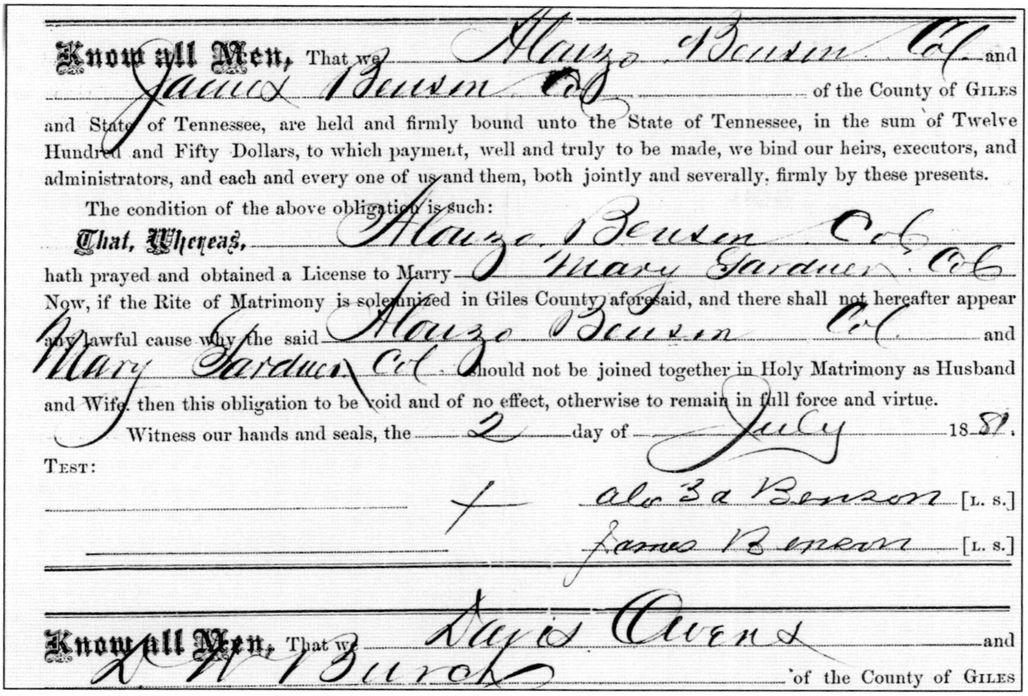

Know all Men, That we Alonzo Benson Col and James Benson Col of the County of Giles and State of Tennessee, are held and firmly bound unto the State of Tennessee, in the sum of Twelve Hundred and Fifty Dollars, to which payment, well and truly to be made, we bind our heirs, executors, and administrators, and each and every one of us and them, both jointly and severally, firmly by these presents.

The condition of the above obligation is such:

That, Whereas, Alonzo Benson Col hath prayed and obtained a License to Marry Mary Gardner Col Now, if the Rite of Matrimony is solemnized in Giles County aforesaid, and there shall not hereafter appear any lawful cause why the said Alonzo Benson Col and Mary Gardner Col should not be joined together in Holy Matrimony as Husband and Wife, then this obligation to be void and of no effect, otherwise to remain in full force and virtue.

Witness our hands and seals, the 2 day of July 1881.

Test:

+ alo Za Benson [L. S.]

James Benson [L. S.]

Know all Men, That we Davis Owens and D W Burch of the County of Giles

This is a $1,250 marriage bond paid by Alonzo and James Benson for the marriage of Alonzo to Mary (Gardner) Benson on July 2, 1881. Alonzo was a well-known carpenter in the community and built many homes in and around Giles County. To Alonzo and Mary's union was born one child, Georgia Lee Benson. The marriage bond was to be used for child and spousal support in case the husband left or died. (Courtesy Giles County Old Records Department.)

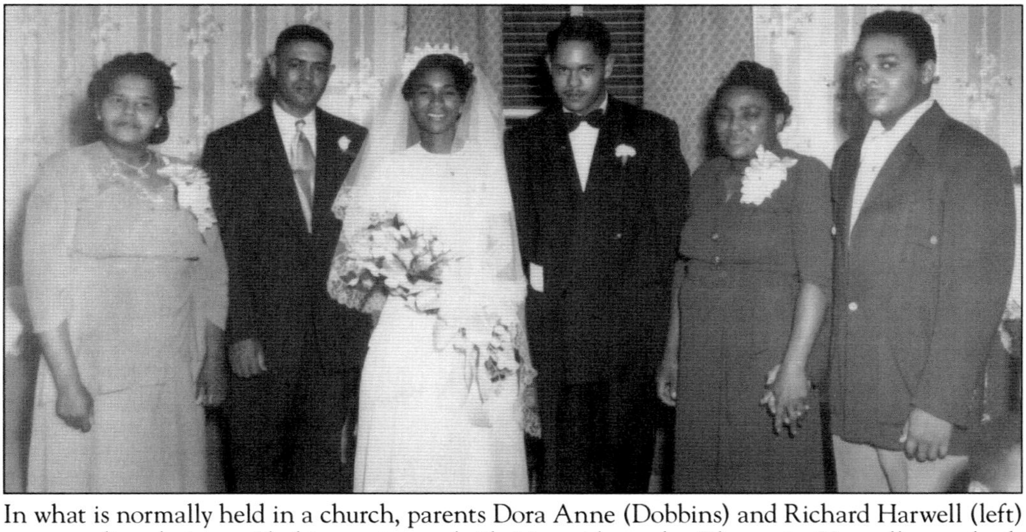

In what is normally held in a church, parents Dora Anne (Dobbins) and Richard Harwell (left) are attending their son Clark's marriage to bride Mary Alexander. The senior Harwells were both raised and educated in the Aspen Hill community. They married on May 5, 1929, and to their marriage came children Richard, Clark, David, Oscar, Ella Mary, Magaline, Ida Lu, and Rose. The other couple in the picture is the bride's parents, John and Cora Alexander. (Courtesy of Clark Harwell.)

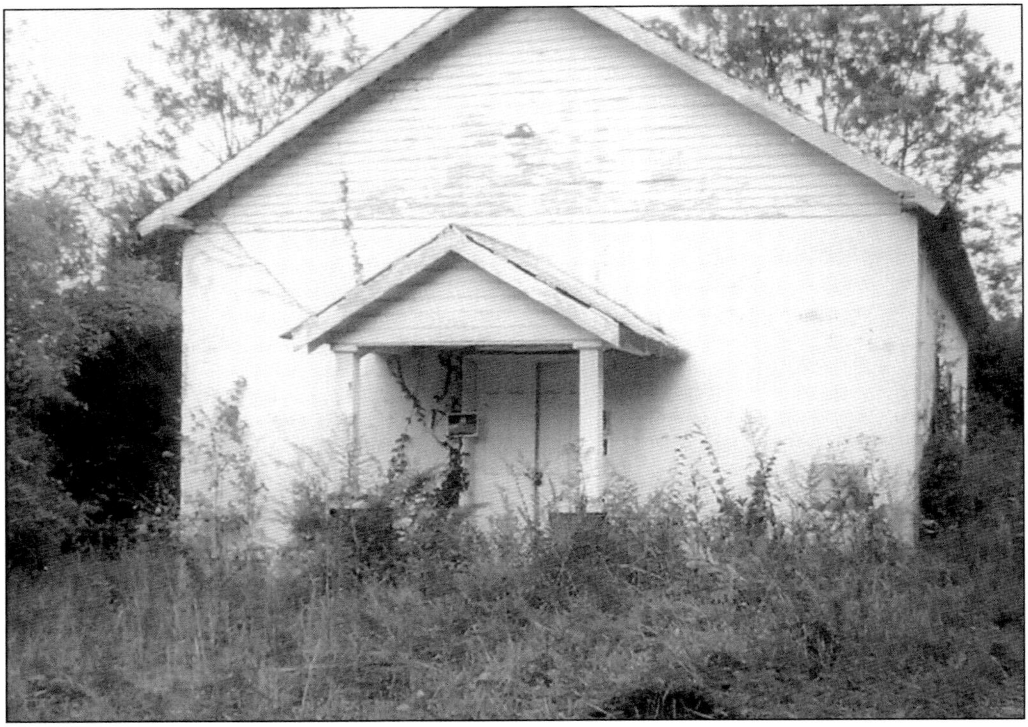

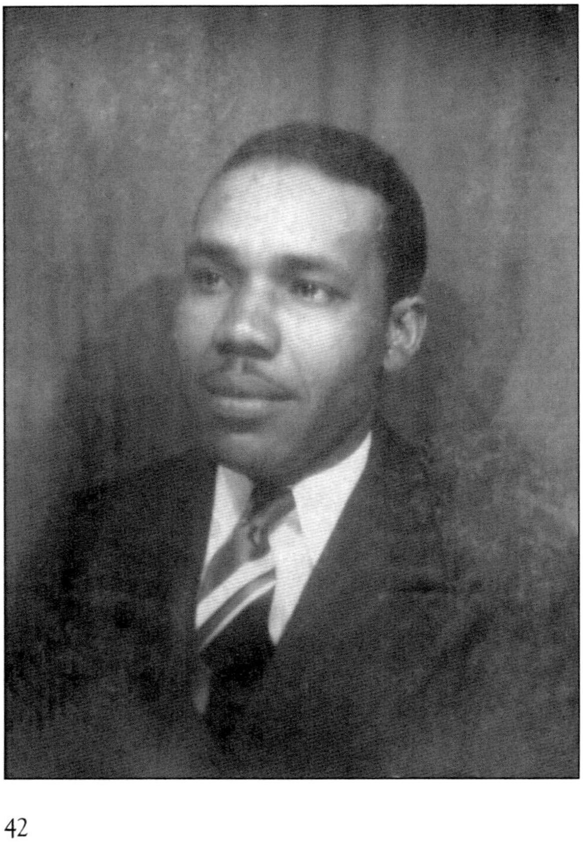

Lilburn Chapel AME Church is located in the Riversburg community. The first building was constructed in 1882 and, like the majority of early African American churches, served as both a church and school. One of the known pastors of the church was D. A. Holbert. Like so many rural churches before, Lilburn Chapel AME Church fell victim to people moving away. (Courtesy of George and Sherry Newman.)

Rev. Shellie Lee Gardner was born on March 20, 1906, in Elkton, Tennessee. His parents were Atha and Ether (Bonner) Gardner. Shellie was raised and educated in Elkton. He was also a U.S. Army veteran of World War II. After the war, he never returned to Elkton to live but came several times a year to visit family and friends.

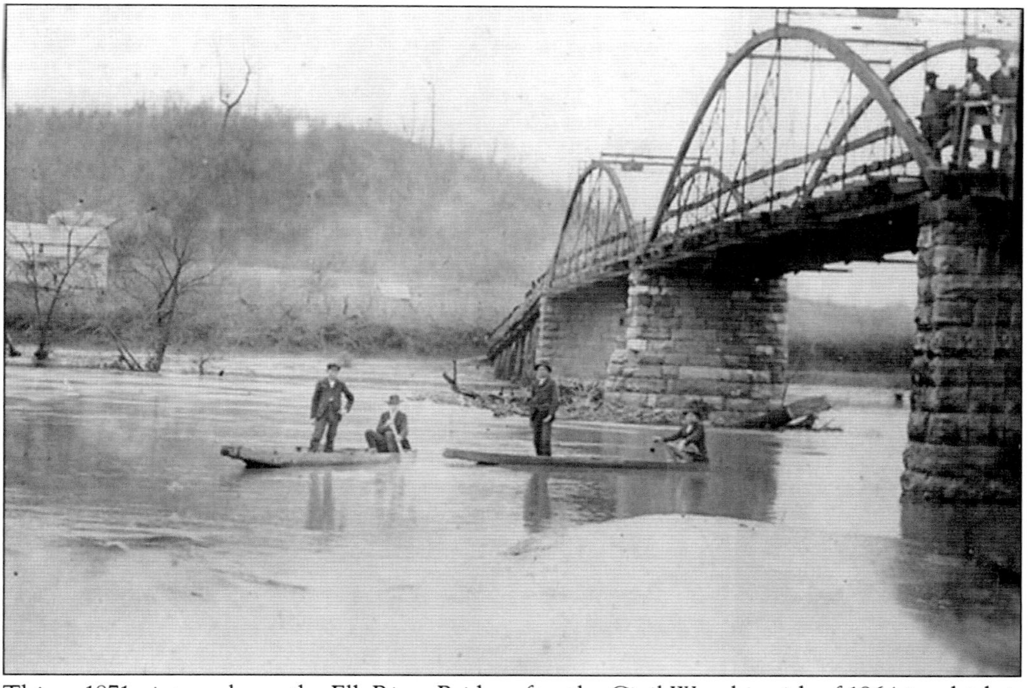

This *c.* 1871 picture shows the Elk River Bridge after the Civil War skirmish of 1864 in which it was destroyed. The Elkton River is where many local African American church baptisms took place. Witnesses lined the banks of the river and the bridge to see loved ones submerged in the water in the name of the Father, Son, and the Holy Ghost and sang that old African American spiritual "Take Me to the Water to Be Baptized." (Courtesy of Ann Smith.)

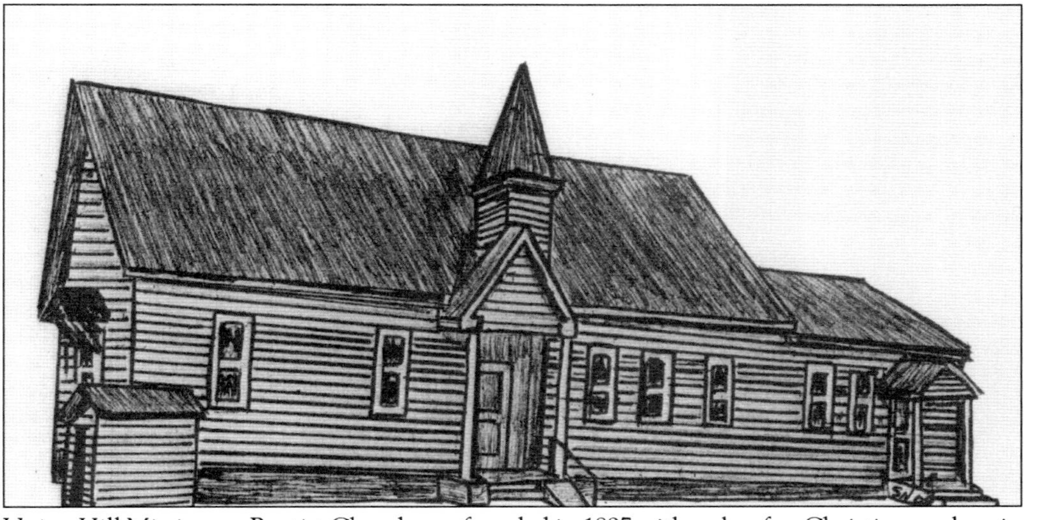

Union Hill Missionary Baptist Church was founded in 1897 with only a few Christian workers in Elkton. The first church was under the leadership of Julius S. Scruggs, who served for many years. The current church is the old historic Rosenwald School for blacks. It was built in 1929, and etched in the wood are the names of the individuals of the community who were helping to build the school on August 31, 1929. Those names are J. T. Phillips, A. McConnell, N. W. Cook, H. Johns, J. Howell, A. Williamson, and Clyde Williamson. (Courtesy of George and Sherry Newman.)

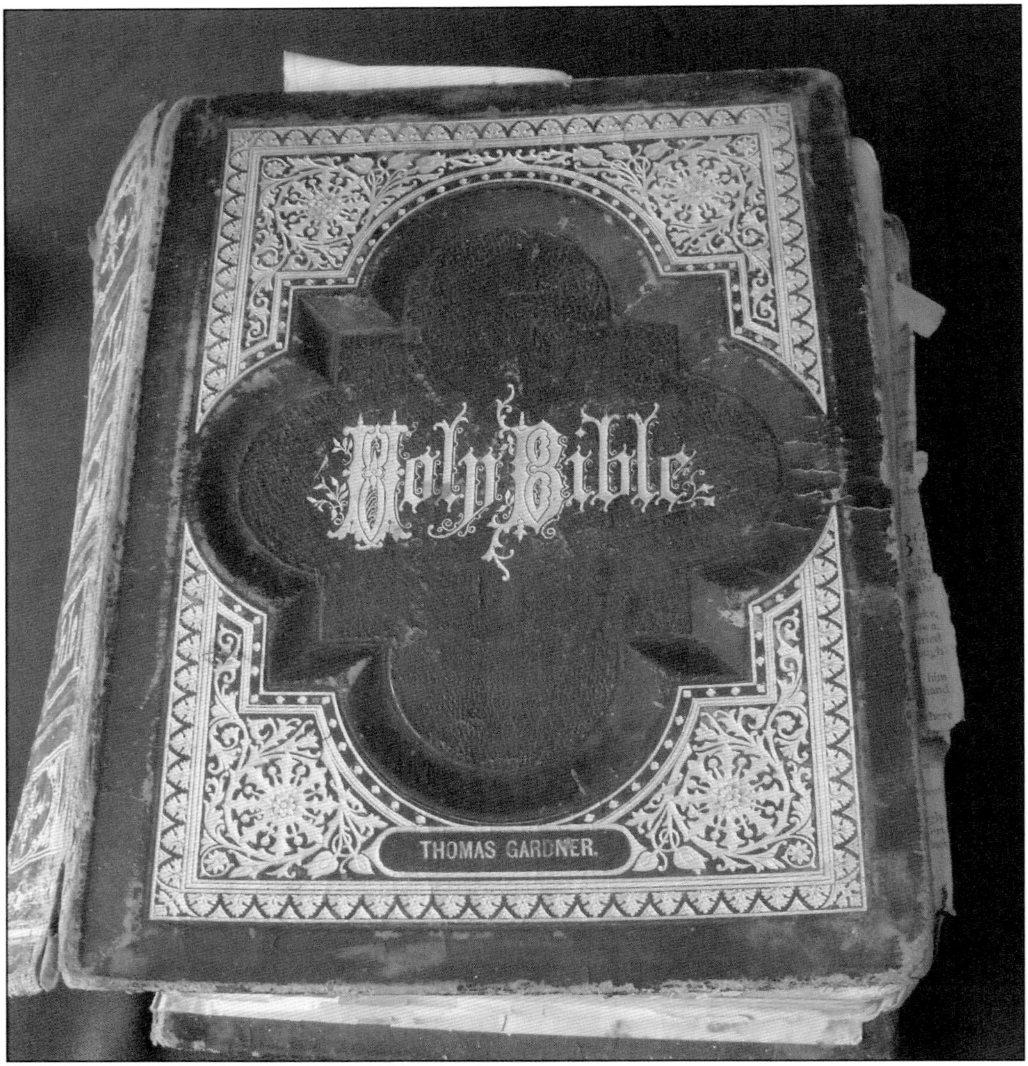

This leather-bound, embossed Bible, inscribed to Thomas Gardner, is over 135 years old. The Peoples Standard Edition Bible contains the Old and New Testaments, the Apocrypha (the hidden books of the Bible), a concordance, the Psalms, and a dictionary. It has over 500 steel engravings and illustrations of Biblical scenery, maps, and events. There are Jewish and Egyptian antiquities, histories of many religious denominations, and so much more. The publishers of the Bible were J. C. McCurdy and Company and P. W. Ziegler and Company of Philadelphia, Chicago, Cincinnati, and St. Louis.

Four

Family and Friends

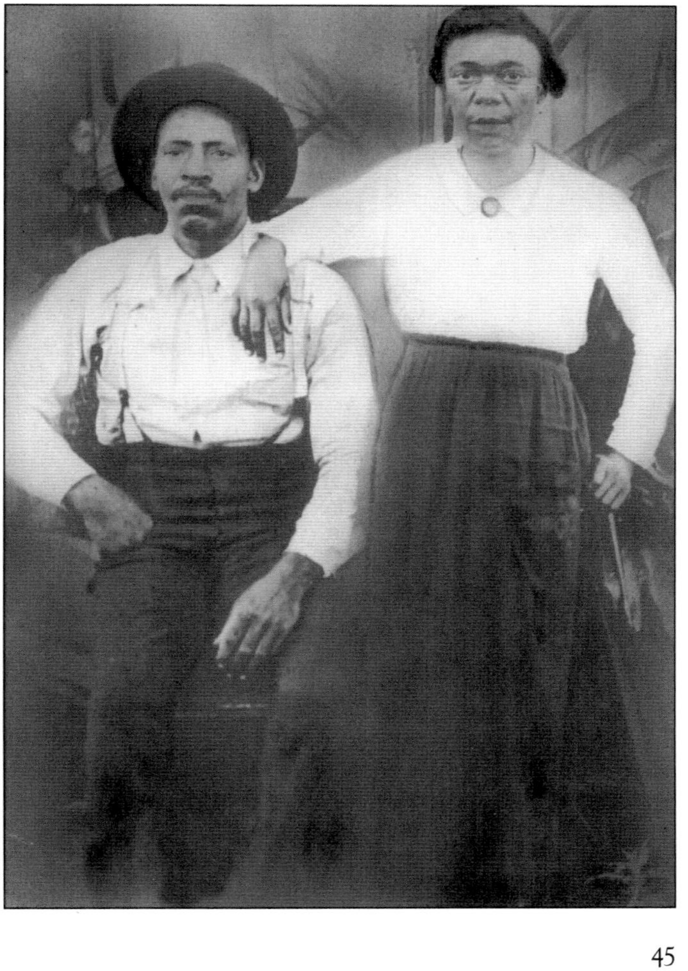

Prince and Georgia (Benson) Stevenson were lifelong residents of Giles County. The couple wed on December 28, 1903. Georgia was born on June 18, 1882, and her mother, Mary (Gardner) Benson, died on January 5, 1885. After her mother's death, she lived with and was raised by her grandparents Tom and Rachael Gardner. Prince was employed as a laborer and was also a farmer, and the couple's children were May Sue, Henry Lee, Alonzo, Eva, and Emma. (Courtesy of Emma Bledsoe.)

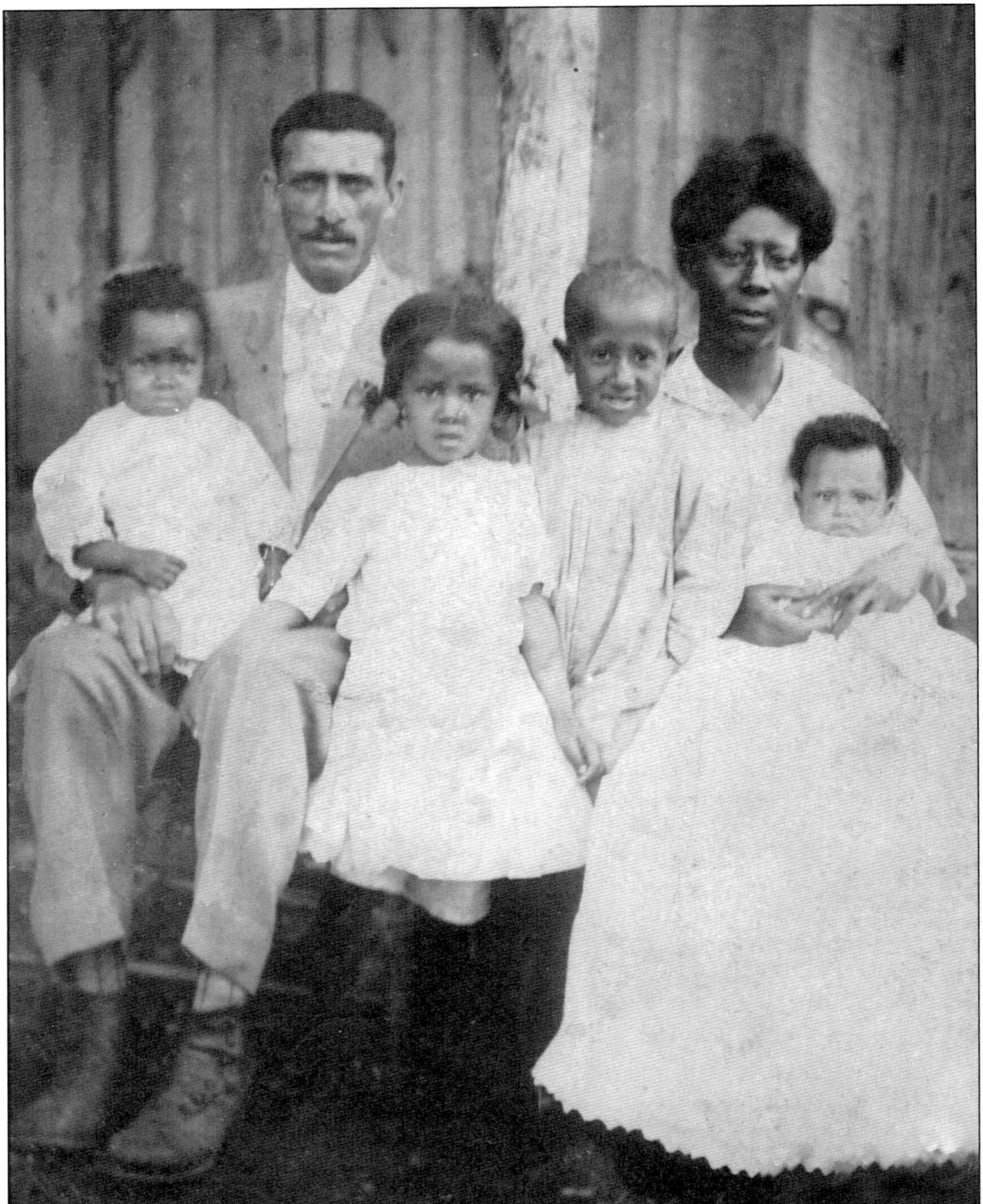

Raymond and Frances Gardner are shown here with their children (from left to right) Katherine "Moose," Henrietta, Lemond, and Clyde "Jack." Raymond attended elementary and high school in Giles County and Tuskegee Institute, in Tuskegee, Alabama. He was going to college to become a teacher when he, like his father, Matt, was called into the ministry. Raymond married Frances Gardner on December 27, 1906. After giving birth to her 10 children—Cleveland, Lemond, Henrietta, Catherine, Clyde, Matt, Madelene, Raymond Jr., Martin, and John Robert—Frances passed away, and Raymond married Beulah King on December 17, 1922. Beulah raised all 10 children as her own.

Richard and Florinda (Holt) Gardner lived in the Dixontown community of Giles their entire lives. Florinda came from a prosperous family in Giles. Richard was a farmer and also came from a prosperous and influential family. Even though Richard and Florinda never had any children together, Richard had three children, Ben, Howard, and Mildred Gardner.

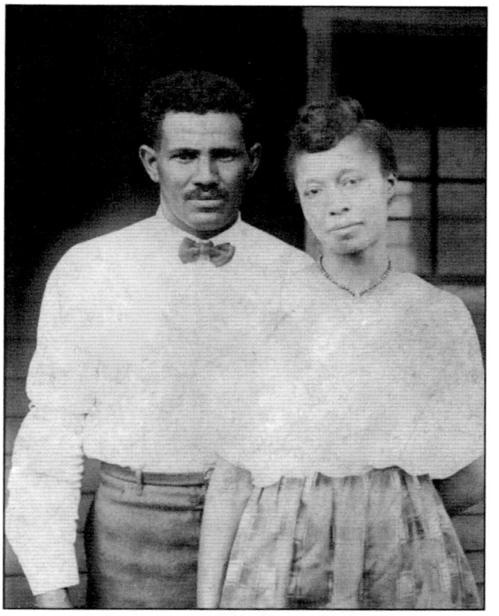

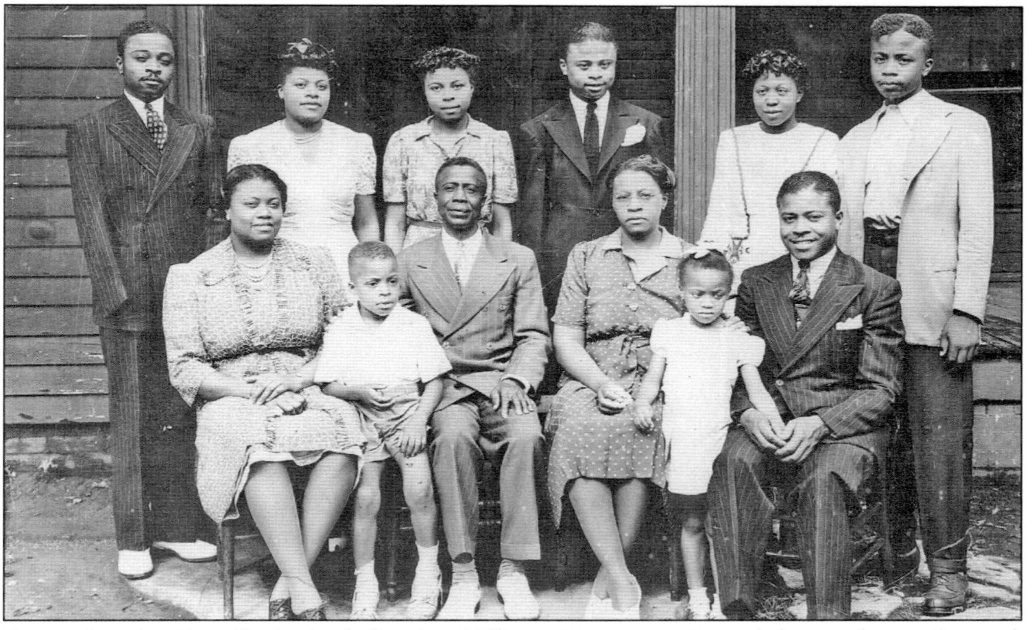

Pictured is the Teao Bridgeforth family of Elkton, Tennessee. From left to right are (sitting) daughter Lura, grandchild Thomas Gardner, Teao, wife Mary, grandchild Davies (Gardner), and son Leroy; (standing) son Oakley, daughters Laura and Lucinda, son Asa, daughter Roberta, and son George. Son John Robert is not pictured. Teao was the 13th child of Sam Bridgeforth and his first wife, Millie (Gardner) Bridgeforth. He was born in 1888 and lived and farmed in the Elkton community. His mother, Millie, died six months after his birth, and his father, Sam, then married Henrietta Reedus. Between his father's two marriages, Teao had 22 sisters and brothers. He married Mary Holt on March 12, 1911. Teao later moved his family to Nashville, where he and his wife continued to raise their family. After taking ill, he moved to Chicago with his daughter and died in 1969. (Courtesy of George Bridgeforth.)

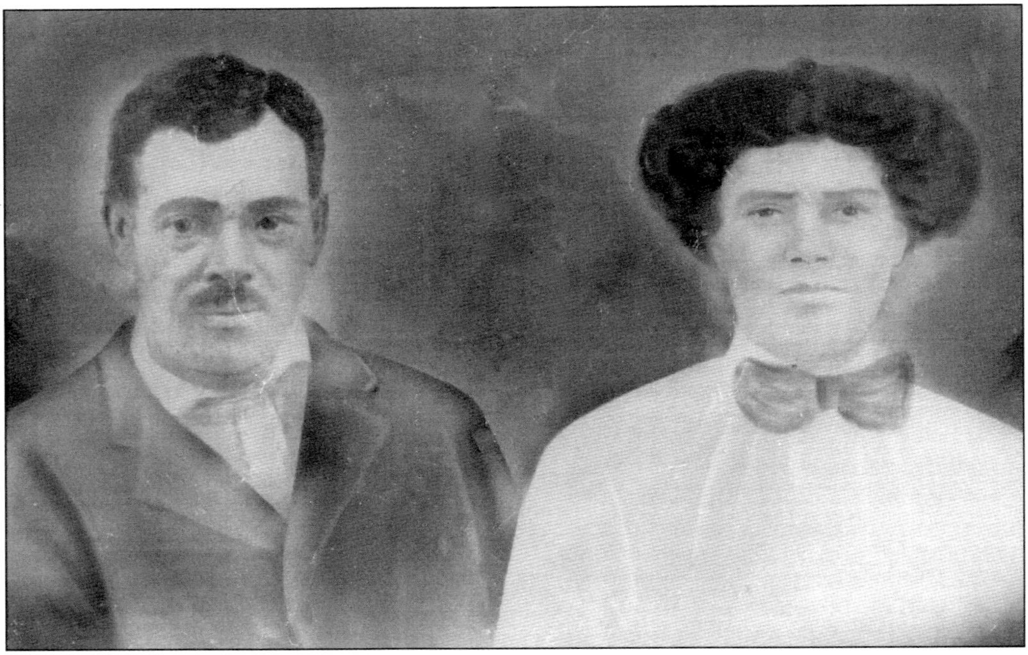

Richard and Mary (Foust) Harwell were both born and raised in the Aspen Hill community. Richard was born in June 1869 and Mary on November 1870. It is believed that Mary's parents were William and Lucinda Foust, and Richard's mother was Mandy Harwell. The couple were married on December 24, 1888, and to their union came 10 children: Louise, Birdie, Emma, Myrtle, Theodore, Blanche, Bessie, Richard Jr., Pinkie, and Susie. (Courtesy of Clark Harwell.)

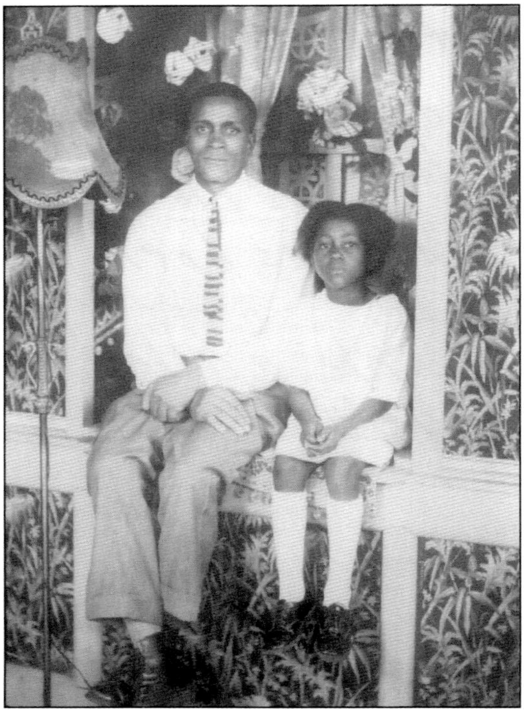

Ervis Vassar is pictured here with his six-year-old daughter, Lillar Mae. Ervis's parents were Martha and Manville "Man" Vassar. Ervis was born and raised in Elkton and went to school there. Ervis married Bertha (Blair) on December 22, 1914. (Courtesy of John Vassar.)

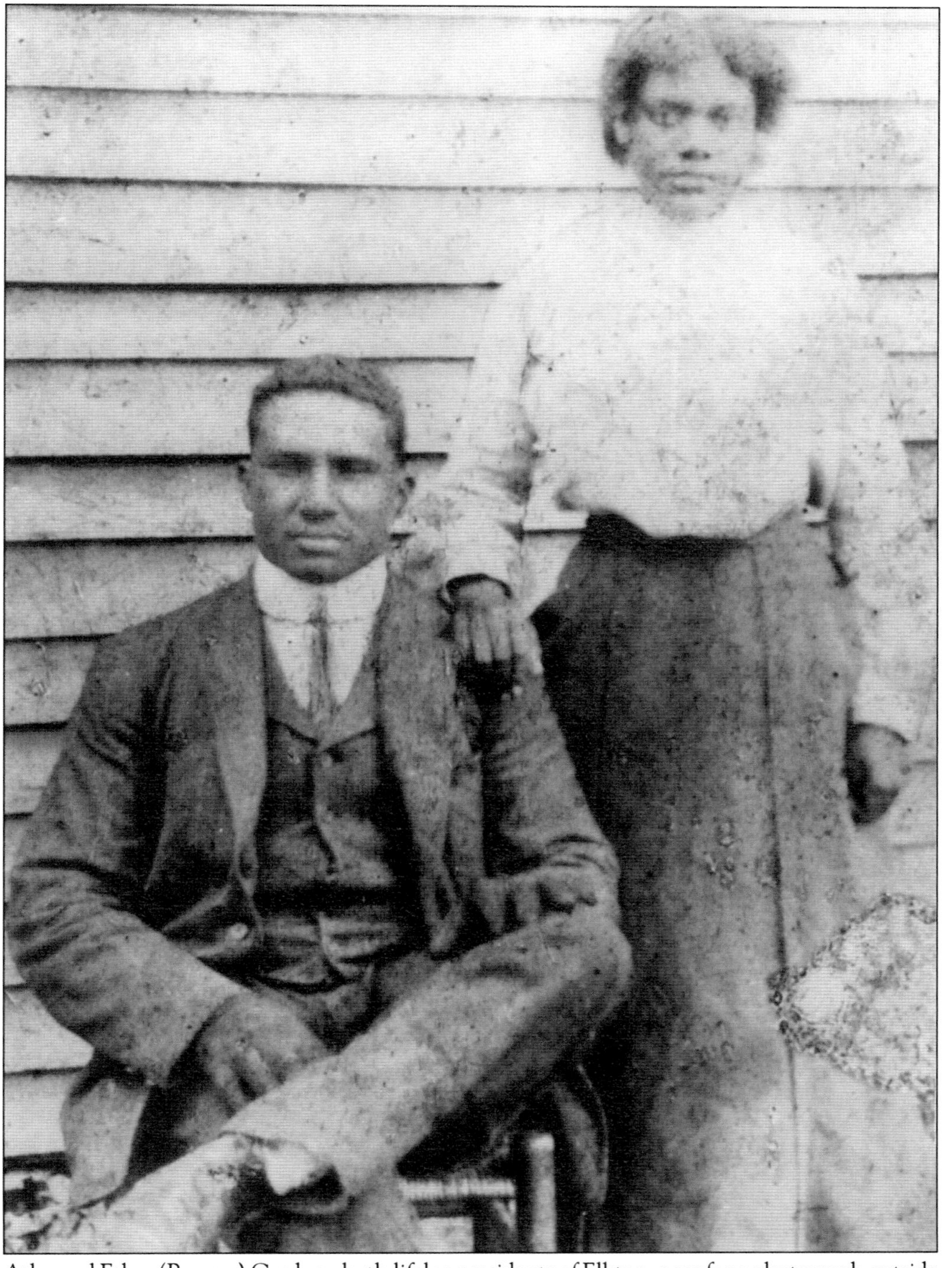

Atha and Ether (Bonner) Gardner, both lifelong residents of Elkton, pose for a photograph outside their residence. Atha was born on September 10, 1877. Ether was born in 1880. It is believed that Atha and Ether were married on December 23, 1897. It is undocumented when Ether died; Atha died on September 7, 1848. The couple's children were A. G., O. C., Joe D., L. Z., Mary I. E., Matt, and Willie T.

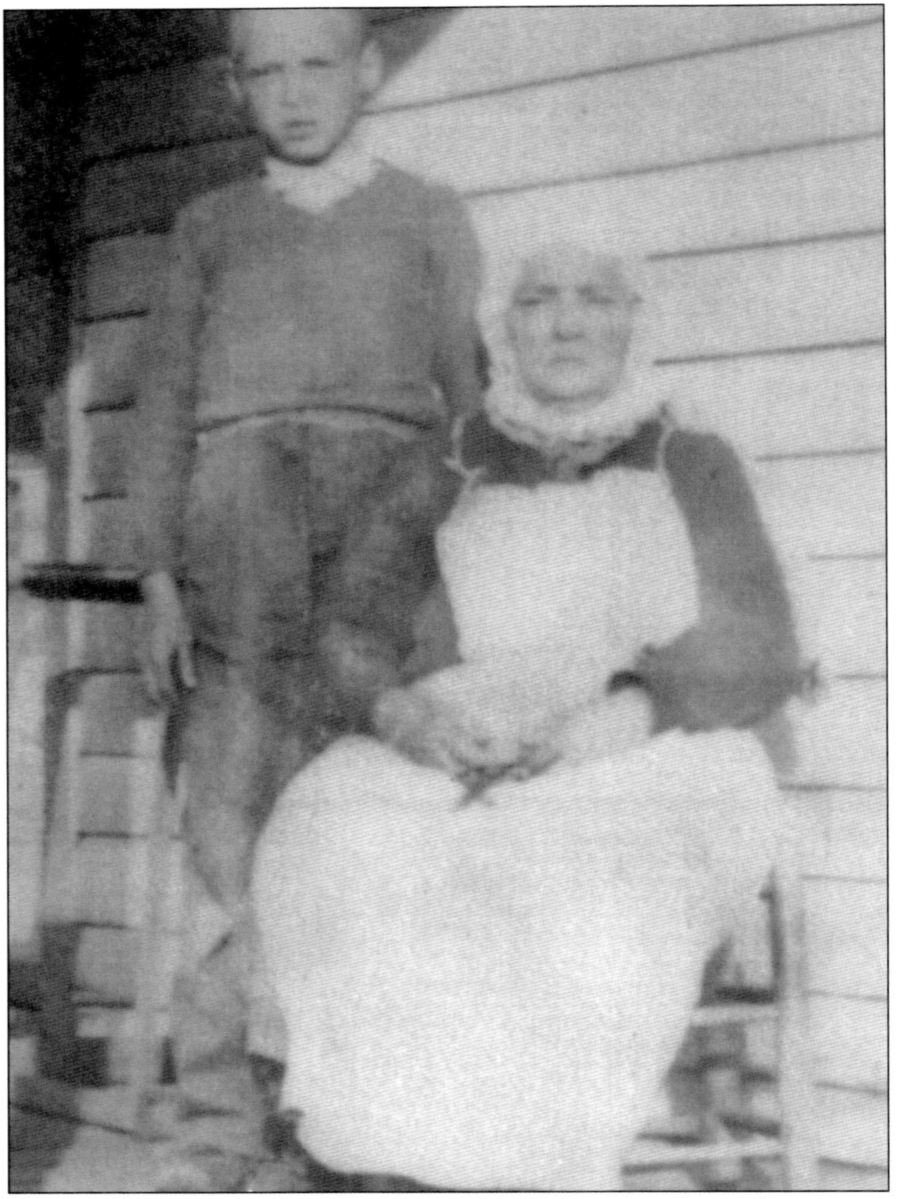

Henrietta (Jenkins) Gardner was born about 1857 to Amanda (Brown) Holt and lived in the Popular Hill community. She was the eldest of six sisters and brothers—Jack, Sam, John, Lula, and Emma. On January 18, 1877, she married Matt Gardner, and together, they became a respected and well-known couple in the Elkton and Dixontown communities. She was affectionately known as "Ritta," a name given to her by her husband. She was a housewife and mother of 11, who were Atha, Raymond, Susan, Mary, Richard, Ellen, Para Lee, John, Clancy, Velma, and Walker. After 56 years of marriage, Ritta passed away; a few excerpts from her obituary appearing in the *Pulaski Citizen* on August 7, 1940, read, "Her home was more than a dwelling, it became a shrine. All races went there, that's where Matt and Henrietta stay and everybody knew for what they stood. Some went for information, others for inspiration. Many went to satisfy their appetites. All felt benefited for having gone. Elkton has suffered a great loss, the Negro race the greatest loss."

Pictured here are Sarah Davis and her daughter, Alice, and son, James Alex, all residents of Pulaski at this time. James grew up and became a preacher. He married Isabella (Pruitt Lewis) Davis on December 13, 1876, and his sister, Alice, married Jeff McKissack on April 13, 1895. Their spouses, Isabella and Jeff, were residents of Giles also. (Courtesy of Philena Morgan.)

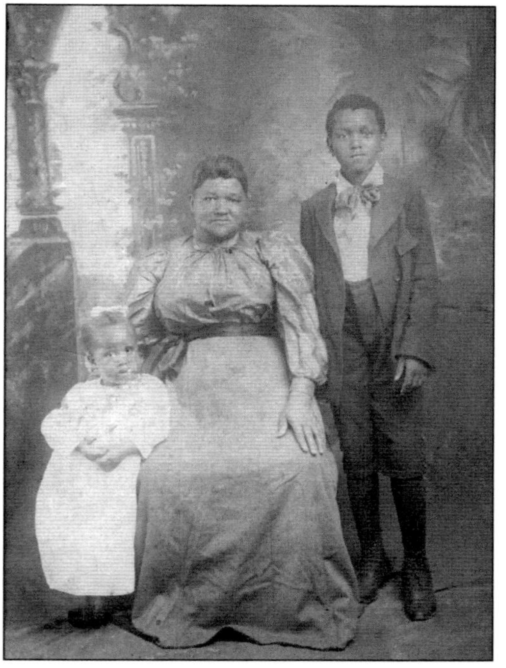

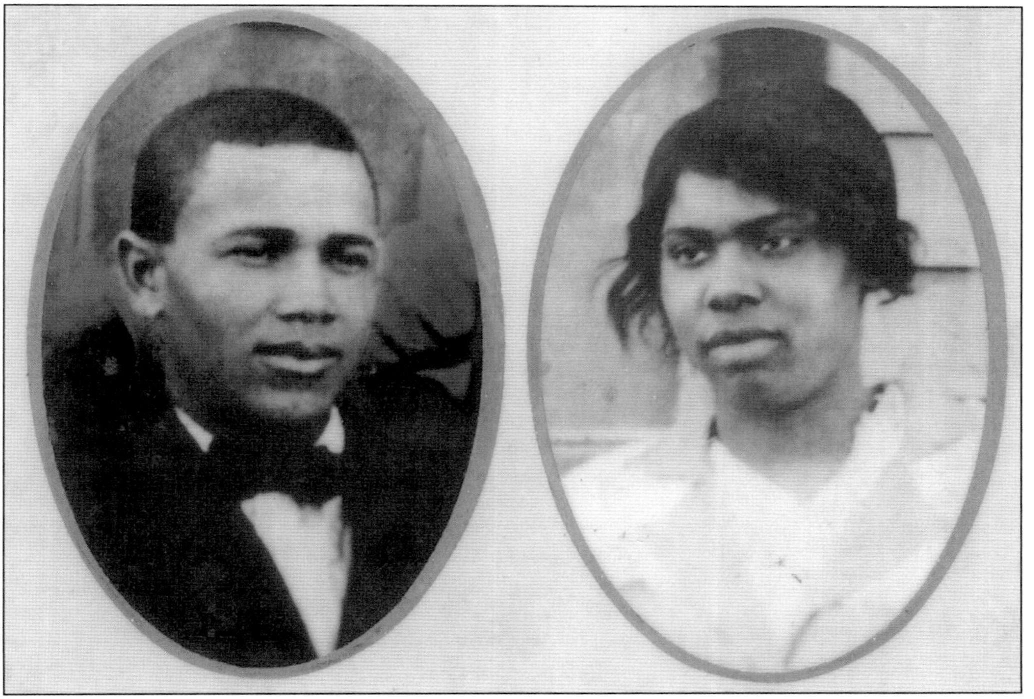

John and Lera (Driver) Gardner were residents of Elkton. Born about 1898, Lera moved to Elkton in 1912 with her parents, George and Tennie (Davidson) Driver. John was born in Elkton on June 29, 1891. On March 29, 1915, elder Howell P. Swinea married the couple, and to their marriage came three sons: John Lewis, Robert Percy, and Will Ross Sr. Lera passed away at an early age and left John a widower. Three years later, he married Alma McClaurine.

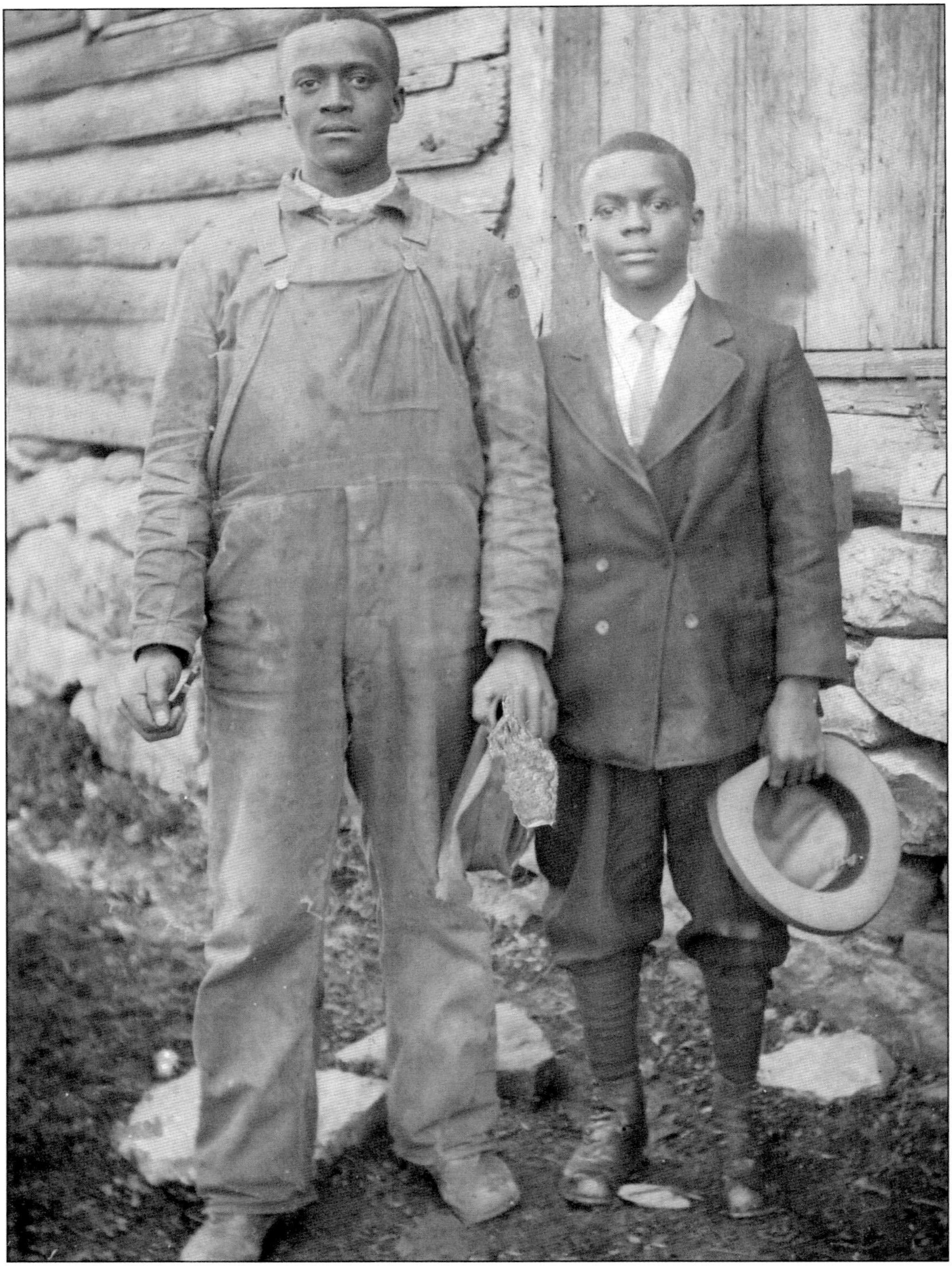

Ellis and Ervis Vasser were the sons of Manville and Martha (Gardner) Vassar. Ellis was born on October 23, 1878, and Ervis was born on November 17, 1893. Even though they were 12 years apart, they were very close, and the younger brother always looked out for his older brother later in life. Other sisters and brothers of Ellis and Ervis include John, Charity, Millie, Mariah, and Emma Love.

Alberta Eddings of Elkton and Carl Sloan of Athens, Alabama, are seen here on a date taking a picture. Alberta, the daughter of Susan (Gardner) Eddings and Willie Eddings, was born on April 24, 1911. She was educated in the colored school of Elkton through the eighth grade. In 1928, Alberta and Carl married, and in 1933, they moved to Indianapolis, Indiana, and their children are Carl Jr., Charles, and Jewel. (Courtesy of Jewel D. Bailey.)

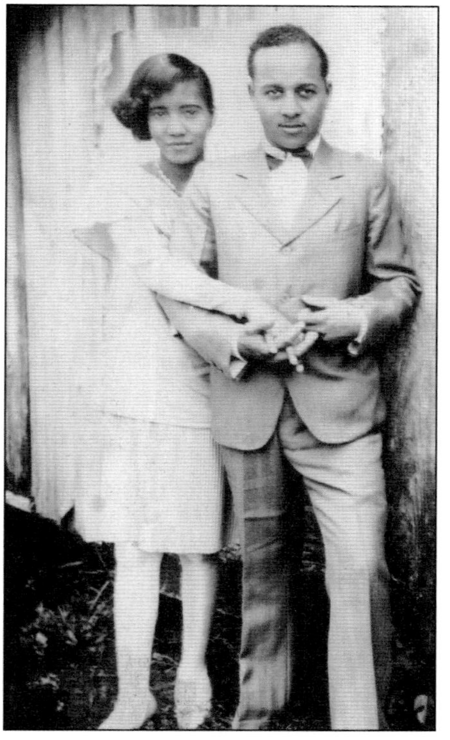

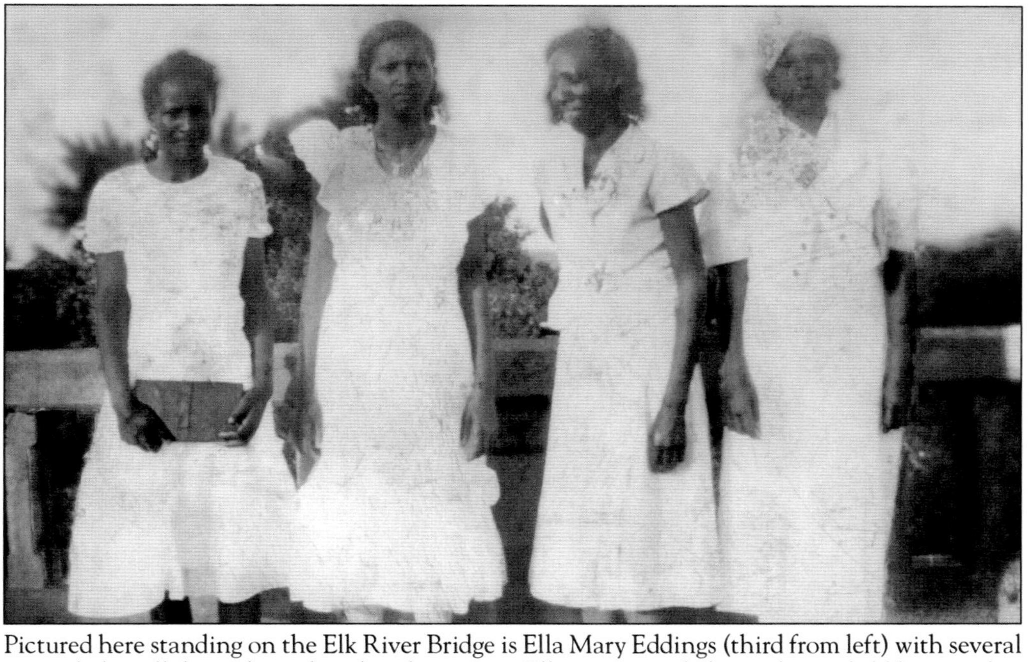

Pictured here standing on the Elk River Bridge is Ella Mary Eddings (third from left) with several young ladies all dressed up after church services. Ella was severely burned as a child because her dress caught on fire as she was kindling the fire in her home. Instead of the stop, drop, and roll method of putting the fire out, she ran out of the house and into the yard, where her mother caught her and covered her to smother the fire. Ella was known as everyone's favorite auntie.

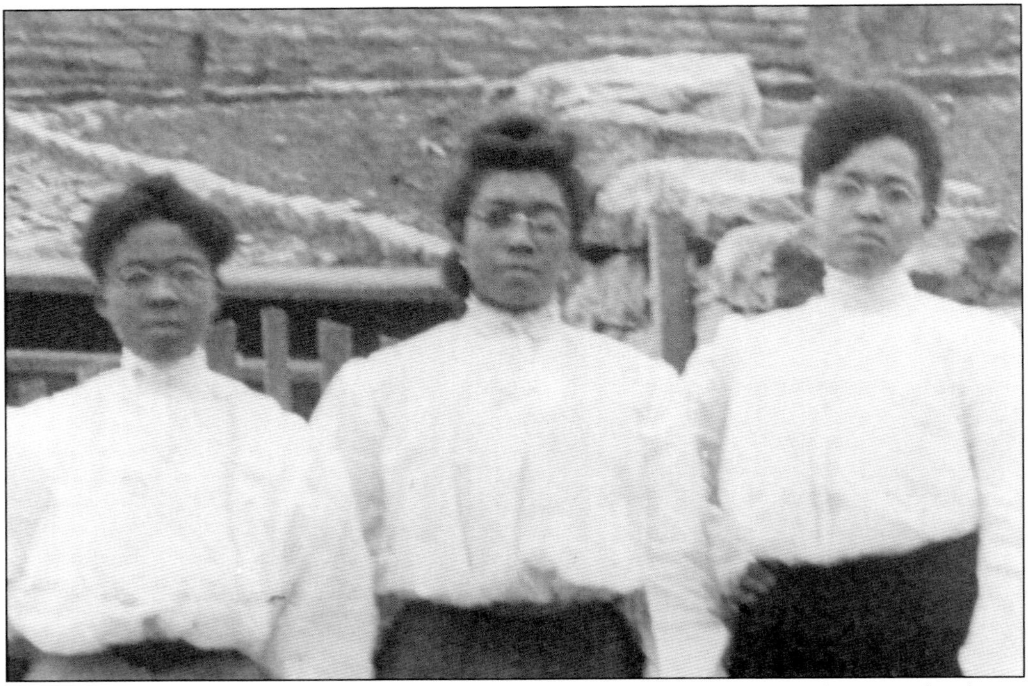

Standing from left to right in front of the Ice House in Pulaski are Sally (Pruitt) Lewis's daughters, Sophie (Pruitt Lewis) Maxwell Price, Nellie (Pruitt Lewis) Maxwell, and Isabella (Pruitt Lewis) Davis. All three were born and educated in the Pulaski community of Giles. Sophie and Nellie married brothers Ben and Dave Maxwell. Sophie and Ben married on March 12, 1892, and Nellie and Dave married on January 14, 1880. Isabella married James Alex Davis. (Courtesy of Philena Morgan.)

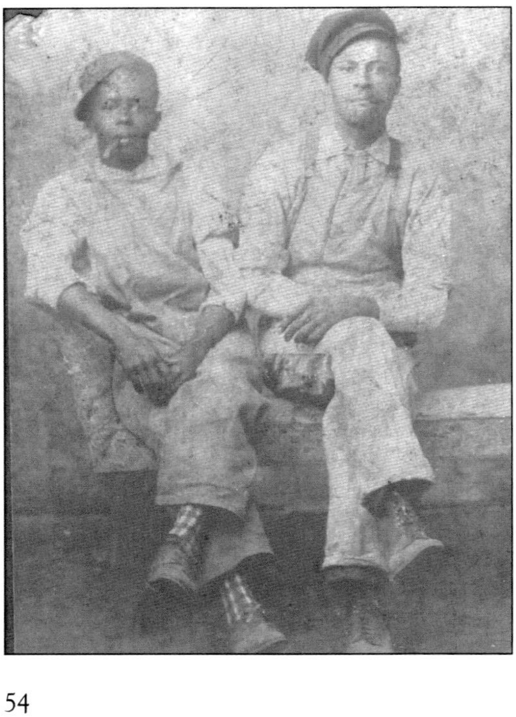

Steven Gardner Jr. (right) and A. D. Bledsoe (left) are seen here as a couple of good friends having some fun in their *c.* 1920 railroad overalls and engineer caps. A. D. was the son of Laura Bledsoe. A. D.'s sisters and brother were Minnie Lou, Mattie, Ella, Lizzie, and D. W. A. D. worked as a sharecropper on a local farm in Giles, and Steven worked on his stepfather Morgan Dunn's farm.

Pictured are Matt Gardner (left), Prince and Georgia Stevenson, and their daughter May Sue (front). Georgia became very close to her uncle Matt after her mother and his sister Mary (Gardner) Benson died on January 5, 1885. They became even closer after the passing of Rachael, his mother, and the grandmother who raised Georgia from the age of three. They are seen here standing in the yard of the Stevenson family with their daughter holding a baby doll and her bike, seen off to the right.

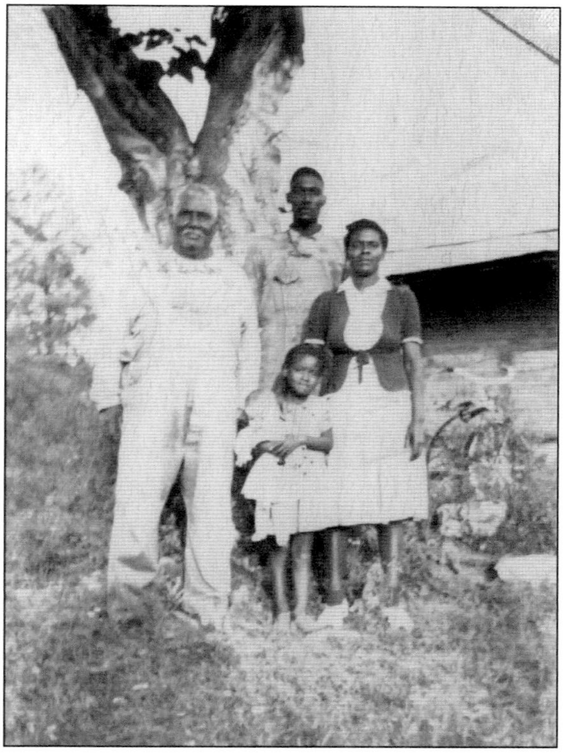

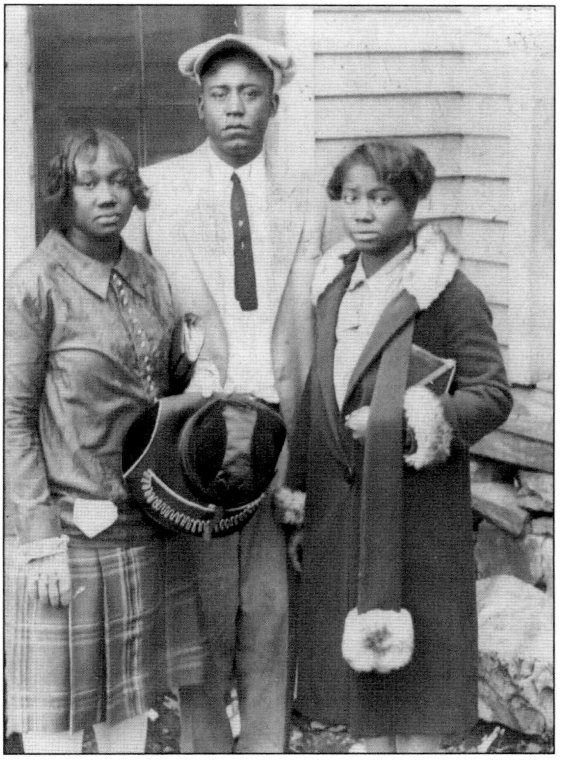

Pictured is James (Lewis) McClaurine, with whom are believed to be two of his sisters. They are the children of Monroe and Roxie McClaurine. Originally from Lincoln County, the family moved in the early 1900s to Giles, where all the children were raised and schooled. James's sisters were Lillie Bell, Ida Mae, Mamie Sue, Alma, and Edna.

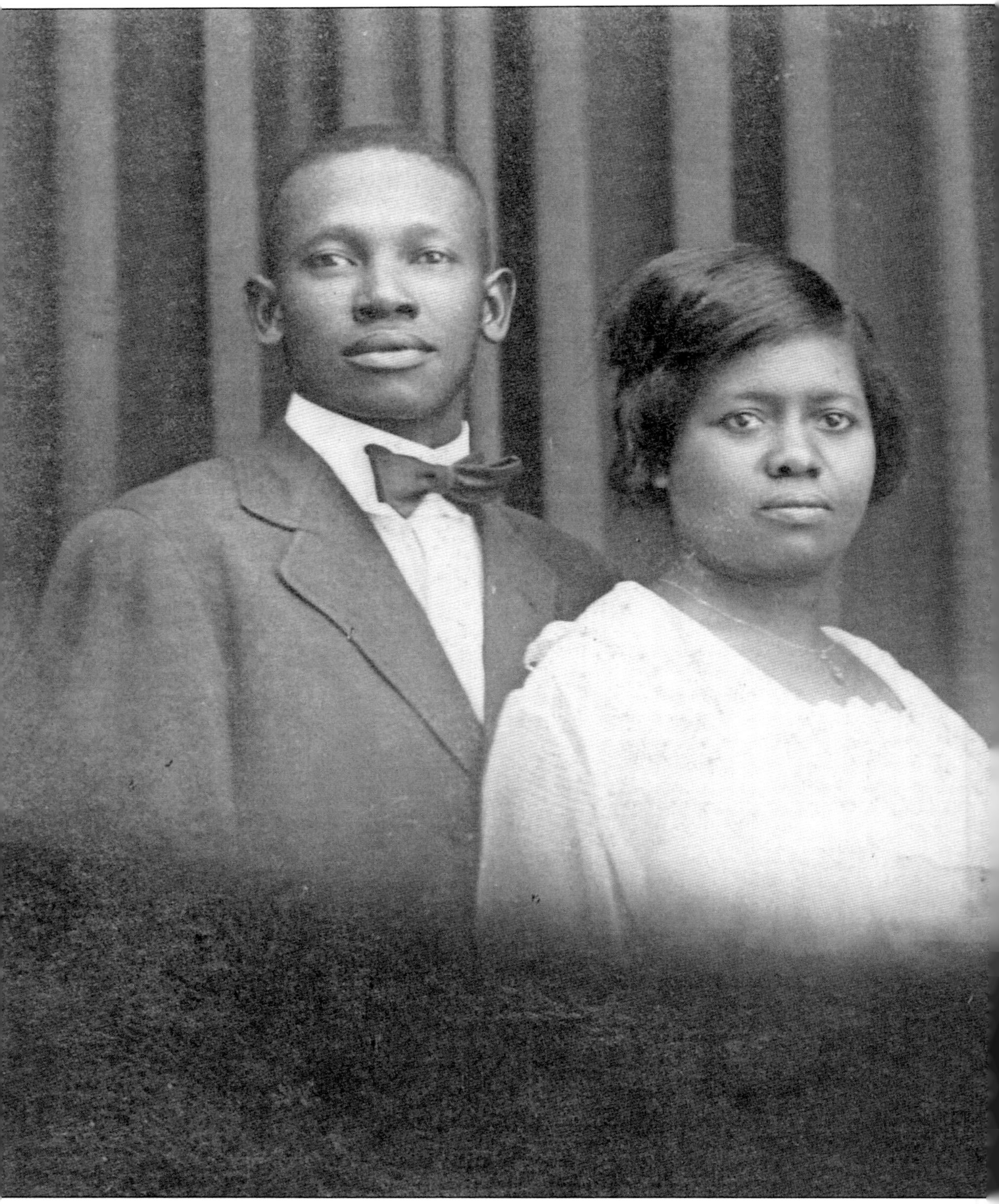

Pictured here are, from left to right, sisters Laverta, Gladys, and Tommie Davis and their brother, Scott. The girls were the children of Thomas Davis and Anna (Caudel) Davis and the grandchildren of James and Isabella (Lewis) Davis, all of Pulaski. Scott was Anna's son. They

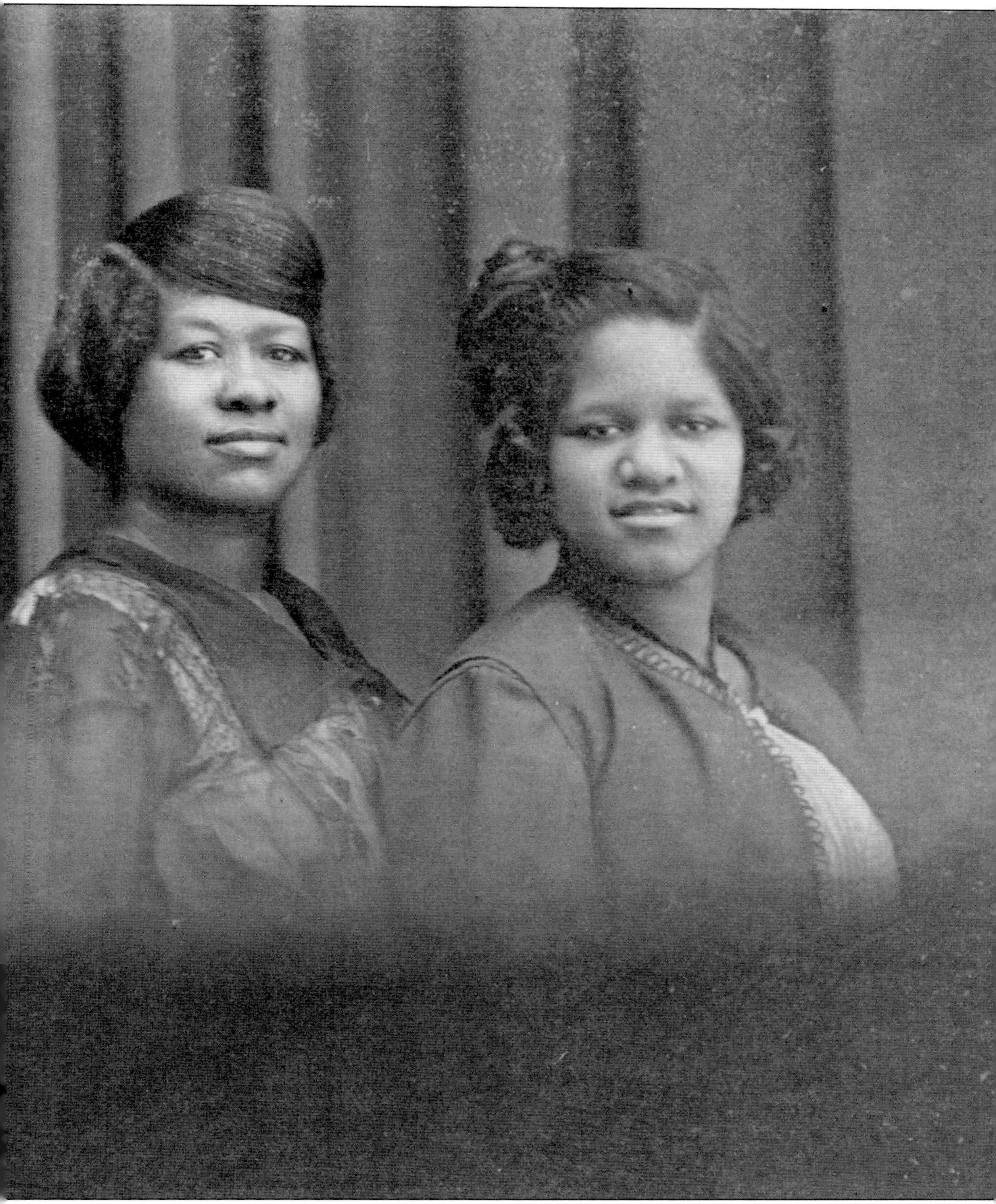

look as if they could be a singing quartet. Over the years, the group of young Davises stayed close and connected to their Giles County roots. (Courtesy of Philena Morgan.)

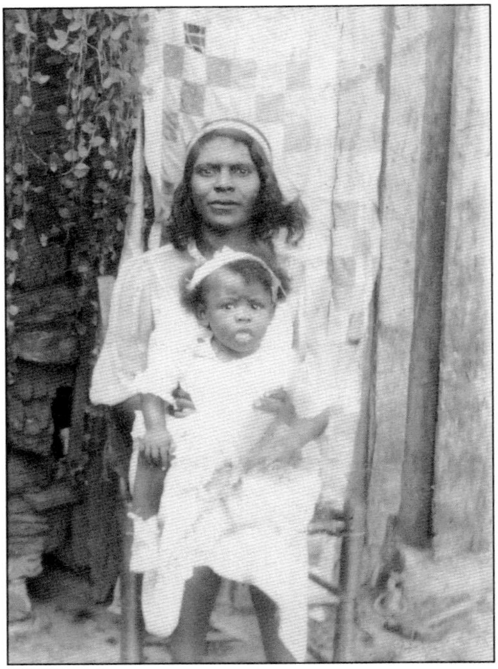

This is a picture of Mary I. E. (Gardner) Clay, and her daughter, Elli Dean Clay. Mary I. E. was born in September 1917, and she was the daughter of Atha and Ether (Bonner) Gardner. Mary I. E. married David Clay, and to their union came the one daughter. Other children of Mary I. E. include Jacqueline and Thomas.

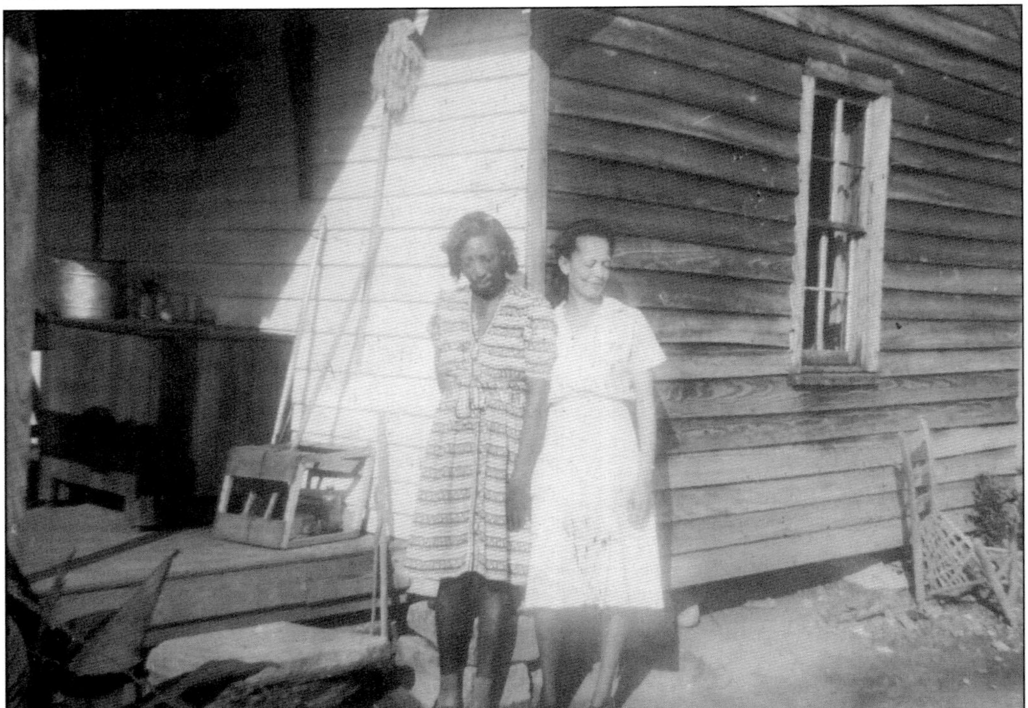

Cousins Ella Mary Eddings (left) and Ellen (Gardner) Cooper are pictured on a sunny day hanging around Ellen's house on Dixontown Road and U.S. Highway 31 in Elkton. The cousins lived next door to each other. Ella was the daughter of Susan (Gardner) Eddings, and Ellen was the daughter of Mary (Gardner) Gardner.

The Coleman brothers are, from left to right, (seated) Robert "Boots" and John "Billy;" (standing) Roosevelt and H. Wood. These brothers were all born, raised, and educated in the colored school in Elkton, Tennessee. They were the sons of Andrew and Emma (Love) Coleman. Their only sister was Minnie Bell Coleman. Somewhere between 1920 and 1930, the family moved to West Virginia seeking employment. Their father and H. Wood were laborers, John and Roosevelt were drillers, and Robert was a machine operator, all in the West Virginia coal mines. (Courtesy of Margaret Cleveland.)

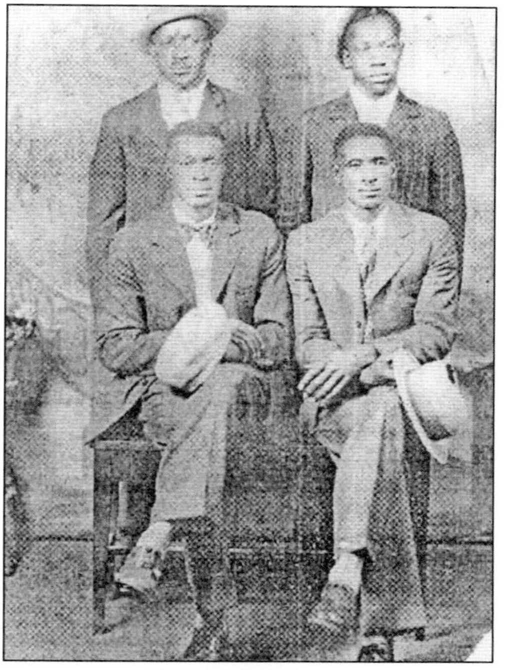

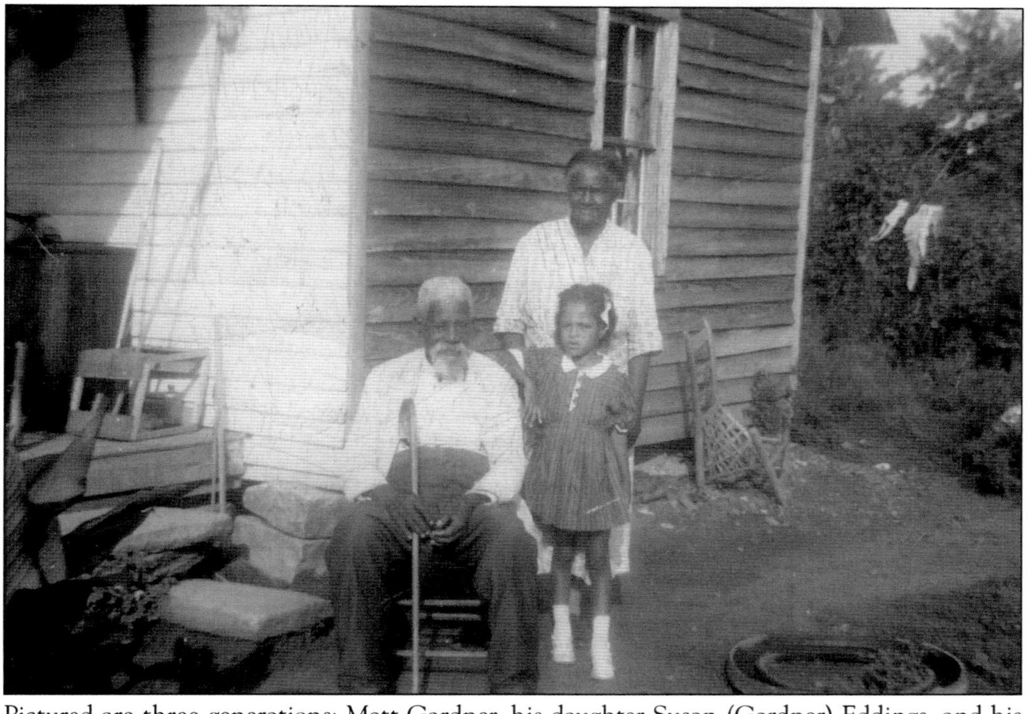

Pictured are three generations: Matt Gardner, his daughter Susan (Gardner) Eddings, and his great-granddaughter Marie (Phelps) Thornton. Marie was the daughter of Iwilla (Gardner) Phelps. Because Iwilla lived and grew up in Giles, she made Marie farm twice a year, once in the spring and then again in summer. Her mother wanted her to know her grandparents and other family members as well as experiencing a farm life.

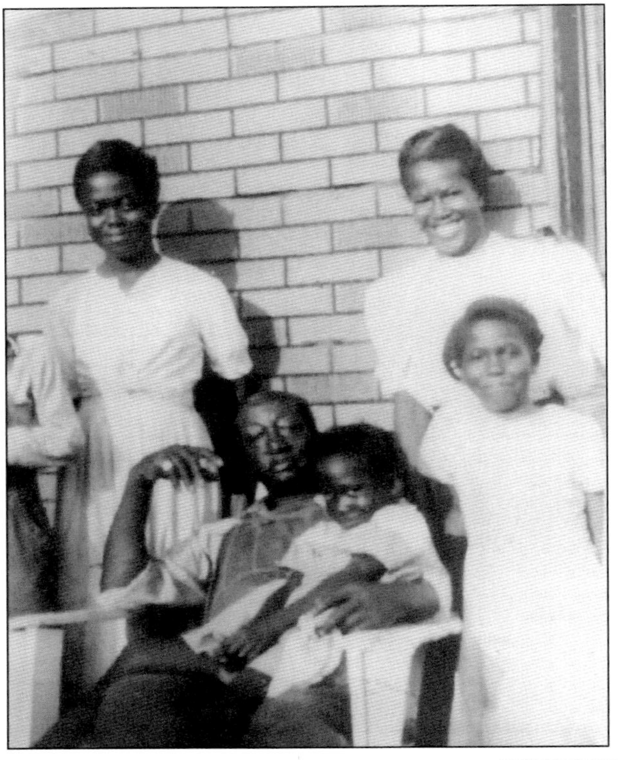

Tobe McLin is pictured here with his granddaughters, from left to right, Martha, Edith, Louise, and, in his lap, Marie. Tobe was born and raised in Giles, and on August 31, 1898, he married Martha (Bridgeforth). To the couple came 13 children: Polly (McLin) Brown, Tommy, James, Laura (McLin) Nivins, Rachel (McLin) Grisby, Drewcilla, Everett, Wiley, John, Charlotte (McLin) Smith, Robert, and twins who died at birth. Tobe often gathered the girls and told them about the good old days. (Courtesy of Louise [McLin] Kitchen.)

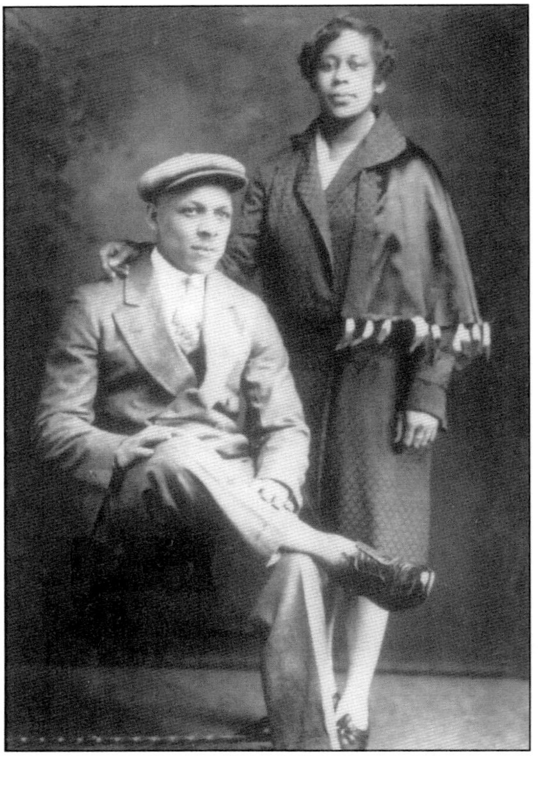

M. D. Chainey is seen with his wife, Lillie Belle (Gardiner) Chainey. M. D. was born on October 18, 1904, and Lillie Belle was born on December 4, 1904. The couple was married on June 26, 1929, and they were blessed with 10 children: Helen, Rose, Henry, Gladys, Shirley, John, Sally, Penny, Sandra, and David. Lillie Belle died on November 13, 1969. (Courtesy of Helen Mays.)

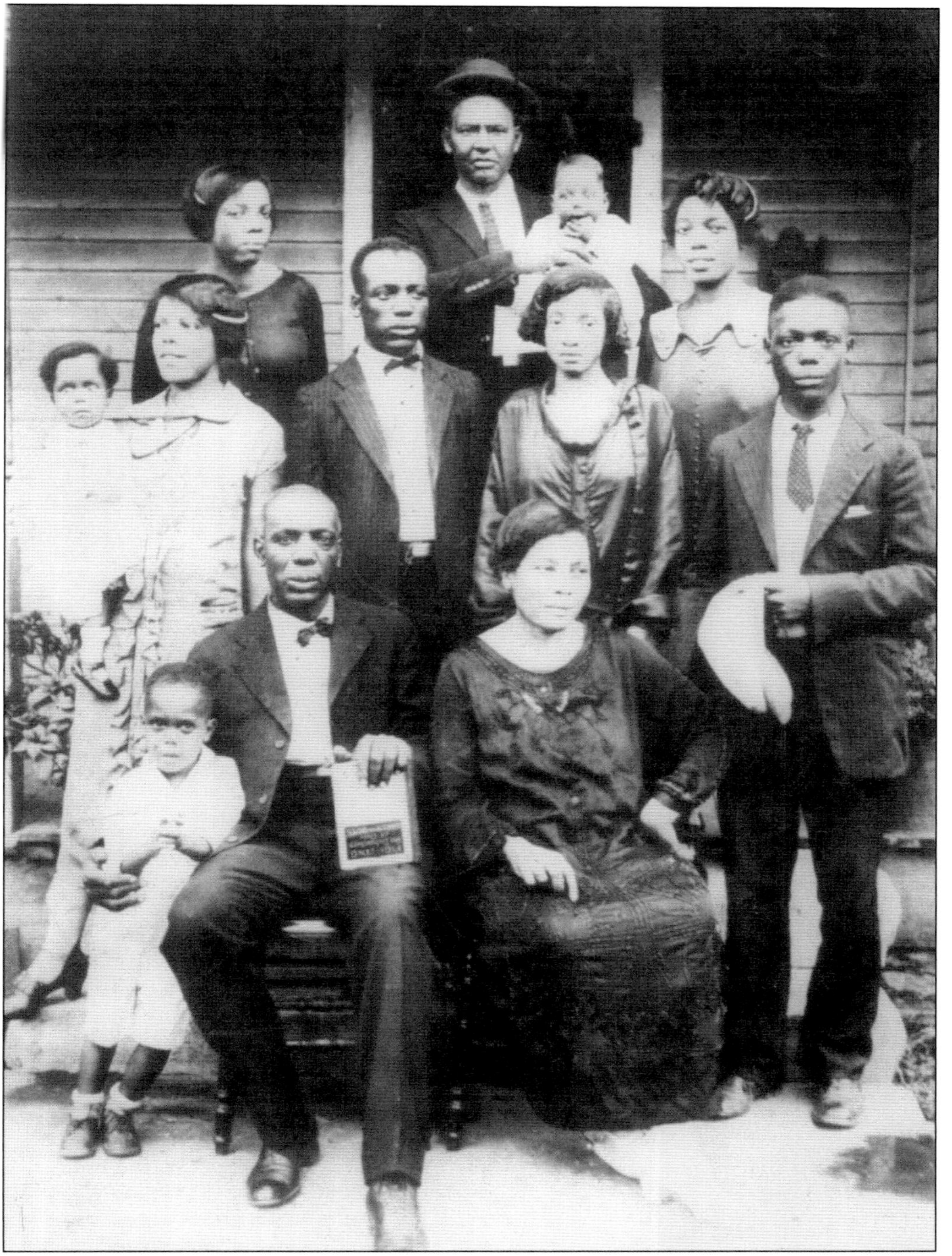

Members of the James T. Bridgeforth family are, from left to right, (first row) grandson Clinton Nelson; James Thomas; and wife Mattie; (second row) granddaughter Mattie; daughter Susie; son Maceo; Maceo's wife, Eleanor; and son John; (third row) daughter Roberta; son-in-law Tom Ballentine; grandson Thomas; and daughter Lenora. (Courtesy of Agnes Bridgeforth.)

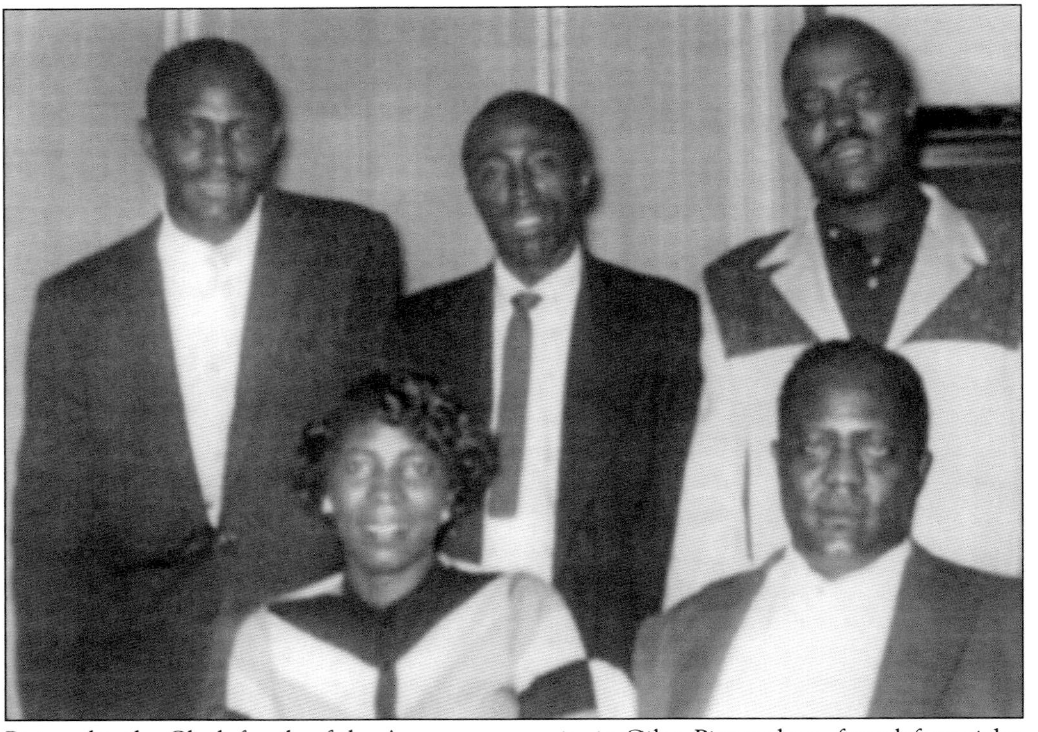

Pictured is the Clack family of the Agnew community in Giles. Pictured are, from left to right, (first row) Mary Eliza (Clack) Dangerfield and Edward Allen Clack Sr.; (second row) Archie Eugene Clack, Albert Lee Clack, and Buford Freeman Clack. Their parents, William Bill and Mattie (Johnson) Clack, were married on December 3, 1905. Other children of William and Mattie not pictured include William Jr. and Claude. (Courtesy of Elmorie Miller.)

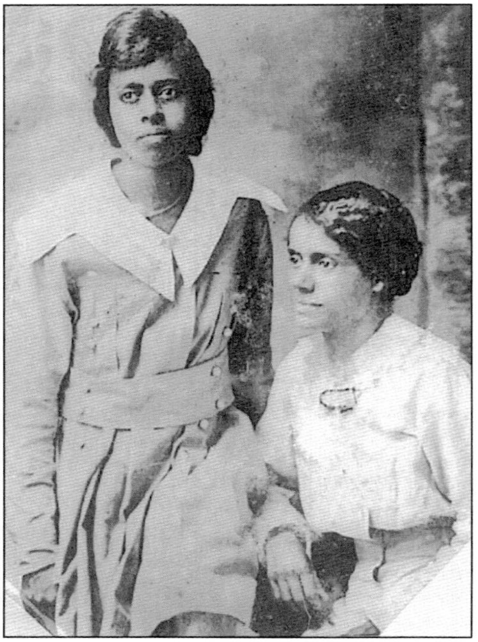

Alice and Mamie Smith were the daughters of Jones and Mattie (McKinney) Smith. Both were born and educated in the Pulaski community of Giles. Mammie (sitting) was born in November 1879, and she married a gentleman with the same first name as her father, Jones Woodson, on March 8, 1898. To their union came 11 children. Alice was born on February 14, 1890, and she later met and married William Cline. She and William moved to east Tennessee, and together they raised six children. (Courtesy of Renelda Walker.)

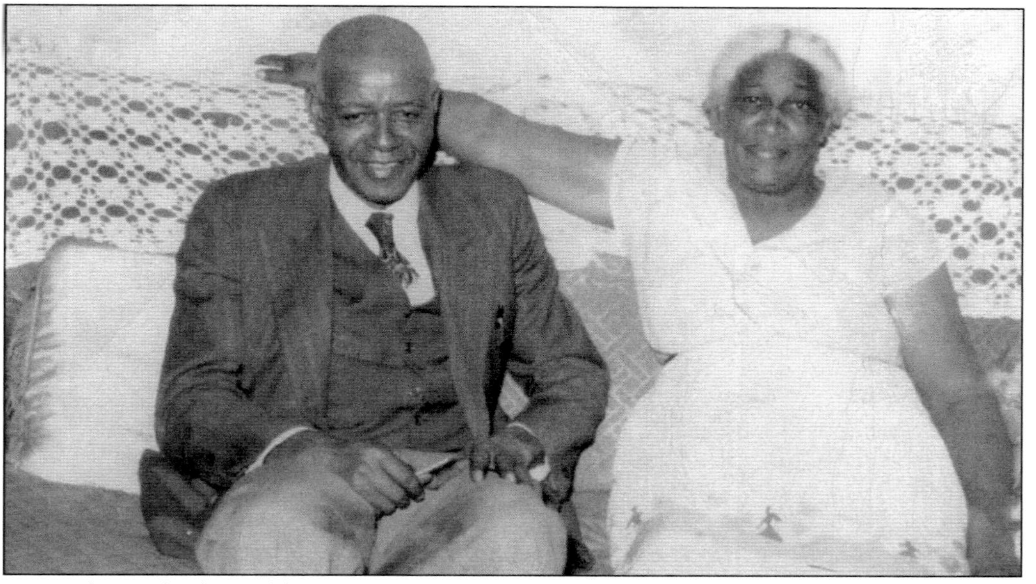

Pictured are Charles and his wife, Parlee (Gardner) Coleman. Charles was born in Ardmore, Alabama, on November 11, 1898. He later moved to Giles County, Tennessee, where he met Parlee in the town of Elkton. The couple was married on December 23, 1911, and they were blessed with eight children: Mary E. Lois, Malion, Charles Bufford, John Thomas, Winston, Flossie, Thurmond, and Blanche. In the late 1920s, the family moved to West Virginia, but they always claimed Giles as their home. (Courtesy of Thurmond Coleman.)

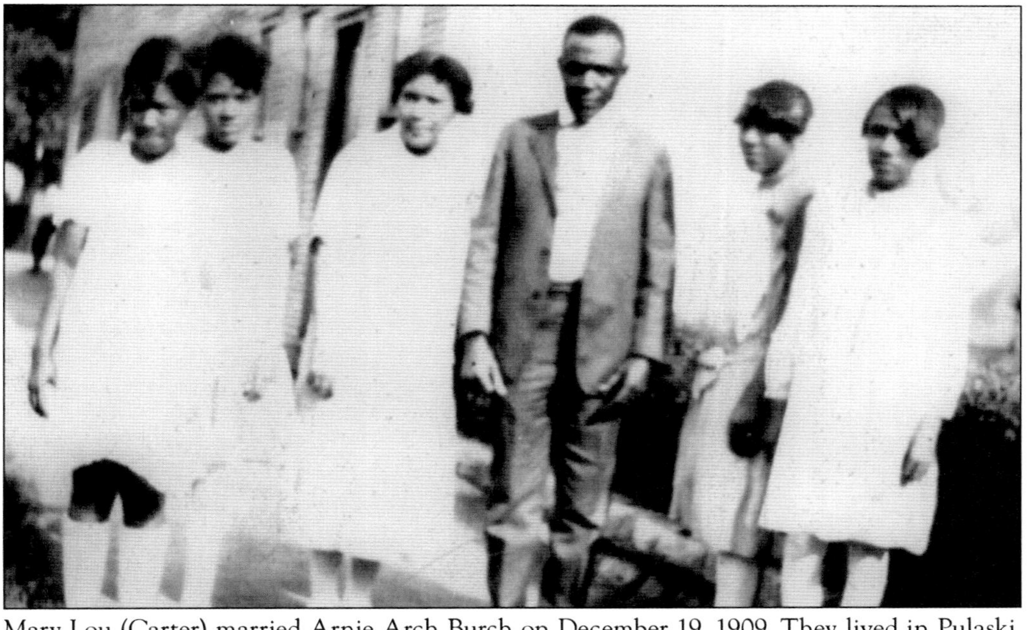

Mary Lou (Carter) married Arnie Arch Burch on December 19, 1909. They lived in Pulaski, Tennessee, where Arch, as he was called, was a shoe cobbler and ran his business in the Bellview community. Mary Lou was a housewife until later years, when she worked as secretary for Queen Anne Funeral Home. Arch and Mary Lou had four daughters, Agnes, Lou Alice, Amanda, and Weeta, who all were teachers. (Courtesy of Agnes Bridgeforth.)

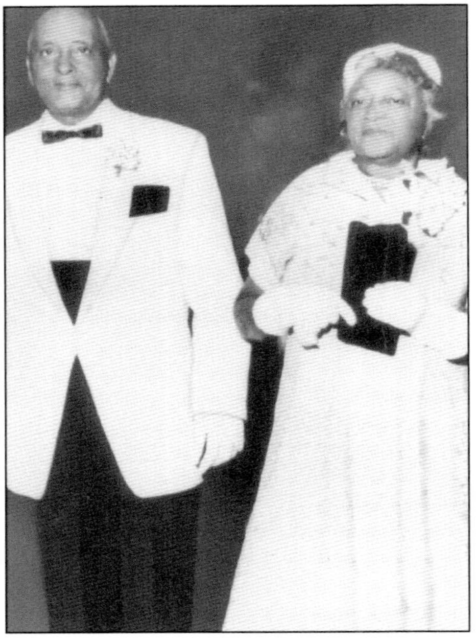

Lex and Ethel (Bridgeforth Holt) Driver were both lifelong residents of the Elkton community. They were married on November 6, 1914, and into their marriage came six children: Maruine, Ridgeway, Millie, Leroy, Edith, and Lizzie Bell. Lex was also a father to Ethel's three other children—Katherine, Thaddeus, and Samuel Holt—when she became a widow after the death of their father, Lee Holt. (Courtesy of Joyce Hague.)

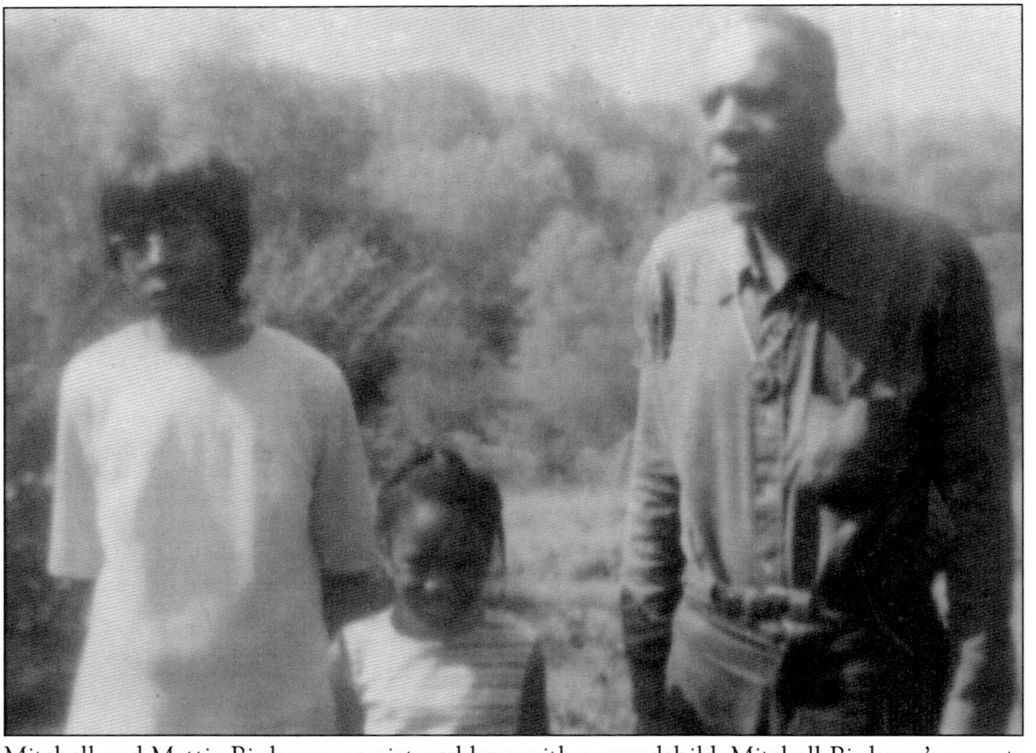

Mitchell and Mattie Birdsong are pictured here with a grandchild. Mitchell Birdsong's parents were John and Alice Birdsong. Mitchell was born in 1910, and his wife, Mattie, was born in 1905. The Birdsongs lived in the Bryson community, and they had nine children—six boys and three girls. Mattie and the children did all the farming while Mitchell commuted everyday to work in Nashville until he retired in 1955 at the age of 45. (Courtesy of the Birdsong family.)

Walker Gardner and daughter Lura Mae were the husband and daughter of Lizzie Mae (Hogan) Gardner. Lura Mae grew up in the town of Elkton but later in life moved to Chicago. Living in Chicago prevented her from visiting her parents and other family members in Giles for long periods of time. They are seen here smiling as they catch up on lost time and memories. Walker Gardner is the son of Matt and Henrietta Gardner. Walker was born on February 26, 1898, and married Lizzie Mae Hogan on December 21, 1917. To their union came nine children: Lura Mae, Walker Jr., Jim, Booker T., Adell, Sidney, Buford, Mack Allen, and Albert Lewis. (Courtesy of Gloria McLean.)

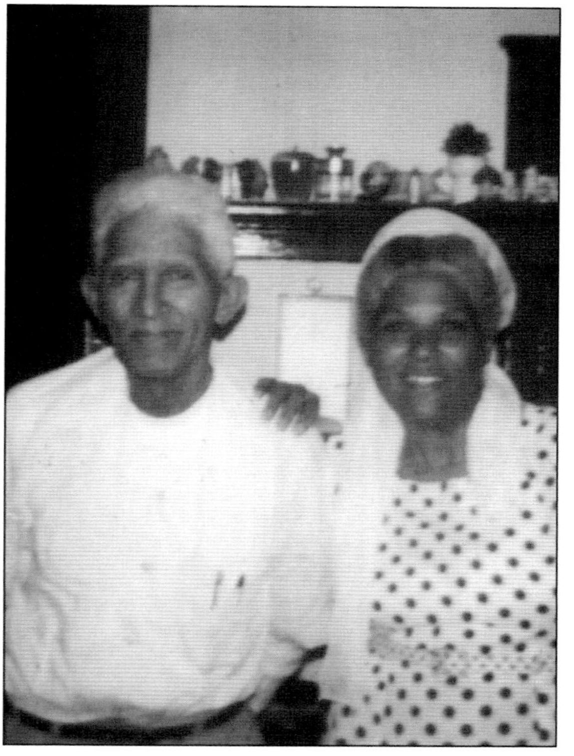

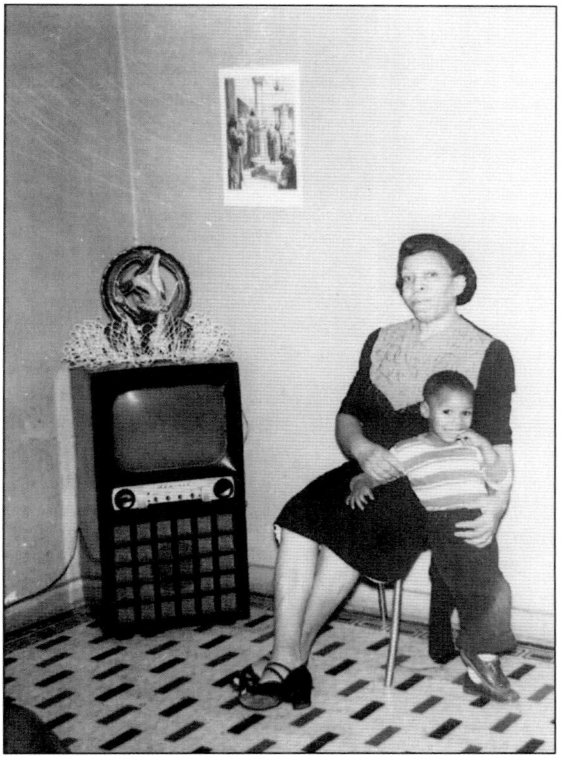

Mary Sue Stevenson is pictured with a grandchild. Mary Sue was born on January 10, 1904, and her parents were Prince Stevenson and Georgia (Benson) Stevenson. Mary's husband's name is unknown, but he worked for the railroad and traveled most of the time. Mary Sue had one daughter, Georgia Lee, who she named after her mother. (Courtesy of Emma Stevenson.)

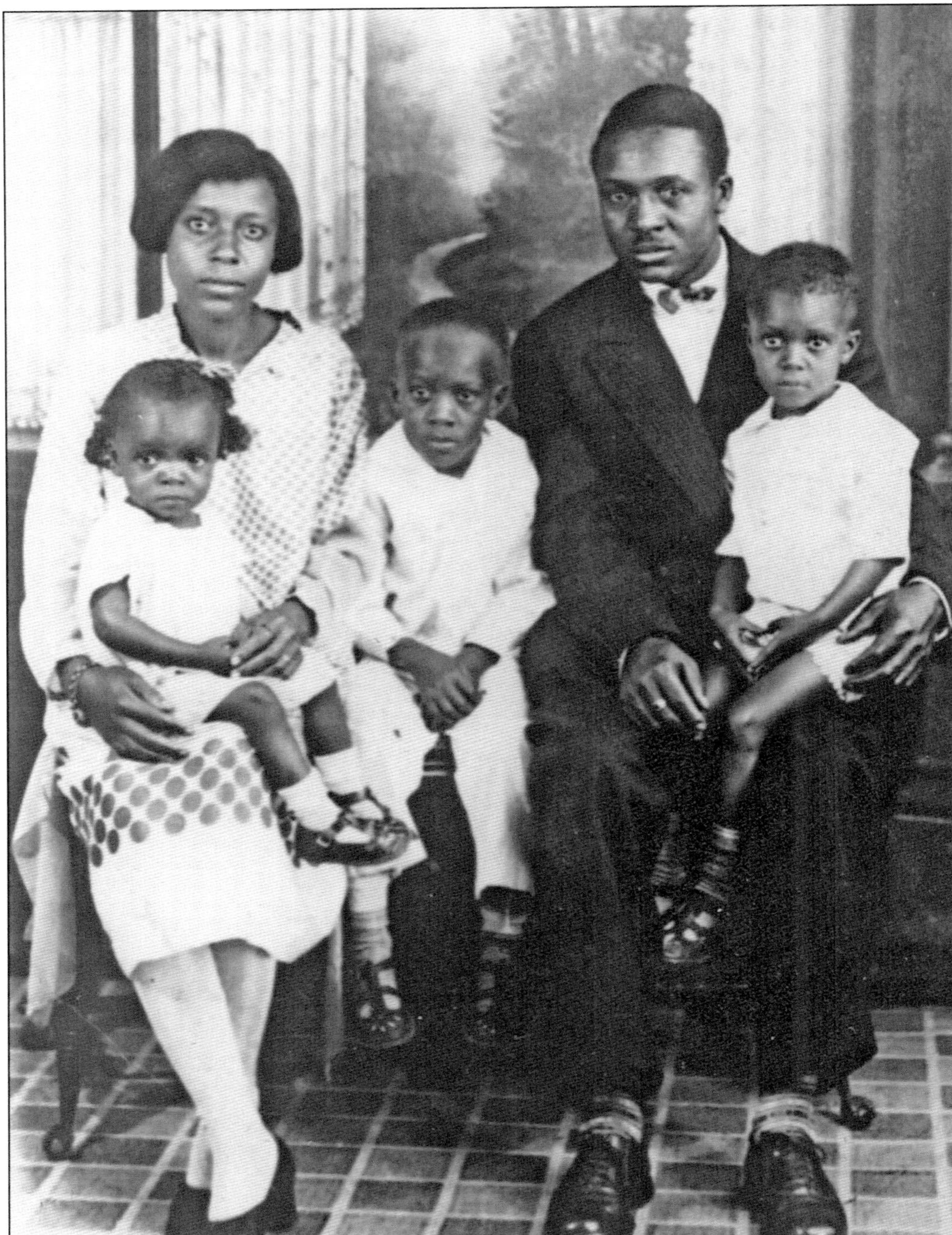

Isaiah Sr. and Lizzie Bea (Bledsoe) Bridgeforth were both born in Giles and are seen here with their children, from left to right, Mary Helen, Alan, and David. The couple was married for 27 wonderful years and were blessed with a total of 12 children. The other children are William, Craymore, John, Marcella, Isaiah Jr., Anna, Regina, Hezekiah, and Joyce. When Isaiah passed away in 1947, Lizzie was left to raise her children alone, and she did a great job. (Courtesy of the Lizzie Bridgeforth family.)

Five

Military Heros

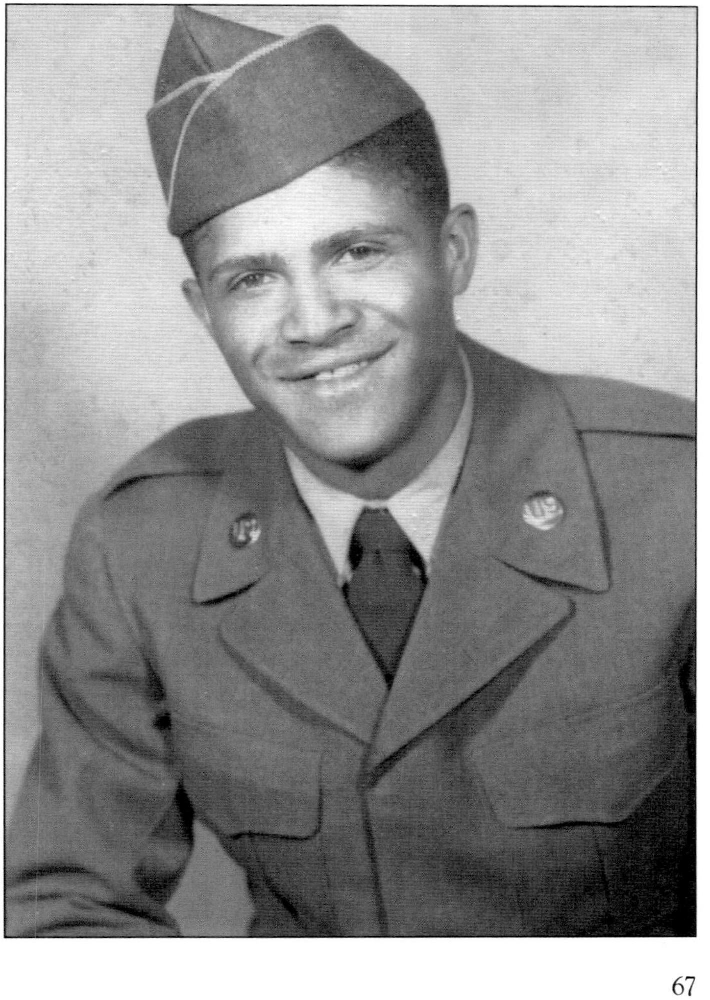

Booker T. Gardner was born on February 1, 1924, in Elkton to Walker and Lizzie (Hogan) Gardner. After completing grammar school in Elkton, he enlisted in the army as a private at Fort Benning, Georgia. When he came out of the service, he moved to Chicago. He had two girls, Shirley and Phyllis, and one boy, Cory. Booker passed away on March 16, 1997.

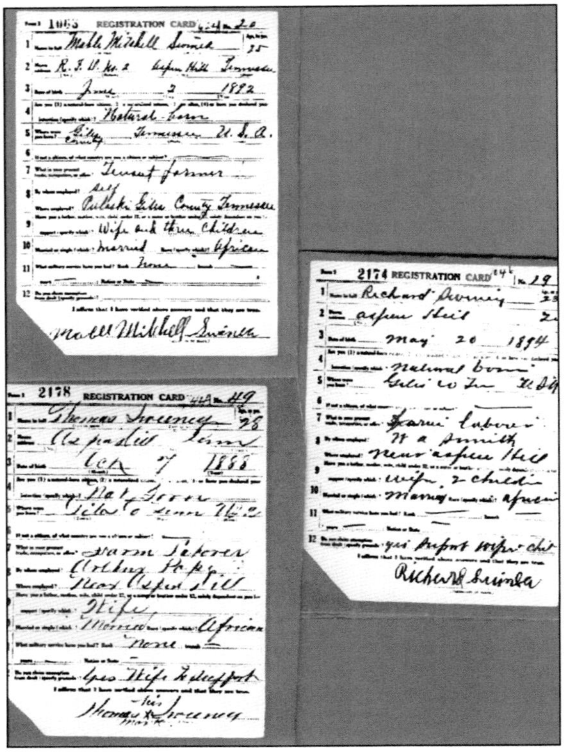
1065 REGISTRATION CARD
Mabl Mitchell Swinea
R. F. D. No. 2 Aspen Hill Tennessee
June 2 1892
Natural born
Giles County Tennessee U. S. A.
Tenant farmer
Self
Pulaski Giles County Tennessee
Wife and three children
Married African
None
Mabl Mitchell Swinea

2174 REGISTRATION CARD
Richard Swiney
Aspen Hill
May 20 1894
Natural born
Giles Co Tenn U S A
Farm laborer
Richard Swinea

2178 REGISTRATION CARD
Thomas Sweeney
Aspen Hill Tenn
Oct 7 1888
Nat born
Farm laborer
Wife
Married African
None
Thomas Sweeney

During World War I, men had to complete military registration cards. These cards help African Americans in search of their ancestors to get a glimpse of how their ancestors may have looked, as they offer a description of the person including things such as body build, height, and color of eyes and hair. They give some insight as to the effects of not being allowed to learn, read, and write and having to rely on others for the spelling of one's own name. Pictured are registrations cards for three brothers with three different spellings of the same last name that each family still carries today—Richard Swiney, Thomas Sweeney, and Mitchell Swinea.

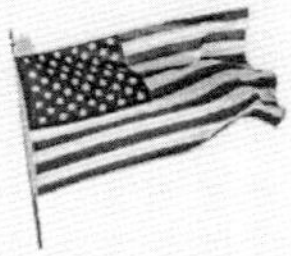
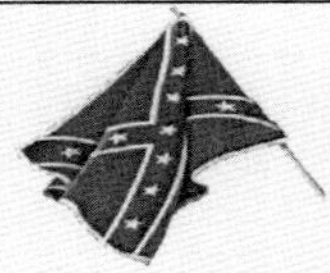

Name	Company & Regiment	Cemetery
Ruff Abernathy	3rd TN Inf. 14	Aspen Hill
Maurice A. Cleveland	Staff Gen. John Adams	Maplewood
David Coleman	Co. I 6th AL Inf. 100	Good Springs
Jacob Coleman	Co. A 11th AL Inf. 2	Neely
Mack Dabney	3rd TN Inf. (Clark)	Brick Church
Nathan Gordon	Co. E 11 TN Cavalry	Waco
Wash Harris	Cheatham's Div. 163	Maplewood
Richard Lester	Co. G 3rd TN Inf. 4	Maplewood
Robert Lester	Co. K 8th TN Inf.	Maplewood
Giles Moore	9th AL & 9th TN Cavalries 22	New Hope
Matt Rivers	11th TN Cavalry 153	County Farm

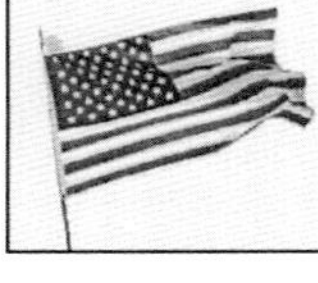
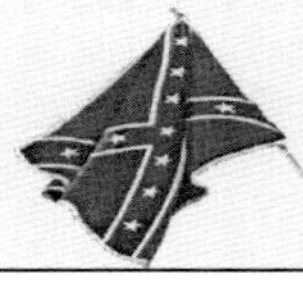

These are names of some African American Confederate soldiers who were from communities across Giles. Buried in numerous cemeteries throughout Giles are African American soldiers who served in the Civil War and received a pension but were not allowed to receive a military headstone or marker, as they did not join of their own free will but came as servants to their slave master. Giles County No. 257 United Daughters of the Confederacy and Gen. John C. Brown's No. 112 Sons of the Confederate Veterans purchased headstones for all the soldiers on this list. (Courtesy of Cathy Wood.)

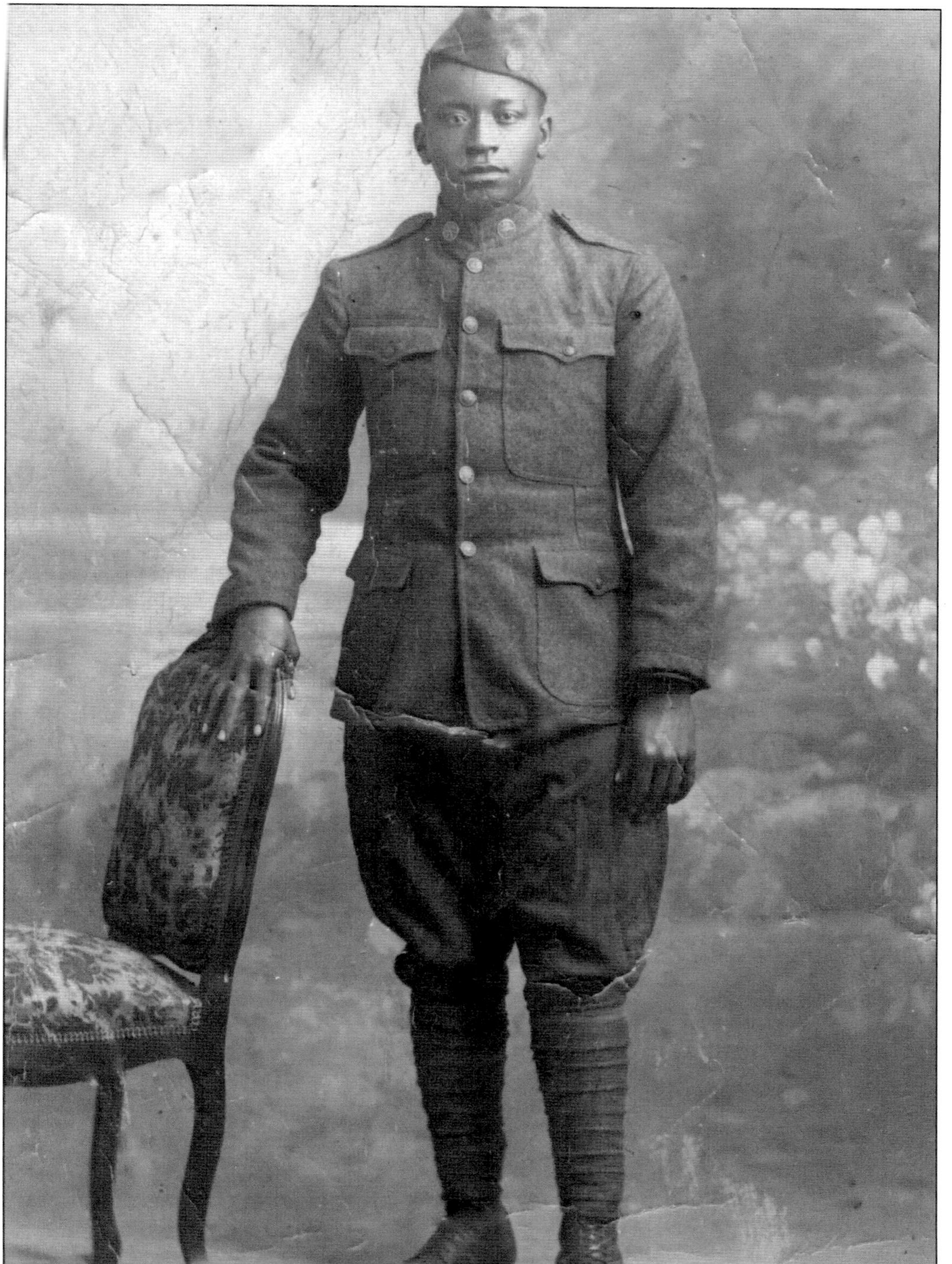

Jodie Daly "Joe D" lived in Elkton, and his first wife was Jennie Daly, who was a teacher and taught in many colored schools in Giles County. Joe D made a living being a handyman. He also had a truck that he used to do odd jobs for people in the community, such as baling cotton and transporting it to the cotton gin in the area. Joe D and Jennie Daly had no children.

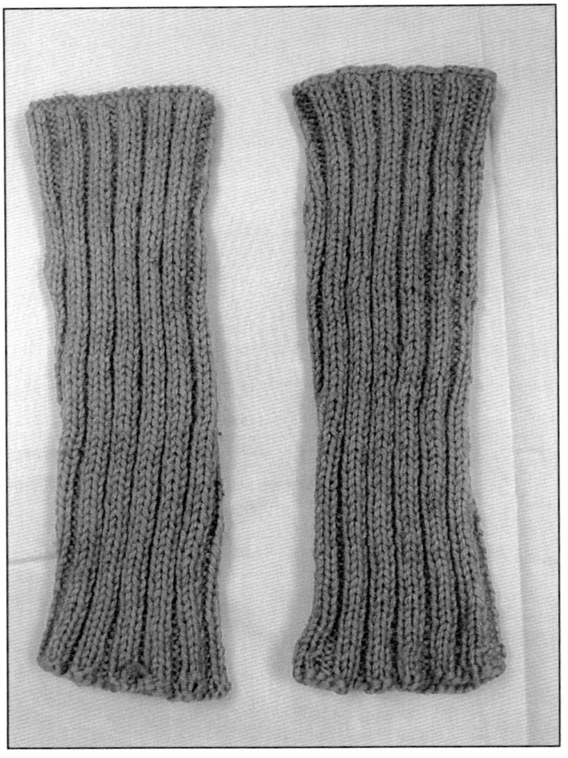

This is a pair of wristlets worn by men at war to keep their hands warm. During the wars, there were groups of white and black women called the Army Comfort League that made sweater kits for the soldiers. The white leagues would make kits for the white soldiers, and the black women would make kits for the black soldiers. Each kit contained a knitted sweater, helmet (a knitted skull cap), and wristlets. (Courtesy of George Newman.)

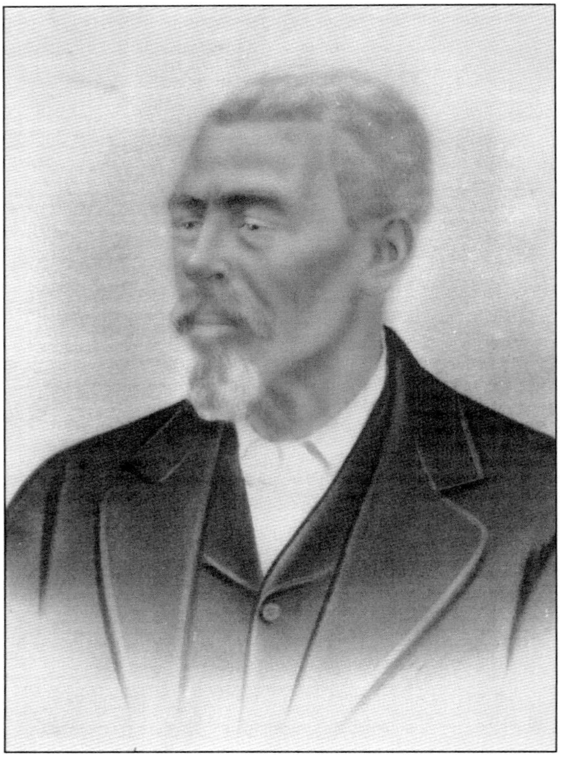

Howell P. Swinea served in the Civil War as a Union solider. He served in the 110th U.S. Colored Infantry, Company I. He entered the military as a private and was promoted to a corporal. On November 28, 1866, he married Mary Holloway; to their marriage came one son, Yancy, and one daughter, Mary, who married Morgan Dunn. Swinea, also a minister, served as pastor of St. Elizabeth Primitive Baptist Church from around 1879 until 1887 before moving to another church. (Courtesy of Bob Swinea)

Pictured are Clyde Gardner and his wife, Cathy. Clyde Gardner's parents were Raymond and Frances Gardner. Born in 1913, he went to grade school and high school in Elkton. Clyde joined the U.S. Navy at the age of 18 and never retuned to Giles County except to visit his family. Cathy Gardner is wearing a unique paisley-printed dress with a heart-shape gathered bodice accented by a flowered stovepipe hat.

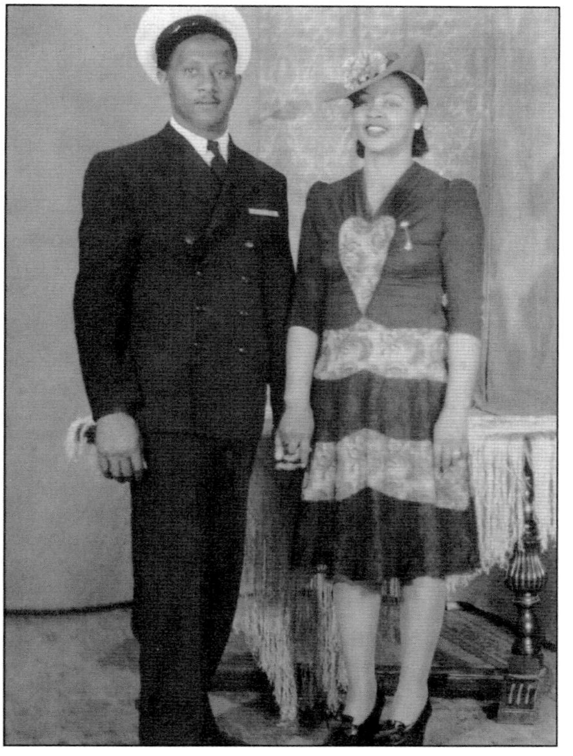

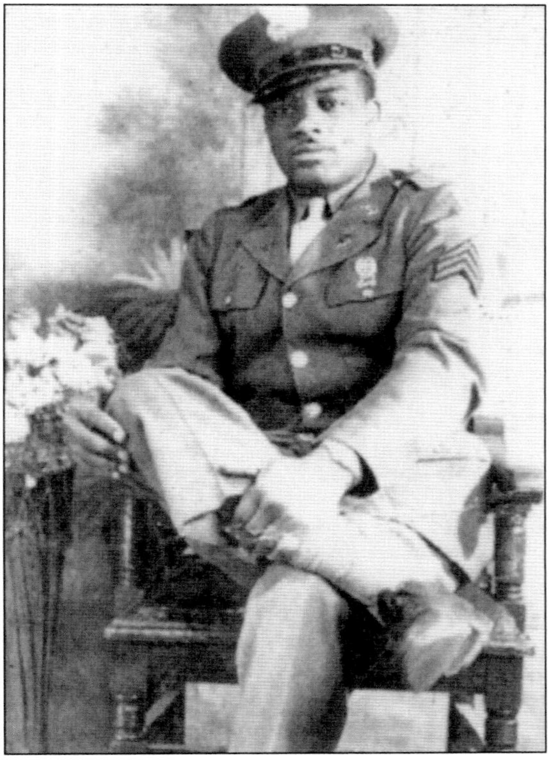

Greatus "Jeep" Vance was born on January 17, 1917, in Elkton, Tennessee, and was the fourth child of Philmore and Ethel (Bailey) Vance. Greatus had a natural talent for art and was a sergeant in the army. His art skills are shown in the drawing of his father, Philmore, in this book on page 104. He was nicknamed "Jeep" because of an incident he had falling from a Jeep. Greatus departed his life at the early age of 48. (Courtesy of Michiko Bailey.)

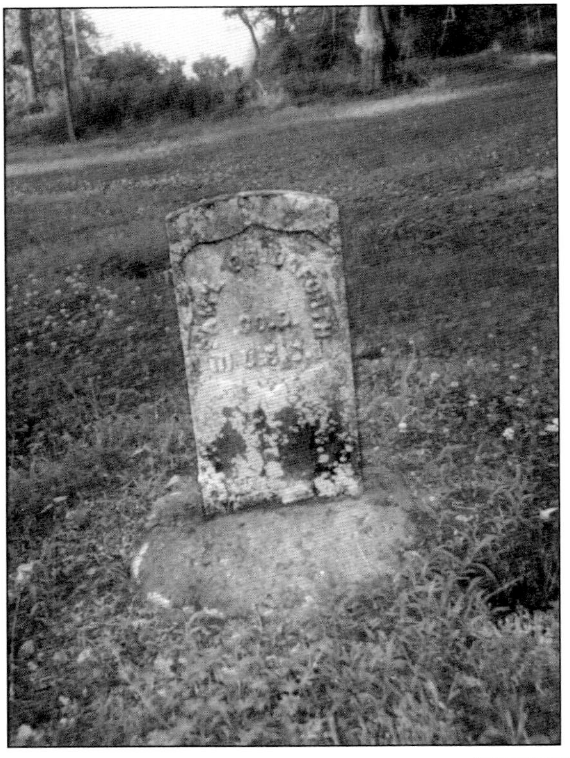

This is the headstone and grave site of Samuel "Sam" Bridgeforth. When the 111th U. S. Colored Infantry regiment was organized on June 25, 1864, Sam was recruited. He became a private in Company D and served until the unit was mustered out on April 30, 1866. He received an invalid pension, known today as a disability pension, from the Civil War. He was a farmer and a Baptist minister of two churches, St. Mark in Elkmont, Alabama, and St. Elizabeth in Elkton, where he was pastor for 27 years until 1914. He was the first black person to drive a hearse carriage, pulled by horses, for Austin Brothers Funeral Home. Sam died on March 23, 1918. He is buried in Union Hill cemetery in Elkton. (Courtesy of Lula Bridgeforth.)

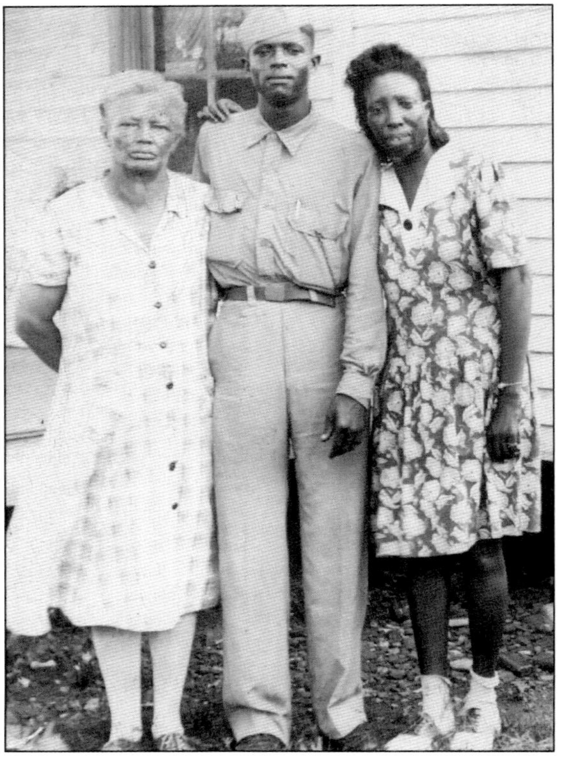

Mary Gardner is standing with her nephew Walker "Jack" Gardner Jr. and niece Ella Mary Eddings in this picture taken when Walker was home in Elkton visiting his parents, Walker and Lizzie Gardner, while on leave during World War II. Ella Mary Eddings was the daughter of Susan and Willie Eddings of Elkton.

Six

A FASHION BLAST FROM THE PAST

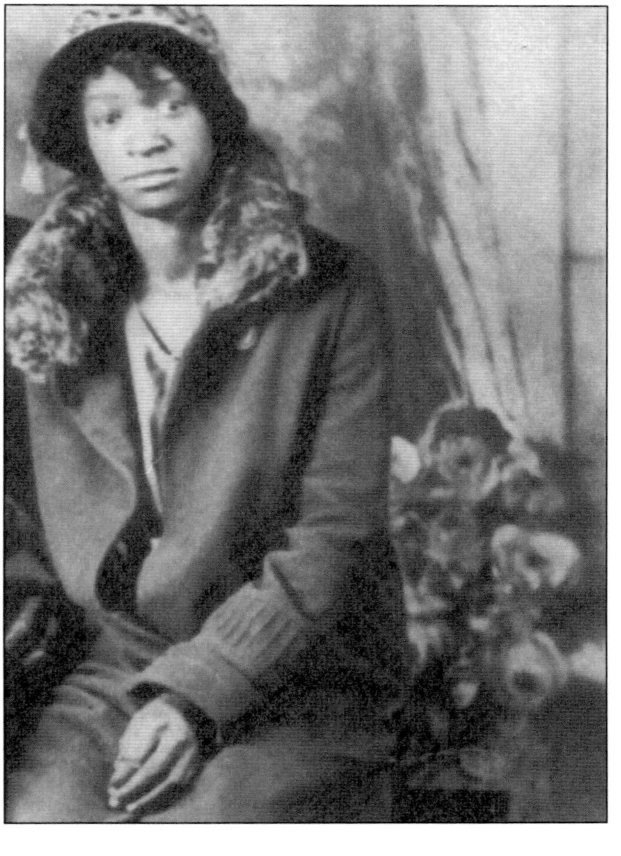

Minnie Bell (Coleman) Smith is seen here wearing a pinched-cuff-sleeve, fur-collar coat with matching hat. Born in Giles, Minnie Bell was the daughter of Andrew Coleman and Emma Love. Her mother, Emma, was born on April 9, 1877, and her father, Andrew, was born about 1876; the couple wed on December 23, 1893. Minnie Bell, born in February 1904, was the couple's only daughter. She had four brothers: Robert, Roosevelt, John, and H. Wood. The family later moved to Logan, West Virginia, where Minnie married Eddie Richard Smith. (Courtesy of Shirley Wimbley.)

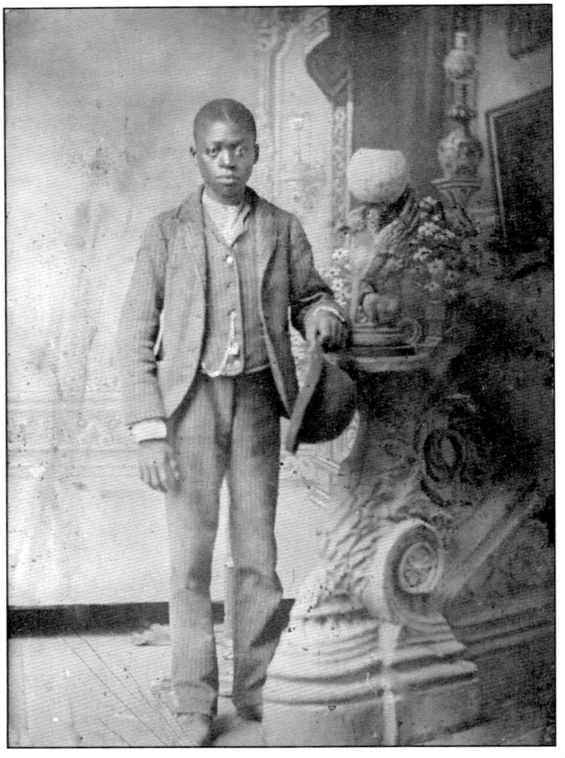

This is a tintype of an unidentified young man of the Giles community. He is posing for his picture wearing a pin-striped three-piece suit with a white mandarin collar shirt, the classic pocket watch of the time, and a derby-style hat in his hand.

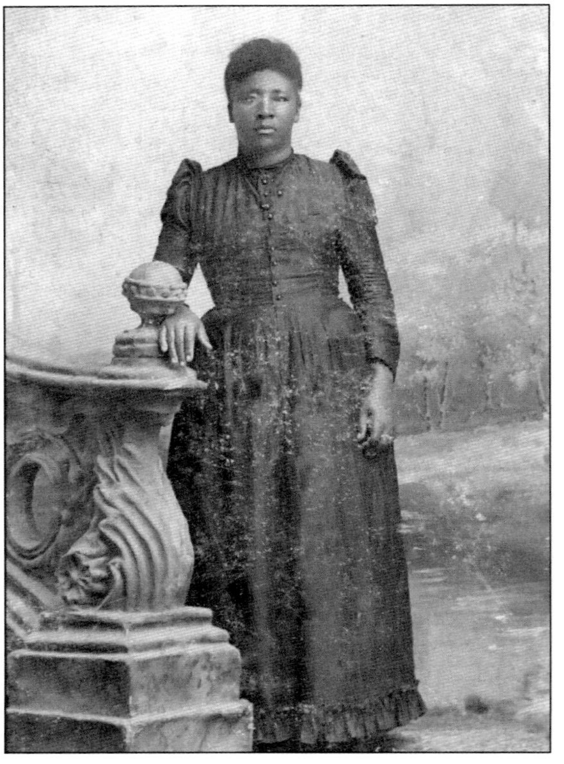

This picture is believed to be of Mary (Gardner) Benson in what was known as a day dress. It has a fitted waist with puffed and tapered sleeves. Mary was the third child of Rachel (Vasser) and Tom Gardner. She was born on December 3, 1866, and married Alonzo Benson on July 2, 1881. The couple only had one child, daughter Georgia. Mary's siblings include Millie, Martha, Ida, Matt, Stephen, and Lizzie.

Velma (Gardner) Braden is seen wearing a silk skirt and blouse with matching cuffs and bodice. The outfit is accompanied by a pair of high-top lace boots, and Velma has a side-swooped pompadour hairstyle. She was born on May 5, 1895, in Elkton to Matt and Henrietta (Jenkins) Gardner. On December 27, 1919, she married Robert Braden. To their union came three children: Magnolia, Robert Jr., and Frances.

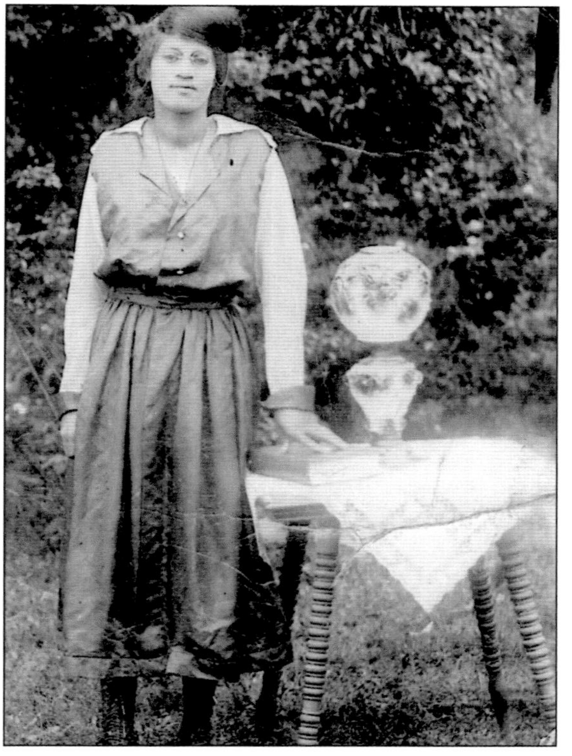

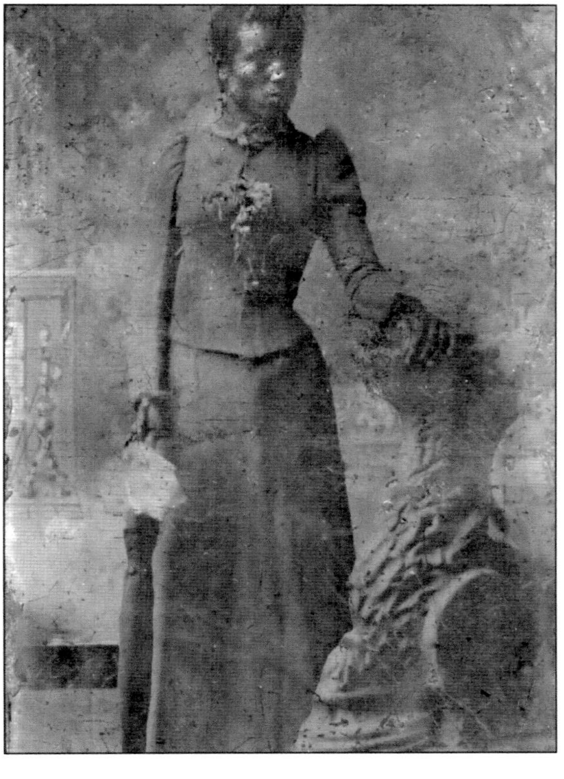

This is a tintype of an unidentified person in the community. She is wearing a dressy day skirt with a tapered and fitted high-neck blouse. The blouse is accented with what seems to be crocheted rosettes, and she is styling a pulled-back pin-up hairstyle. Lastly, she has her parasol umbrella by her side.

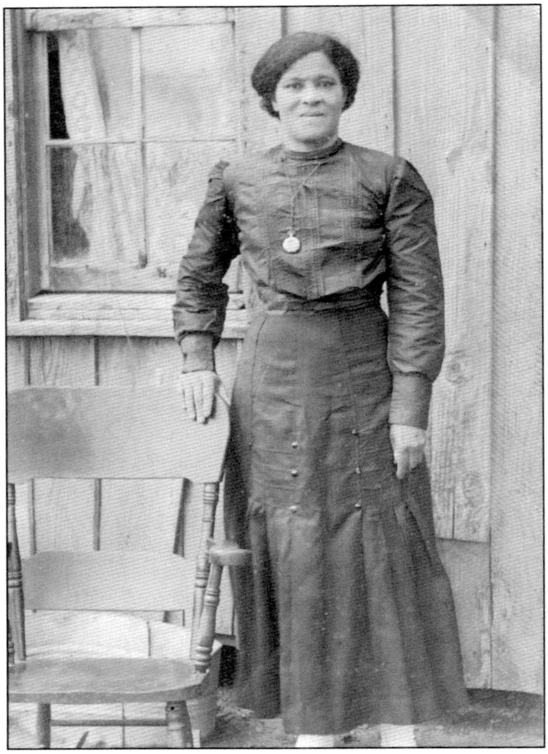

Lula (Holt) Freeman is seen in a c. 1900 lady's high-collar, long-cuff shirtwaist top and a six-button, five-gore skirt with a 1900s picture locket around her neck. Lula was born about 1875 and raised in Popular Hill near the community of Lick Skillet. Her parents were George and Amanda (Brown) Holt. On January 7, 1894, Lula married Luke Freeman, and their children were Mamie, Susie, Vera, and John. After the death of Luke, she married Lem Harris; they had no children.

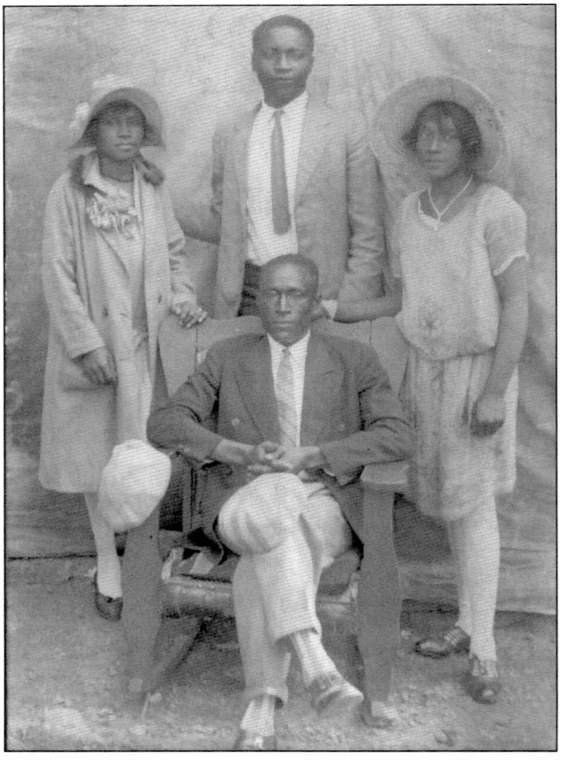

Millie Johnson (left), Russell Grisby, Rosetta Beatty (right), and John Ed Holt (seated) all grew up in the Elkton and Prospect communities of Giles County. All are dressed up in their Sunday-best suits, dresses, coats, and hats. It looks as if they could possibly be on a double date. The fashion here seems to be floppy hats for the women and over-sized caps for the men. The cap resting on John Holt's knee is striped and matches his stripped socks. Russell married Millie on April 24, 1930, and John married Rosetta on October 20, 1929.

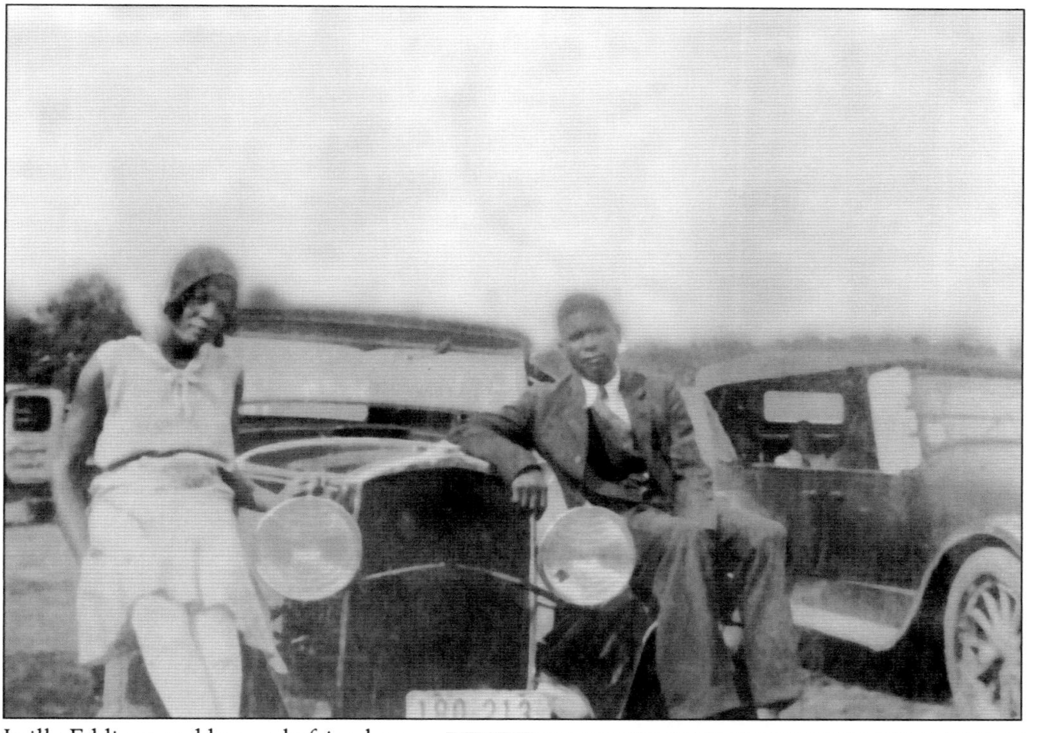

Iwilla Eddings and her male friend are all dressed up and on a possible visit to the local park with other friends after attending Sunday morning church services. They are pictured sitting on the body of a *c.* 1930 Chevrolet while a friend parked next to them is sitting on a *c.* 1927 Ford Model T, two popular, fashionable, American-made cars of the past.

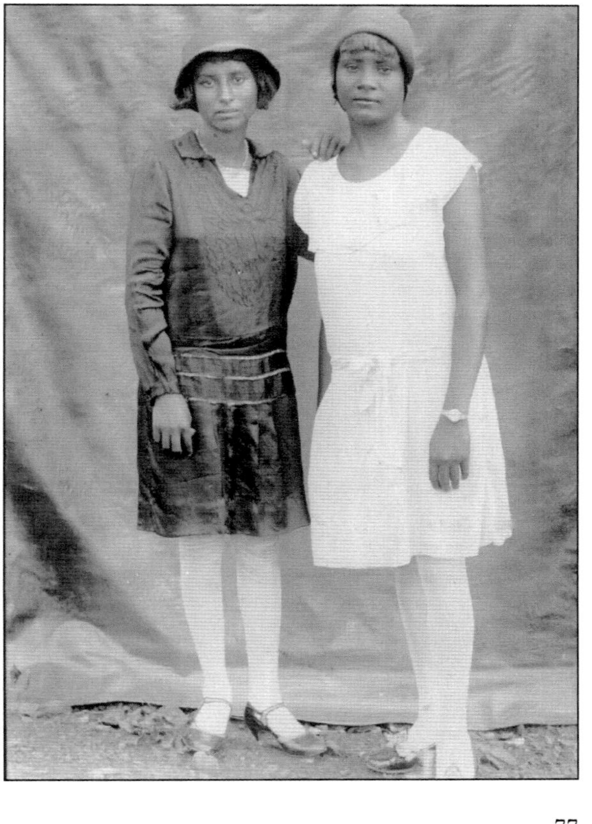

Sweetie Bledsoe (left) and Henrietta "Hen" Gardner are posing for the camera in their cloche hats and drop-waist dresses. Sweetie was the daughter of Herman and Nettie (Sherrill) Bledsoe. Henrietta was on born May 12, 1909, to Rev. Raymond Gardner and his wife, Frances. "Hen" moved to Louisville, Kentucky, where she met Van B. McCray. She and Van married in March 1937, and they had three children, Clara, Frances, and Gladys.

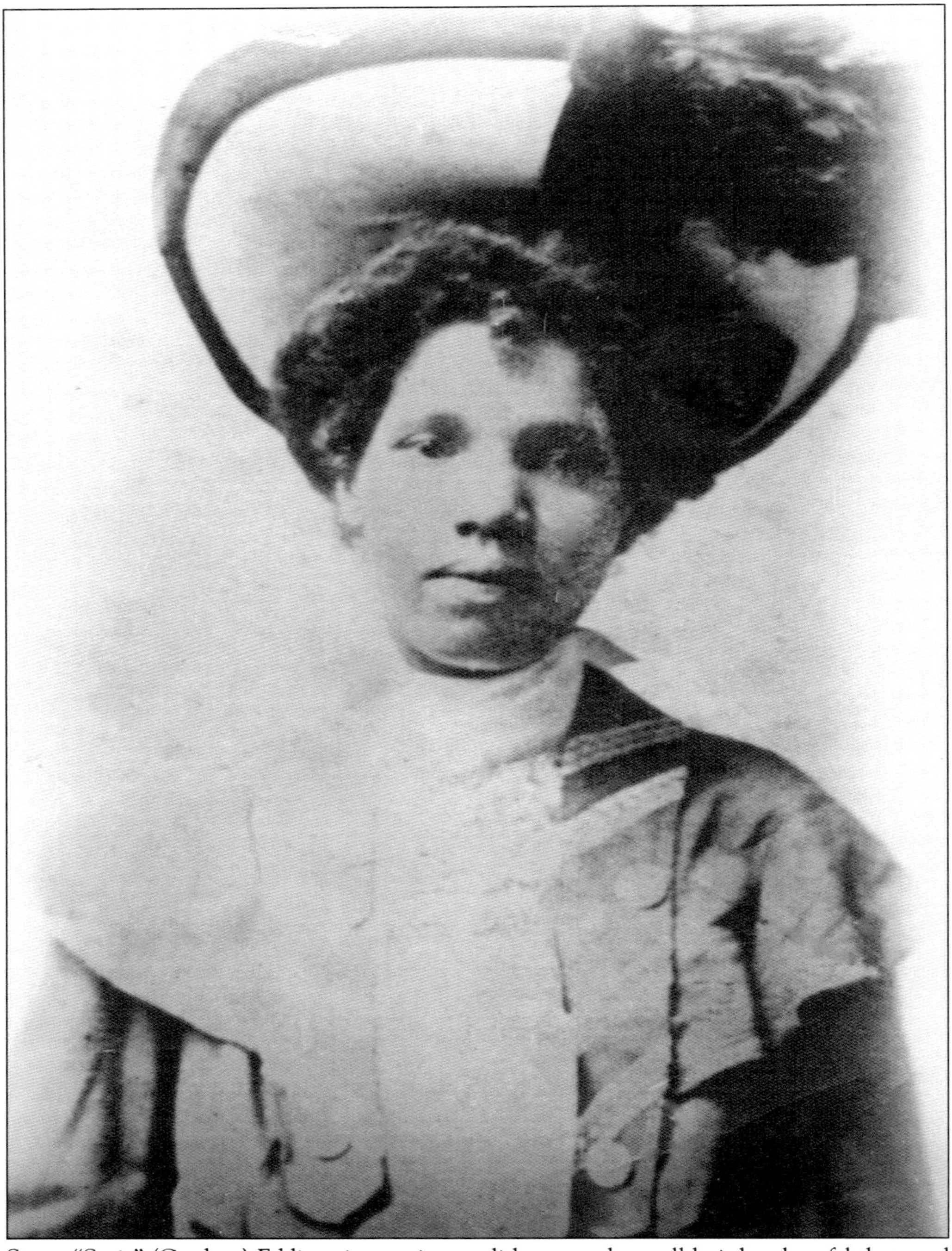

Susan "Susie" (Gardner) Eddings is seen in a stylish pompadour-roll hairdo, plum felt hat, and a traveling jacket. She was the third child of Matt and Henrietta (Jenkins) Gardner. Born on December 25, 1881, she married Willie Eddings on December 22, 1903, and they had four daughters, Ella Mary, Anna Lee, Iwilla, and Alberta. Susie lived and worked at the Gardner farm all her life, and she and her daughter, Ella Mary, took care of her parents until their deaths. Susan Eddings died on April 14, 1975. She is buried in the Union Hill cemetery.

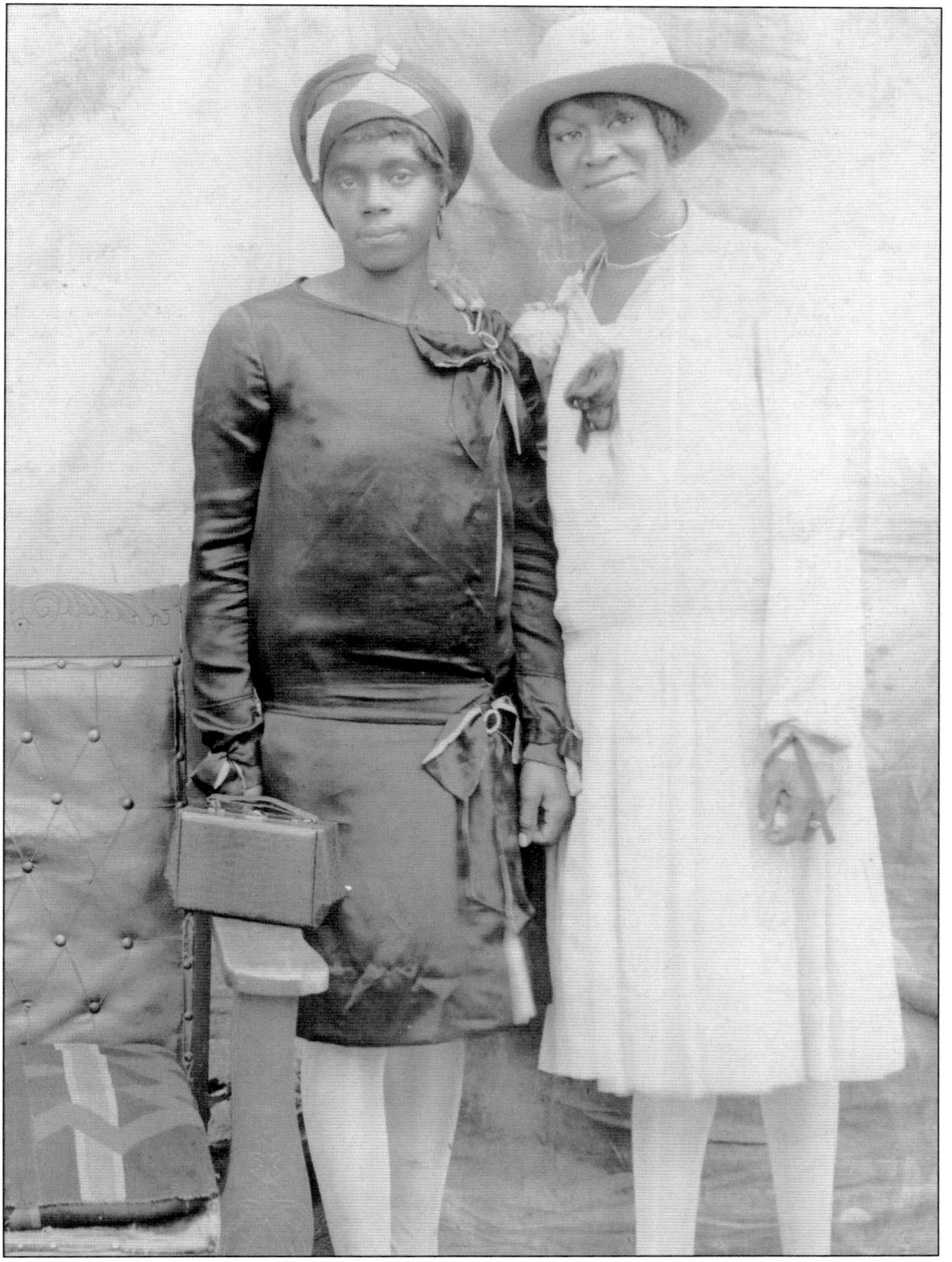

Cousins Rosetta (left) and Martha Beatty were both born and raised in Giles. Both ladies were educated in the colored school of Elkton. Martha is the daughter of Emmett and Charity (Vassar) Beatty, and Rosetta is the daughter of Sunny and Cornelia Beatty. Rosetta has on a satin, 1920s, drop-waist-style dress, turban hat, and a pillbox purse. Martha has on a pleated chiffon dress and a felt bowler hat.

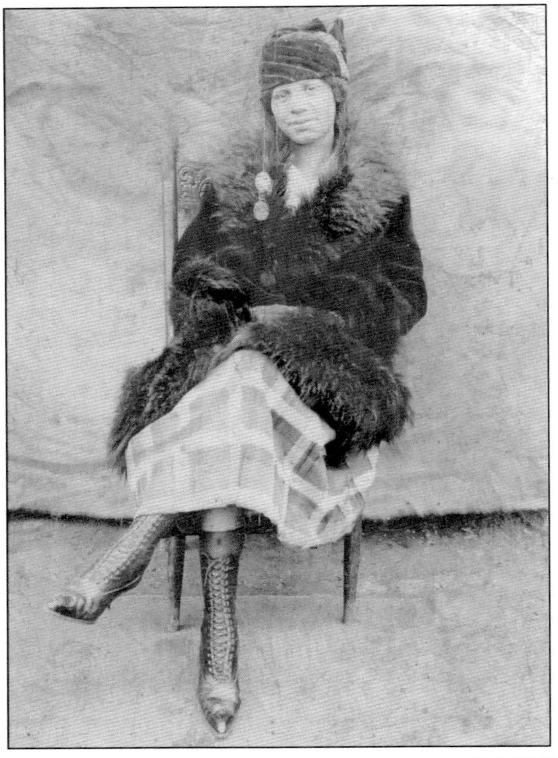

Lura Mae Gardner was born in Elkton to Walker and Lizzie Mae (Hogan) Gardner on September 26, 1919. She is pictured here in fashionable 1940s, three-quarter-length, tuxedo-style coat trimmed in fur; knee-high laced boots; and a cloche hat.

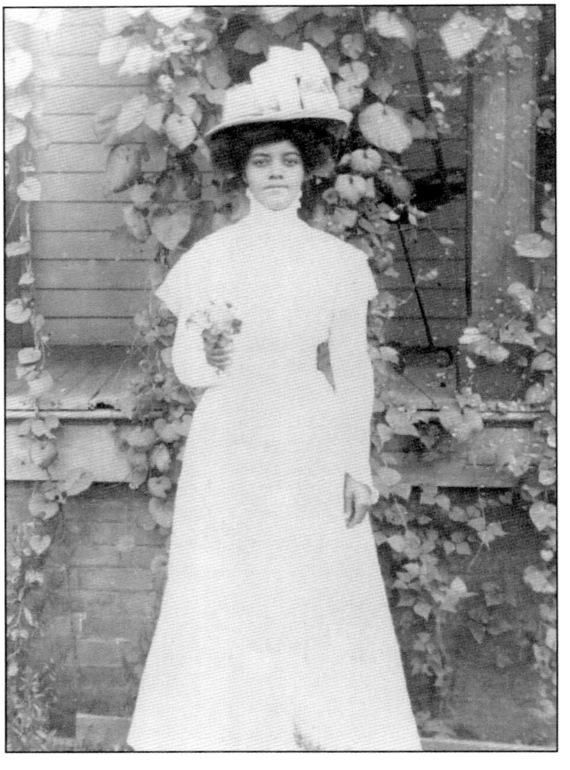

Pictured in her wedding dress is Isabella (Pruitt Lewis) Davis in front of her house in Pulaski. The dress is white with a fitted waist, long sleeves, and a bertha collar. Instead of a veil, she opted for a wide-brimmed ribbon-bouquet hat. She said "I do" to James Alex Davis on December 13, 1876, but this picture was taken in the spring because of the winter marriage. The ivy backdrop makes for a perfect bridal picture. The couple was blessed with kids Gant, Sally, Otis "Champ," and Tommy.

Ellen (Gardner) Vance, pictured with a front-pompadour hairstyle, plaid poplin pinafore skirt, and wide ponytail bow, was the sixth child born to Matt and Henrietta (Jenkins) Gardner in September 1887. On December 28, 1909, her uncle elder Sam Bridgeforth pronounced her and Benjamin Vance husband and wife. To their union came three boys: William, Servier, and Willis. Ellen never got the chance to see her boys grow up, marry, or have children, as she and her husband died at an early age, and the boys were raised by their father's mother, Winnie (Bass) Vance. (Courtesy of Larry Vance.)

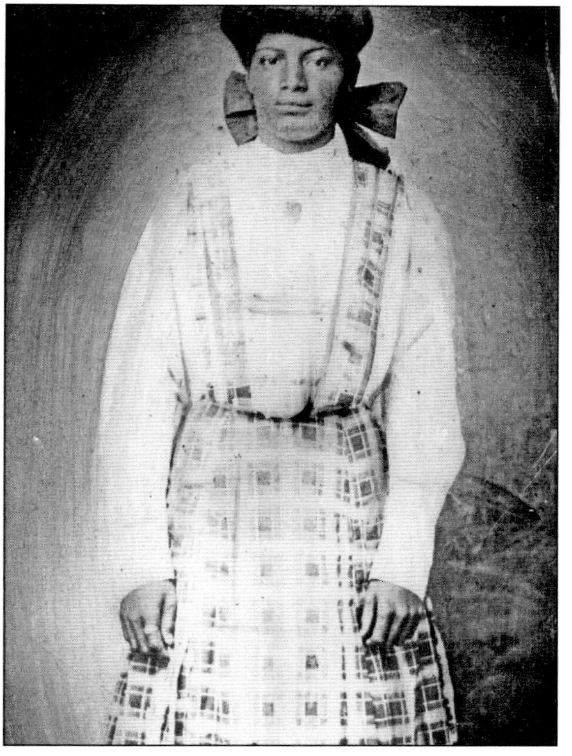

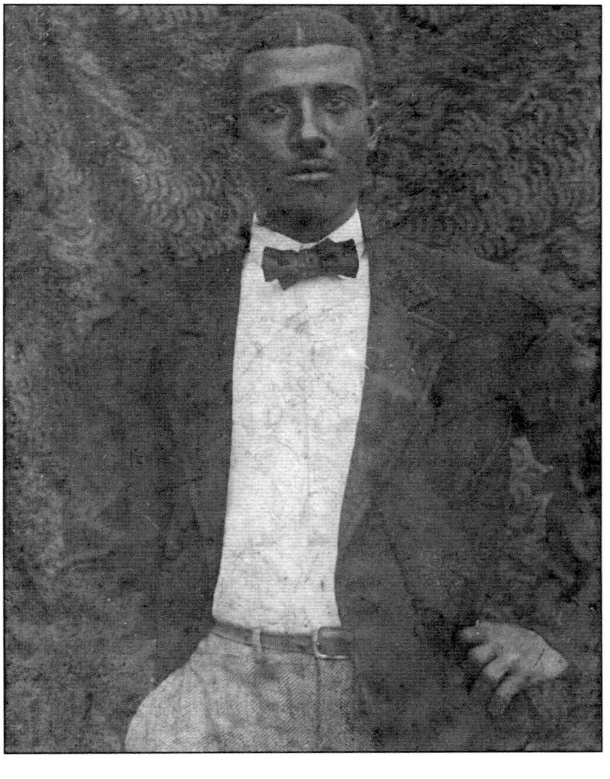

Looking dapper, William Huston Vance is seen in a sport jacket, bow tie, and tweed pants. He was born in 1911 to Benjamin and Ellen (Gardner) Vance. Ben and Ellen married on December 24, 1909. William was always called by his middle name, Huston. His parents died before 1920, and his grandmother Winnie (Bass Vance) Phelps raised him and his brothers. Other siblings of Huston include Servier, born in 1913, and Willis S., born in 1917. Huston's brother Sevier married Flossie Bridgeforth.

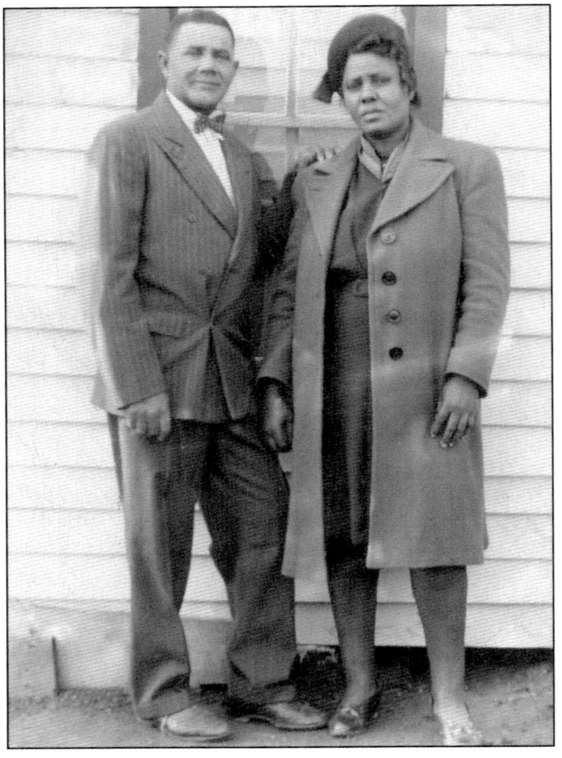

John Gardner is pictured in a double-breasted, pin-striped suit and a bow tie while his wife, Alma (McClaurine) Gardner, is shown wearing a multicolored, button-down coat and lady's-style beret. They were residents of Elkton and on October 1, 1922, were married by John's brother and minister, Raymond. To their union came four children: James Williams, Flournoy, Elizabeth, and Dorothy Jean, and Alma was also mother to John's three older boys, John, Robert, and Will.

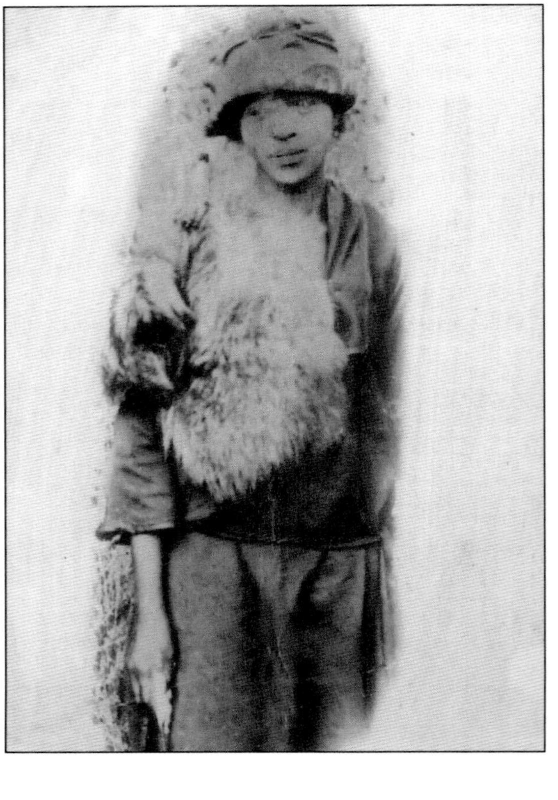

Mattie Flora (Jones) Birdsong was born in 1905 and lived in Giles her entire life. Her parents were William and Tommie Jones, also of Giles. Mattie is seen in this picture with a Kolinsky fur hanging off her shoulder and a cloche hat on her head. Mattie married Mitchell Birdsong on September 21, 1929. The marriage was performed by Rev. E. D. Franklin and witnessed by Mattie's brother Willie Jones (Courtesy of the Birdsong family.)

Ellis Vassar is seen here in a black-and-white plaid, short-waisted jacket. Ellis is the son of Manville "Man" and Martha (Gardner Love) Vassar. Ellis married Lou Sherrell on December 26, 1901, and they were blessed with three boys: Shelton, Collier, and Percy. After Lou's death, he married Sarah Holt and to this union six children were born: Mary Ellis, Ruth, Louise, James, John, and Xie, who died as an infant.

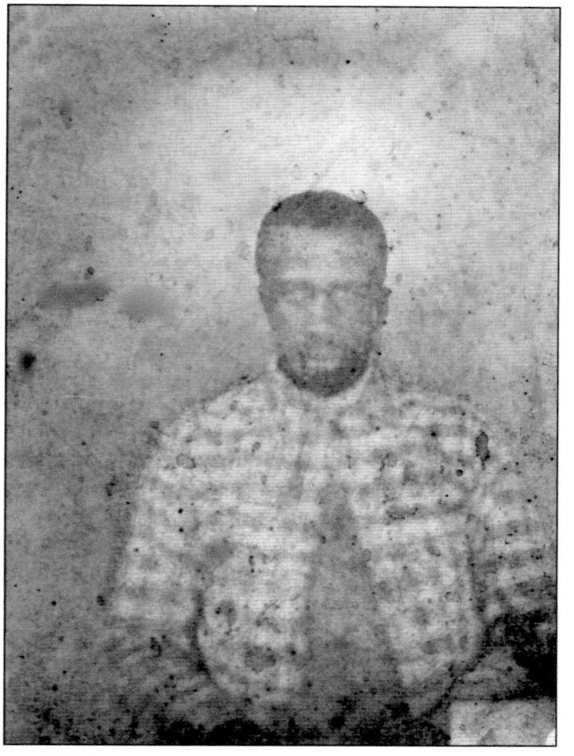

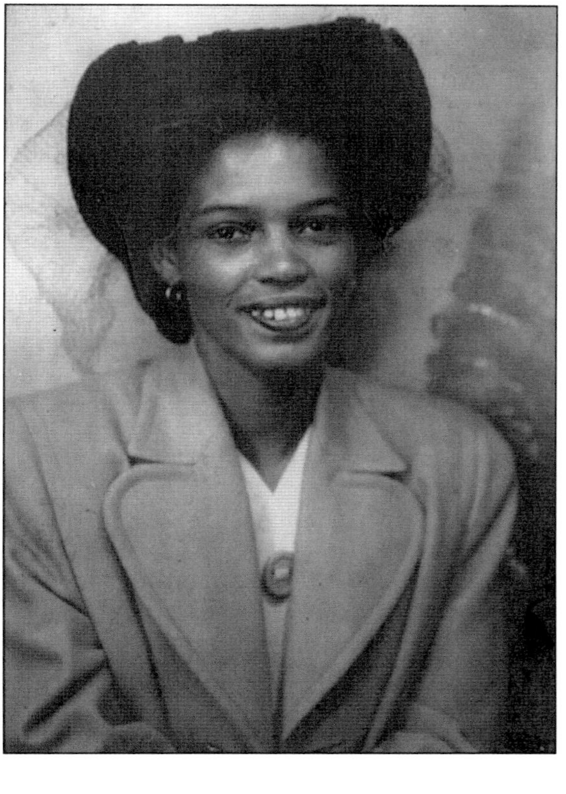

Louise (Vance) Bailey was born in November 1918 in Elkton and named after her grandmother Louise Gardner. Like all the Vances, she carried her own unique personality, and she enjoyed traveling later in life. In April 1947, two weeks after giving birth to her fourth child, Louise died at the young age of 29. (Courtesy of Michiko Bailey.)

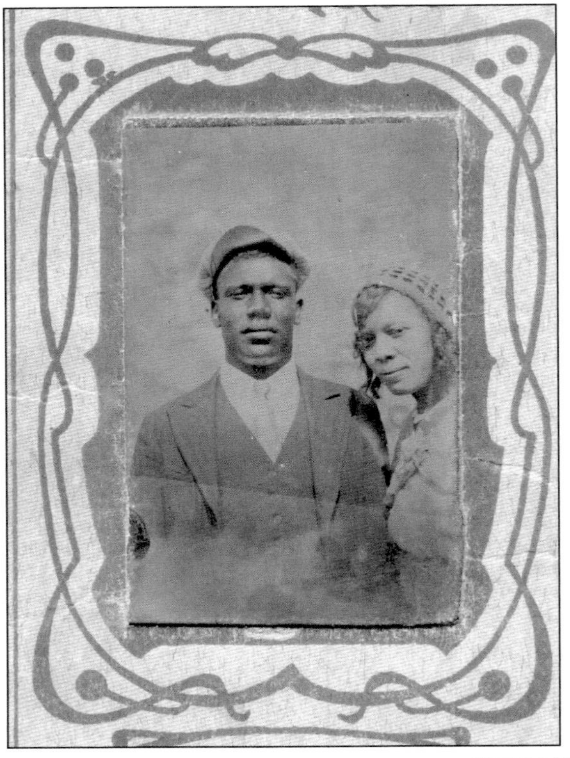

The words "yours forever" written on the picture frame seem to suggest that these individuals will be together forever. Well, they were in the same family and together forever, as these two, A. G. Gardner and Iwilla (Eddings) Phelps, were cousins. Both individuals were born and raised in Elkton. Iwilla moved to Chicago, where she later got married and had three children, Henry, Leon, and Marie. A. G. stayed in Elkton and never married nor had any children.

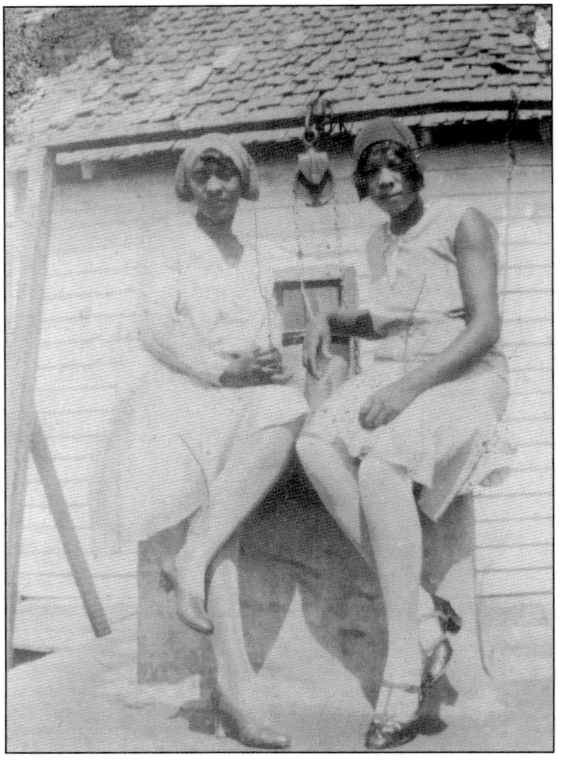

Anna Lee Eddings (left) and a friend are seen striking a pose for the camera. Her friend is wearing a wide-band, flop-down turban, and Anna Lee is wearing a decorative flapper hat. Anna Lee was the daughter of Susan and Willie Eddings of Elkton.

Frank Griffin and Matt Gardner are seen here in their Sunday best smiling for the camera. Griffin is wearing a double-breasted pin-striped suit and striped tie. Gardner is in a light-colored, single-breasted suit and striped tie. Neither man has a handkerchief in his pocket, but each has a lapel pin and a hat. (Courtesy of Joann Gardner.)

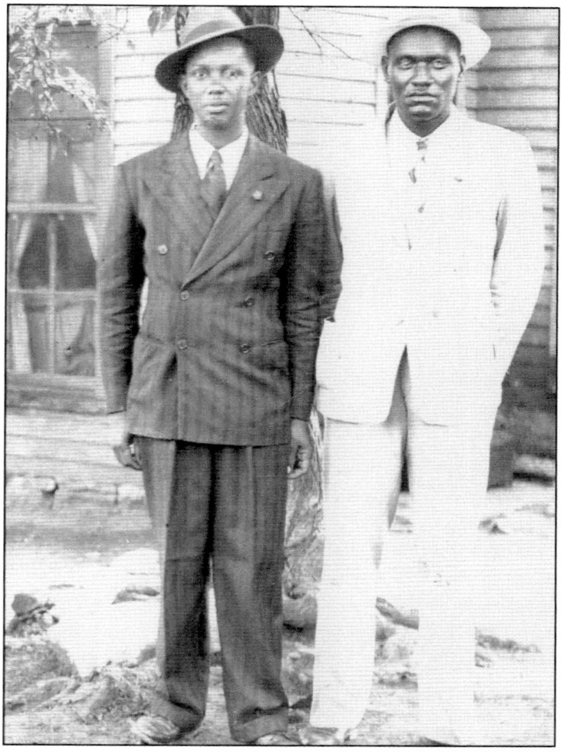

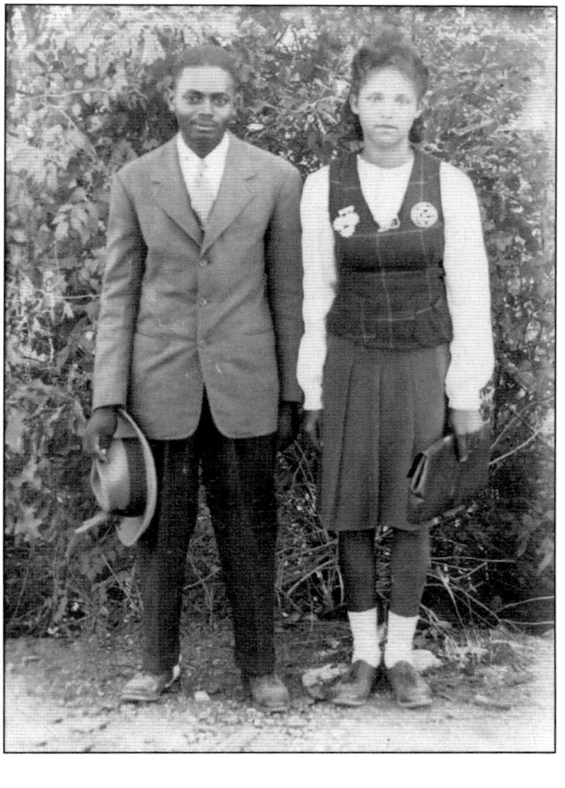

Adelle Gardner and her gentleman friend are dressed for what looks like a date. Adelle was born and schooled in Elkton. She was born on July 26, 1926, to Lizzie Hogan and Walker Gardner. Adelle is wearing a two-pocket velvet appliqué vest, pleated skirt, oxford shoes, and a clutch purse, and her date is dressed in a three-button sports jacket.

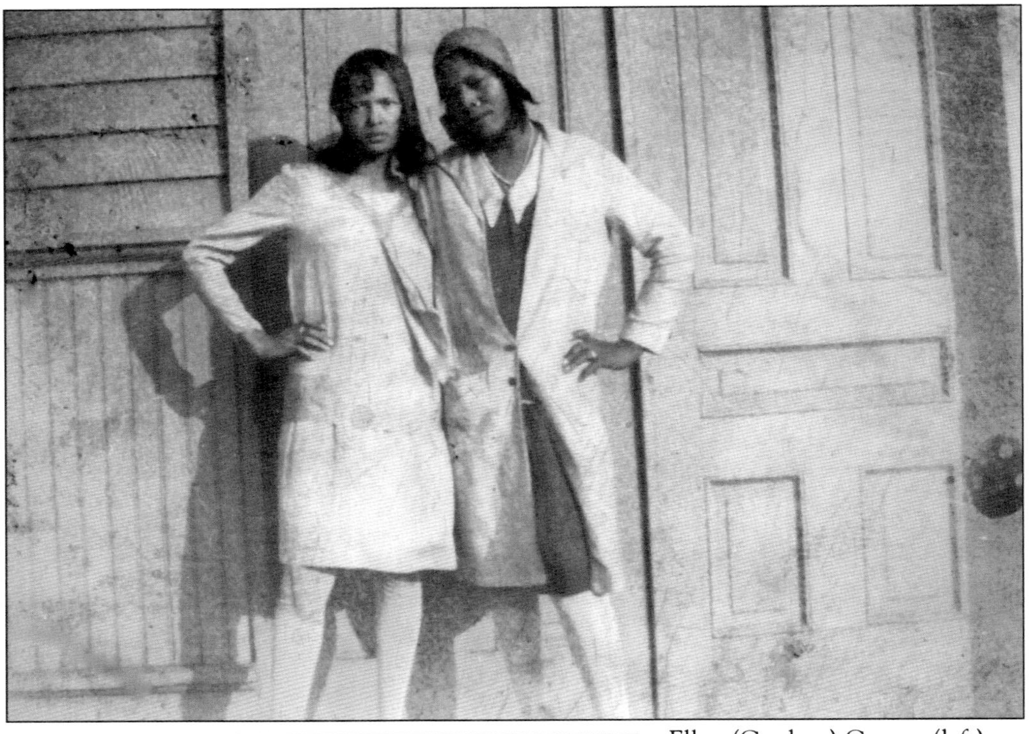

Ellen (Gardner) Cooper (left) and Anna Lee (Eddings) Bledsoe are all dressed up and ready for church. Ellen is in a sailor top two-piece dress, and Anna Lee is in her *c.* 1920 cloche. They are standing in front of what is believed to be the original St. Elizabeth Primitive Baptist Church.

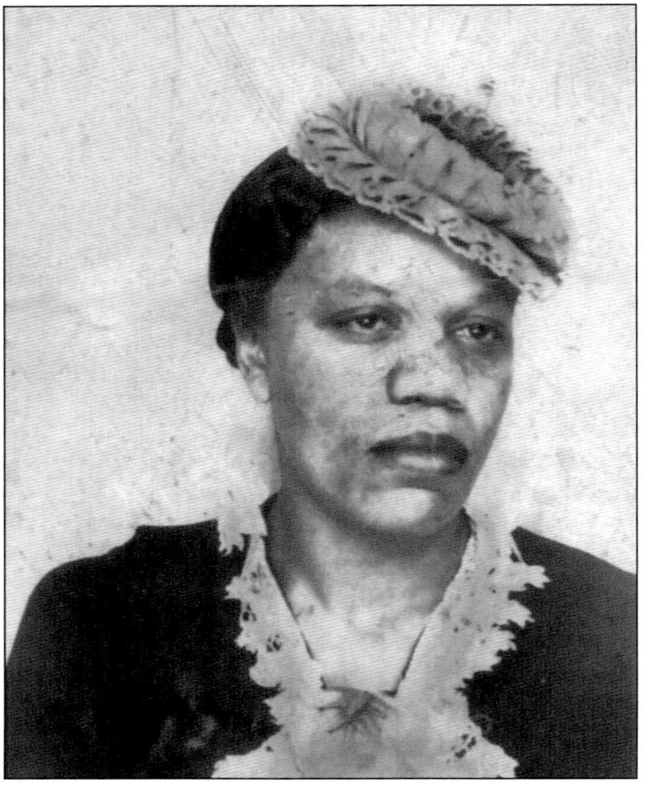

Eva Stevenson is pictured in a matching *c.* 1920 white-lace-collar dress and white-lace-trimmed cocktail hat. Eva was born and raised in Elkton. Born on August 23, 1909, her parents were Prince and Georgia (Benson) Stevenson. Eva married Joe Brown, and together they had no children, but she was a mother to Joe's children. (Courtesy of Emma Bledsoe.)

Seven

The Past Future Generation of Giles

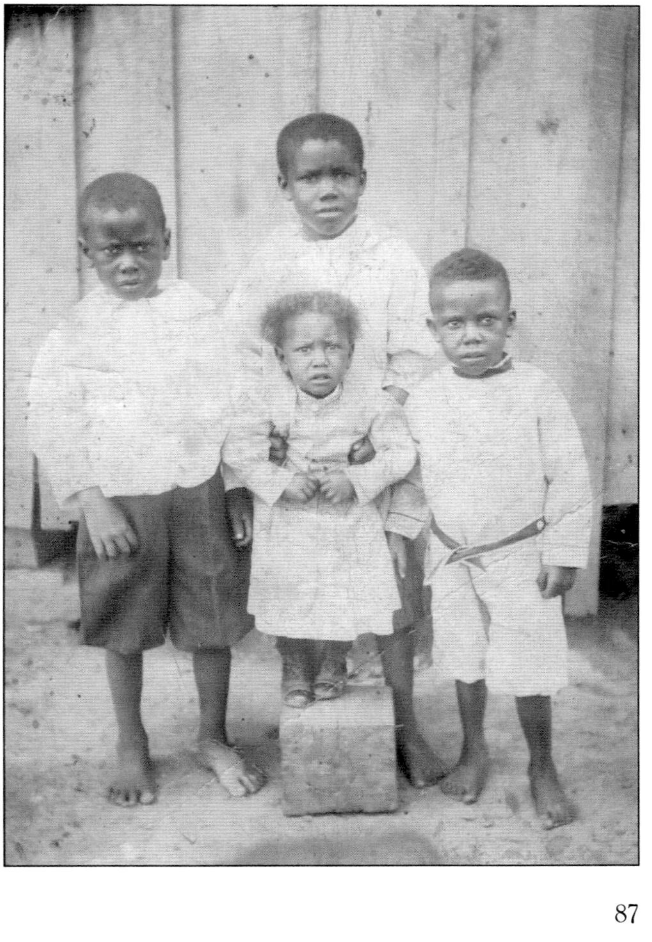

Shown here are the Gardner boys—Shellie Lee (top), A. G. (right), Joe Dee (left), and O. C. (bottom) in what looks like a dress—who were the sons of Atha Gardner and Ether (Bonner) Gardner. The boys were all born and raised in Elkton. Shellie Lee later moved to Louisville, Kentucky, and then went on to the military. After being discharged, he moved to Washington, D.C., where he became a pastor. The other three brothers stayed in Elkton. O. C. and Joe Dee made a living by farming, and A. G. farmed and worked on the railroad.

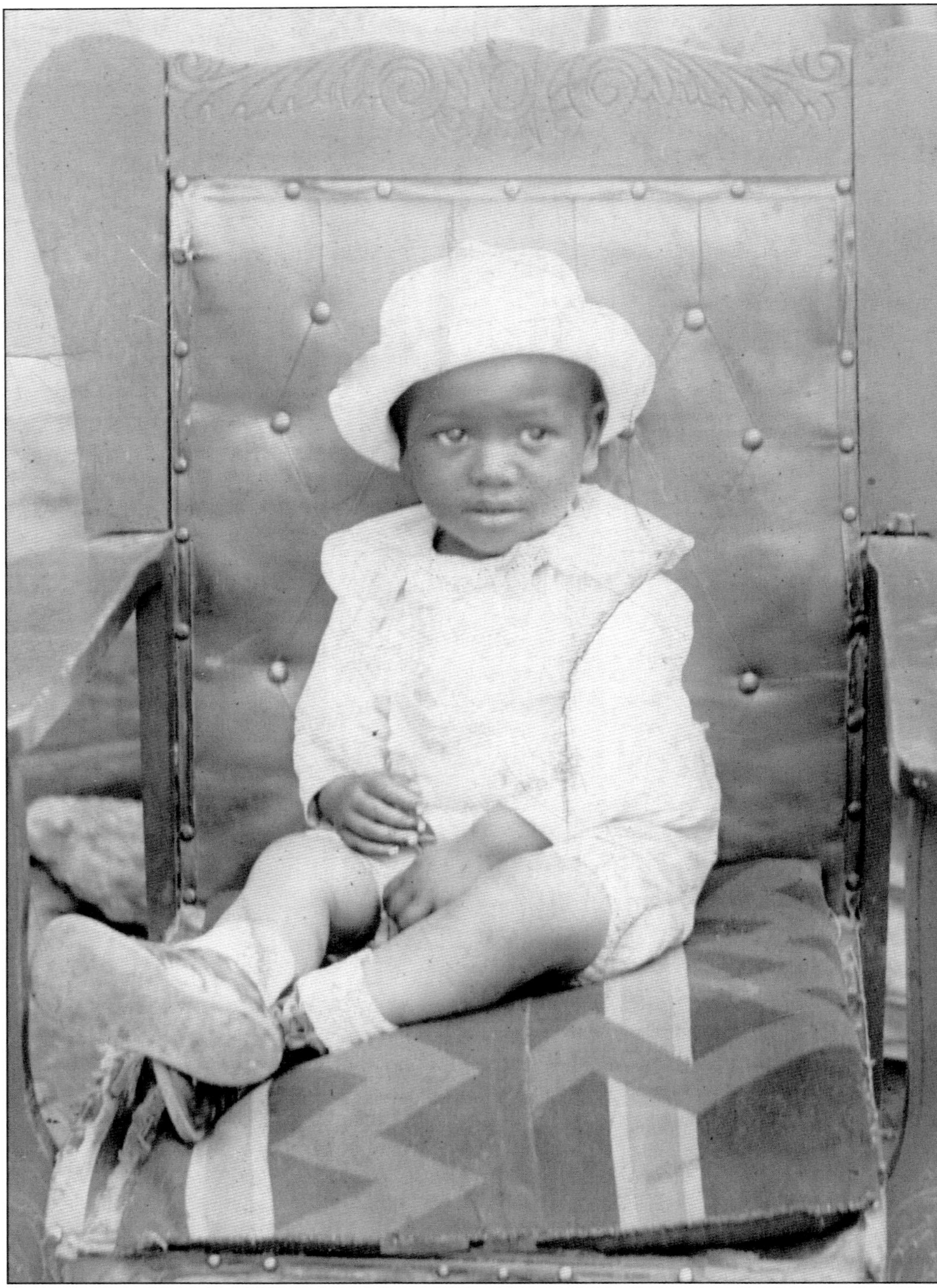

Monroe McClaurine Jr. was born in Elkton in 1927 to Monroe (Vasser) and Charity (Beatty) McClaurine. In this picture, the toddler looks a little unsure about taking a picture. McClaurine later moved to Skokie, Illinois. His siblings include Martha Lear, Clifford, Lula Belle, Emmett Jr., Escott, Sam, and James.

Robert "Dean" Neese was born around 1924, and his parents were Will and Emma (Holt) Neese. Dean was raised and educated in the Popular Hill community. He grew up and moved to Fayetteville in Lincoln County. He had one brother, William.

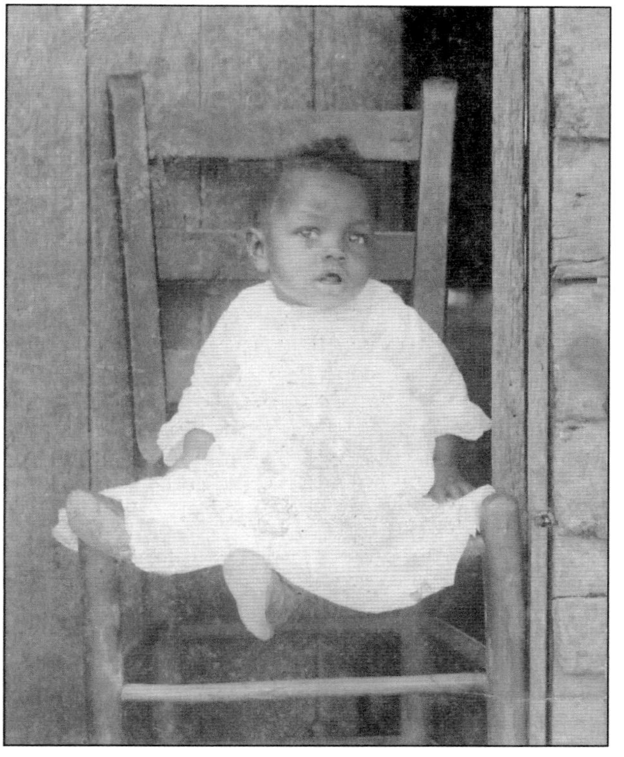

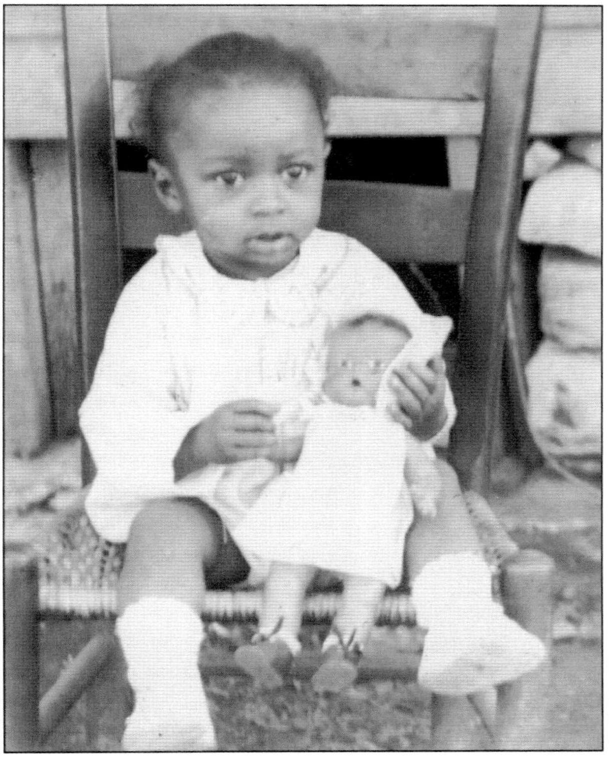

This little girl holding her baby doll is sitting on a porch in Giles. She and the doll seem to be dressed somewhat alike in white-lace-collar dresses, and both have big round pretty eyes.

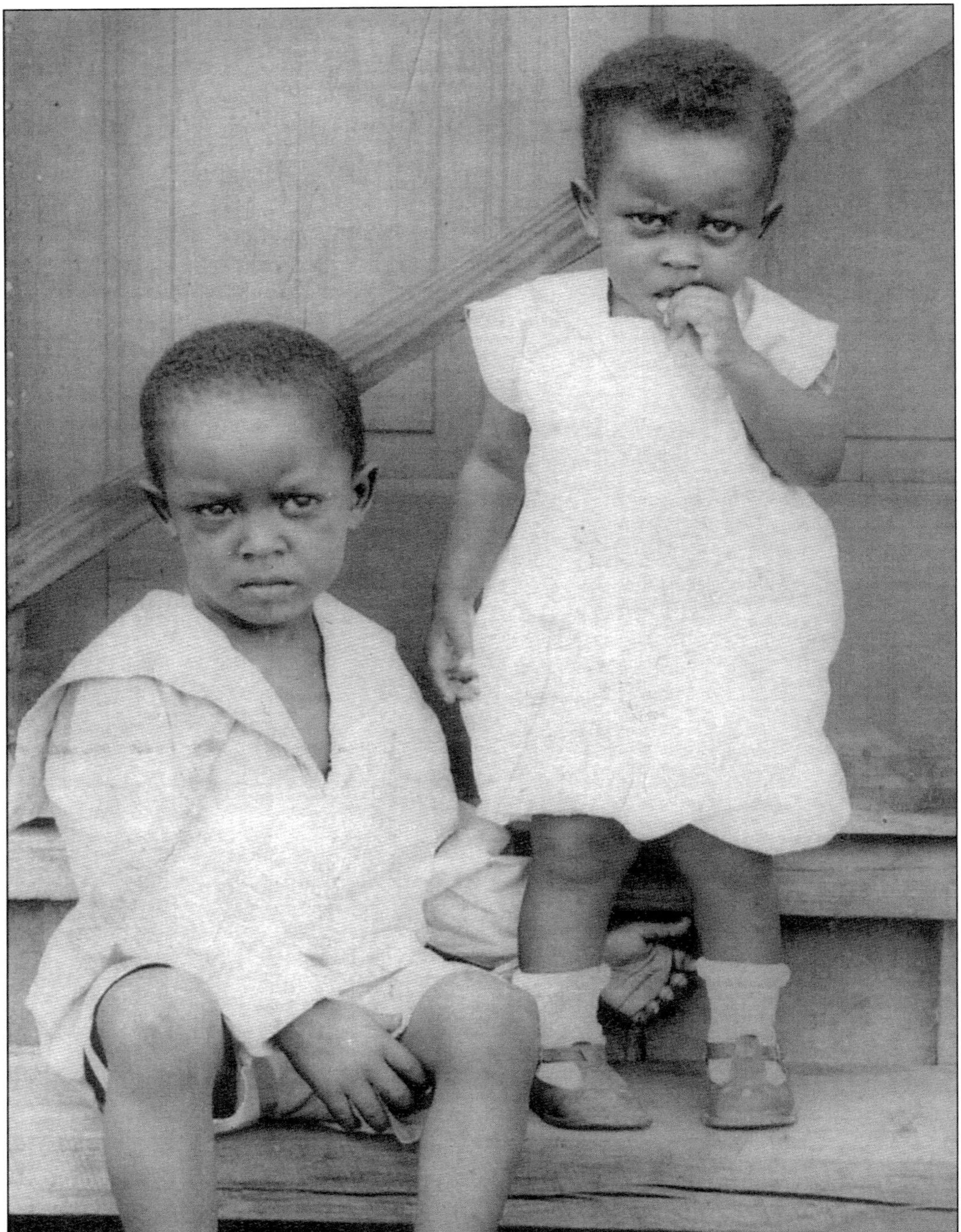

The Moody brothers are Aaron, born around 1922, and Vanderbilt "Van," born around 1924. They were the sons of Aaron Sr. and Maggie (Driver) Moody. Both grew up and were educated in the Wales community along with their sisters, Sally (Moody) London and Katherine (Moody) Ardway. Aaron married Annie, and they had nine children, Jewel, Maggie, Arnette, Connie, Linda, Anita, Cherry, Jerry, and Larry. Van married May Elizabeth, and they had two children, John and Lorrenzia. (Courtesy of Jerry Moody.)

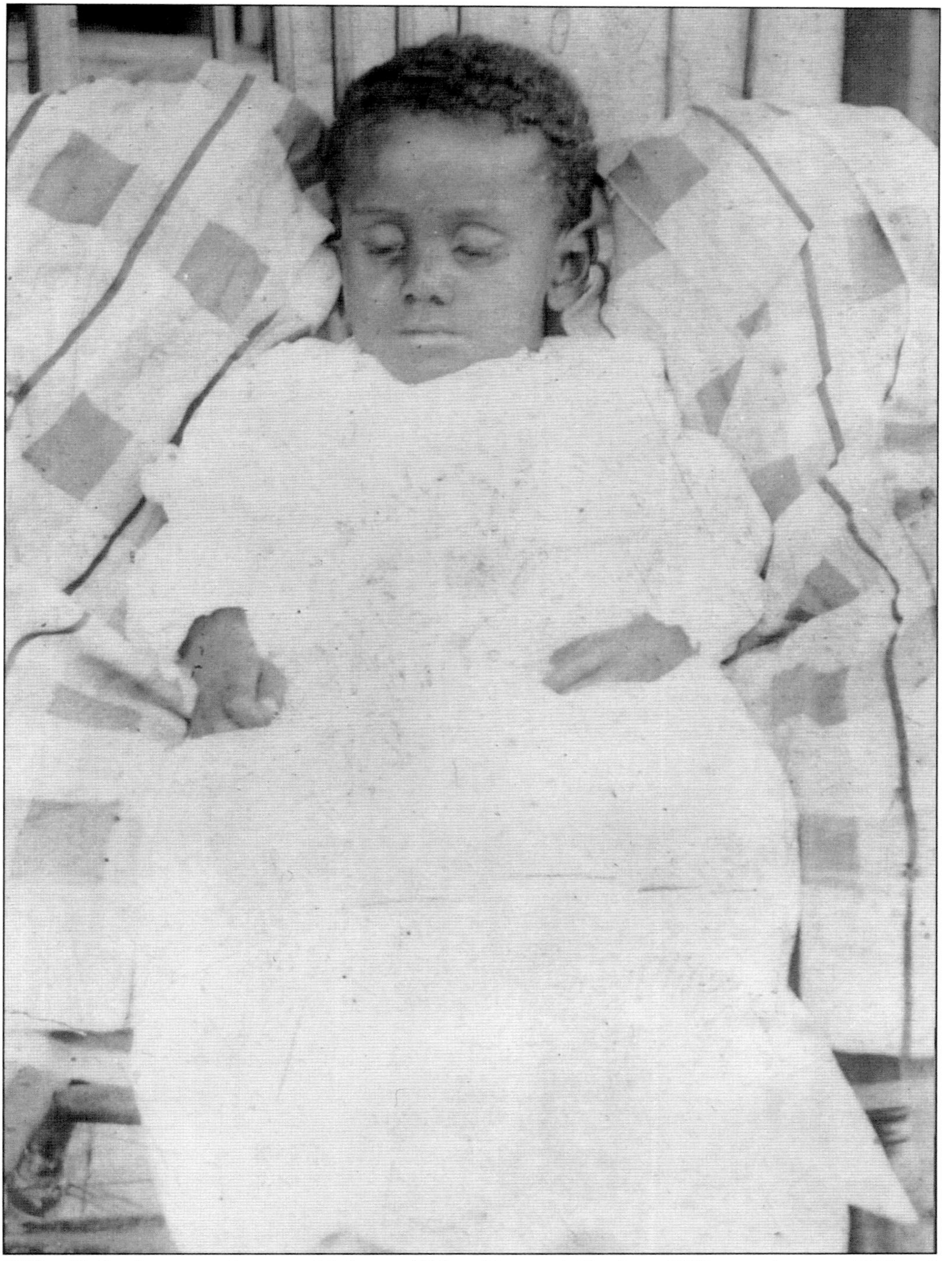

Willie T. Gardner was the son of Atha and Ether (Bonner) Gardner. Willie was born in 1919 and died in 1922 at the age of three. Willie is seen here in a romper as a sleeping angel. This picture was taken at the family home during what African Americans call a wake or "viewing of the body." (Courtesy of Joann Gardner.)

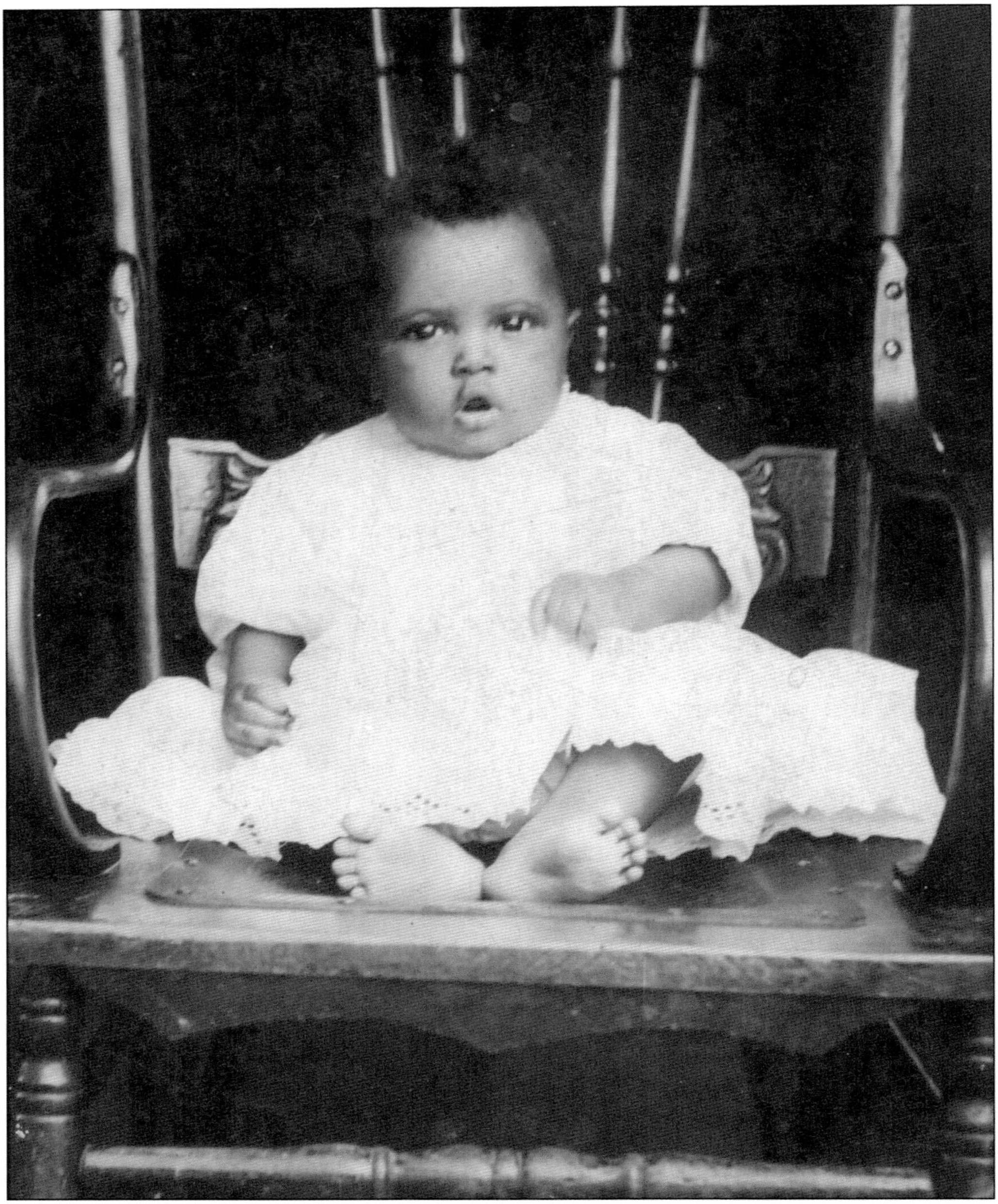

Raymond Gardner, the son of Matt and Henrietta (Jenkins) Gardner, was born on January 19, 1963. He went to grade school in Elkton and high school in Pulaski. He was attending college at Alabama A&I to become a teacher when, like his father, he was called into the ministry. After leaving Alabama A&I, he got married and became a father and a well-known minister in Giles.

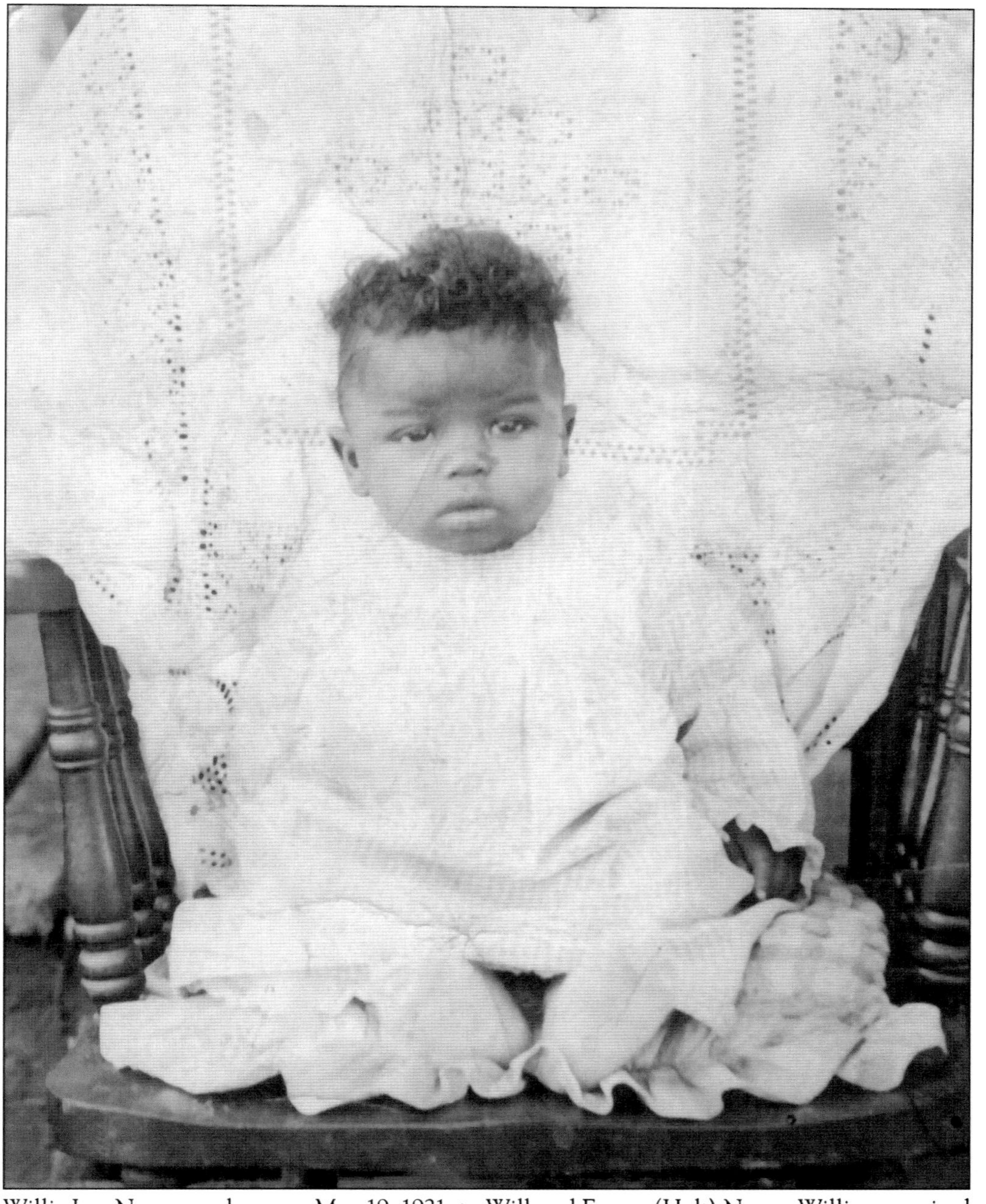

Willie Lee Neese was born on May 19, 1921, to Will and Emma (Holt) Neese. Willie was raised and educated in the Popular Hill community. He later moved to Toledo, Ohio, where he died on September 14, 1996. Willie had one brother, Robert Dean Neese.

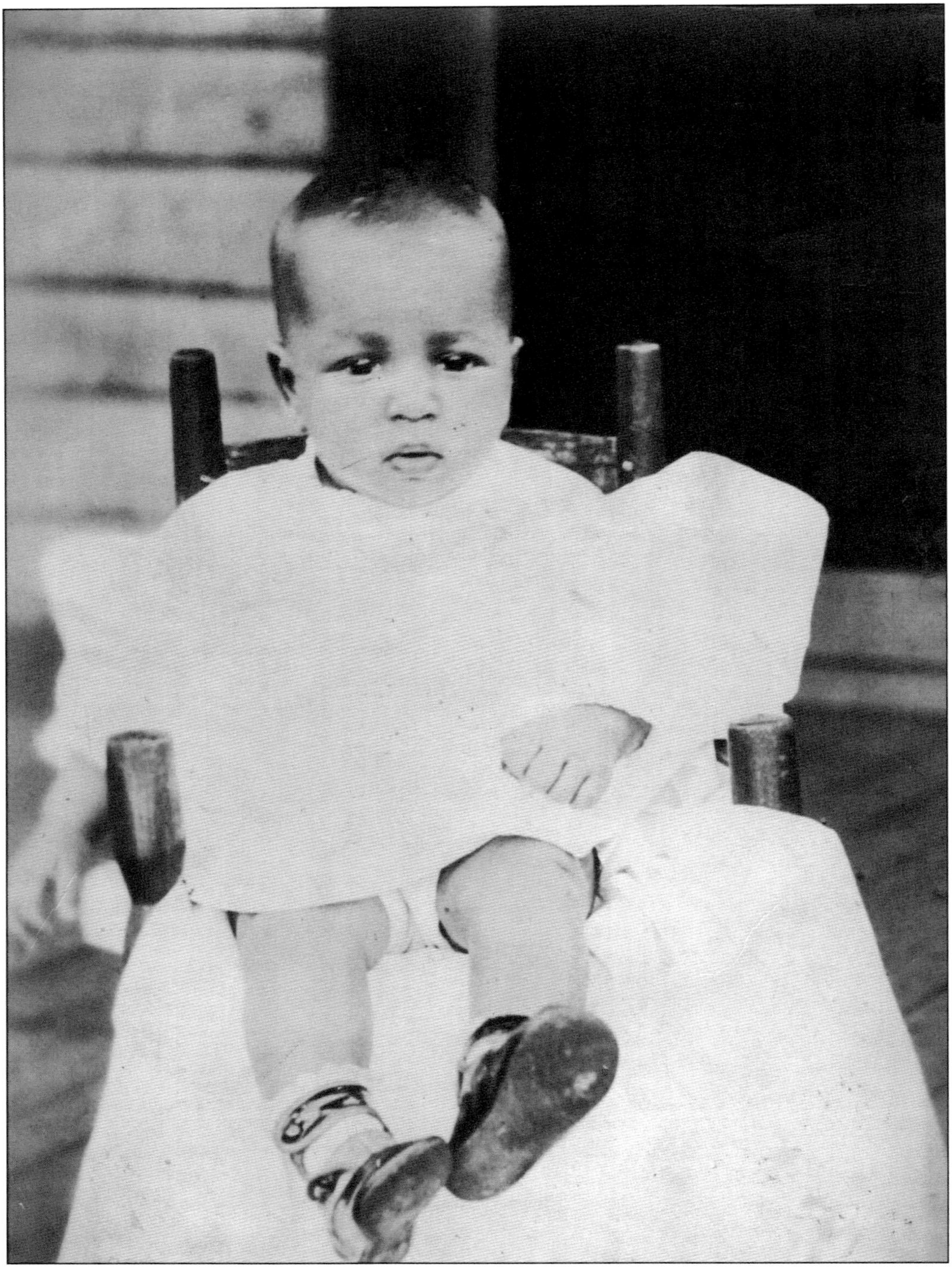

One-year-old Jewel Dean Sloan is seen sitting on her grandmother Susie Eddings's porch in Elkton. Her parents were Carl and Alberta (Eddings) Sloan. She moved to Indianapolis, Indiana, but always stayed connected to her Elkton family roots. Her children are Susan (Dunn) Brown and Carla (Storey) Jones.

Flournoy Gardner Sr. was born on January 24, 1926, and died on December 3, 2005, in Elkton. He was the son of John Matt Gardner and Alma (McClaurine) Gardner. He attended school in Elkton and high school in Pulaski. He was also a World War II veteran and served in the U.S. Air Force. He married Bessie Mae McNairy on October 27, 1958, and to this marriage came Sheila, Suzanne, Lisa, Flournoy Jr., and Michael. (Courtesy of Bessie Gardner.)

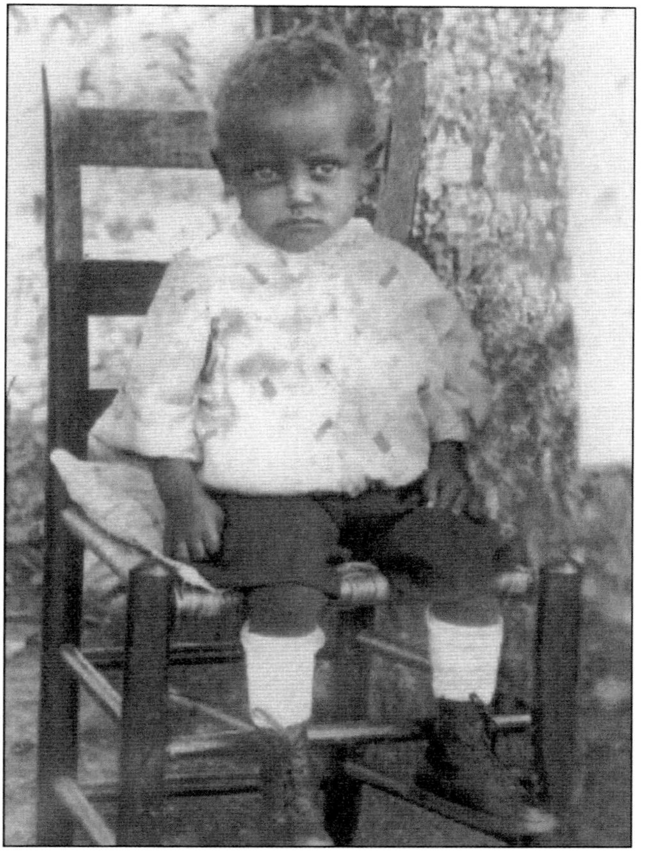

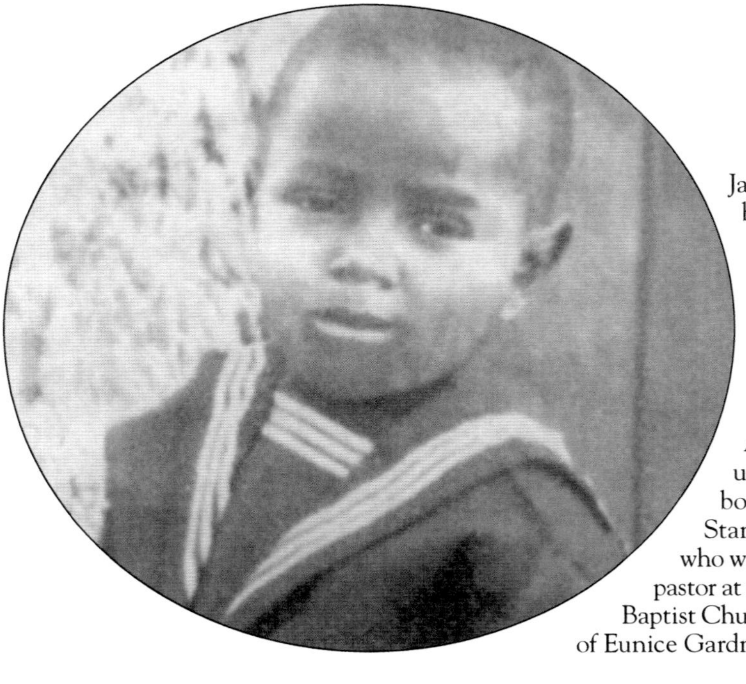

James William Gardner was born on August 10, 1923, and died on March 10, 2008, in Elkton. He was the eldest son of John Matt Gardner and Alma (McClaurine) Gardner. He was united in marriage to Eunice Thompson on August 2, 1952, and to this union five children were born: James, Gary, Glenda, Stanley, and Nelson. Gardner, who was also a minister, served as pastor at the Oak Grove Missionary Baptist Church for 16 years. (Courtesy of Eunice Gardner.)

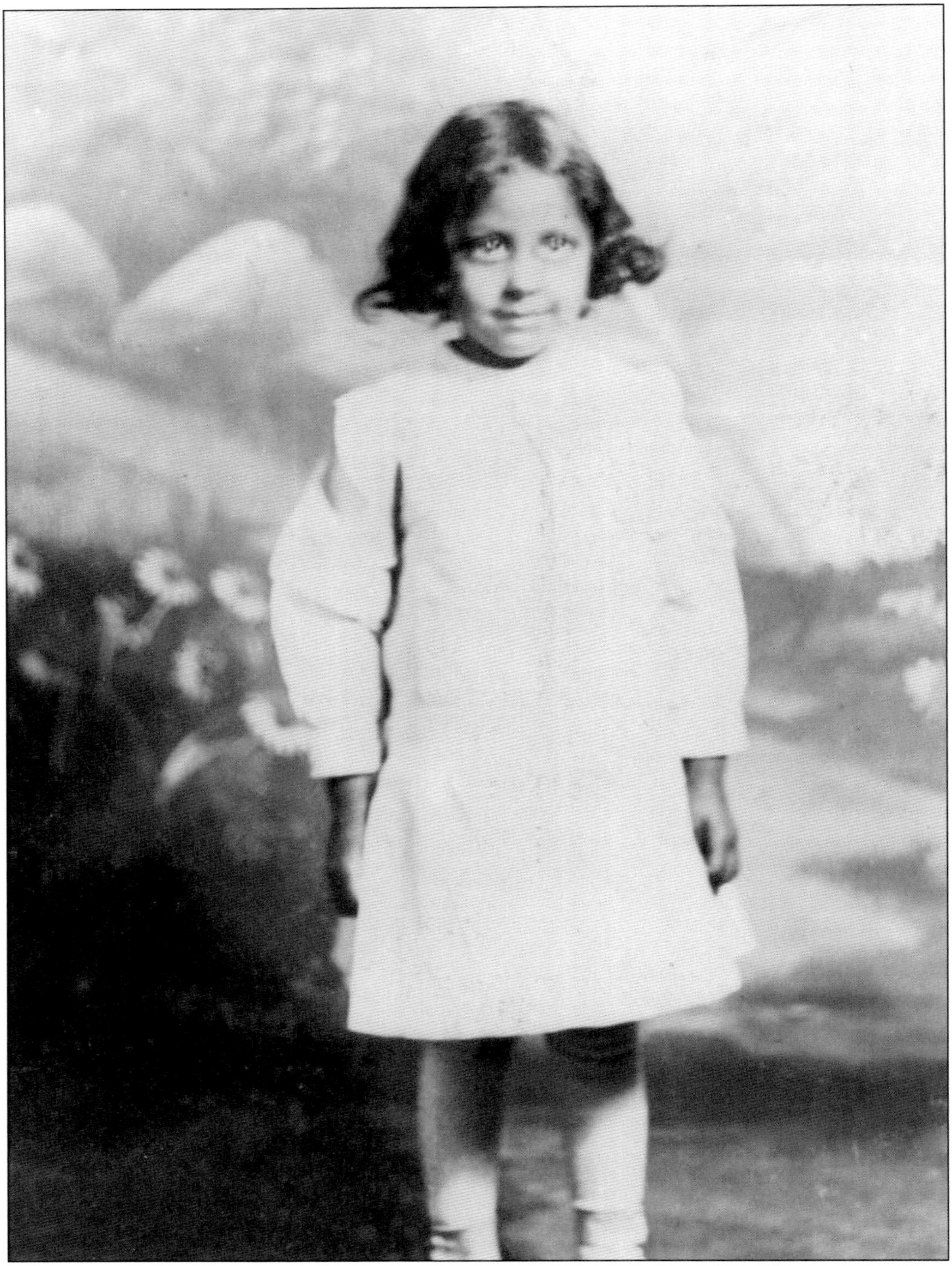

Laverna Davis is seen here looking innocent and standing patiently to have her picture taken. Laverna was born in Pulaski in 1908, and her mother was Sallie (Davis) Carter. Laverna had two sisters: Hattie Mae Carter, born in 1898, and Edie Bee Carter, born in 1900. (Courtesy of Philena Morgan.)

Eight

Community

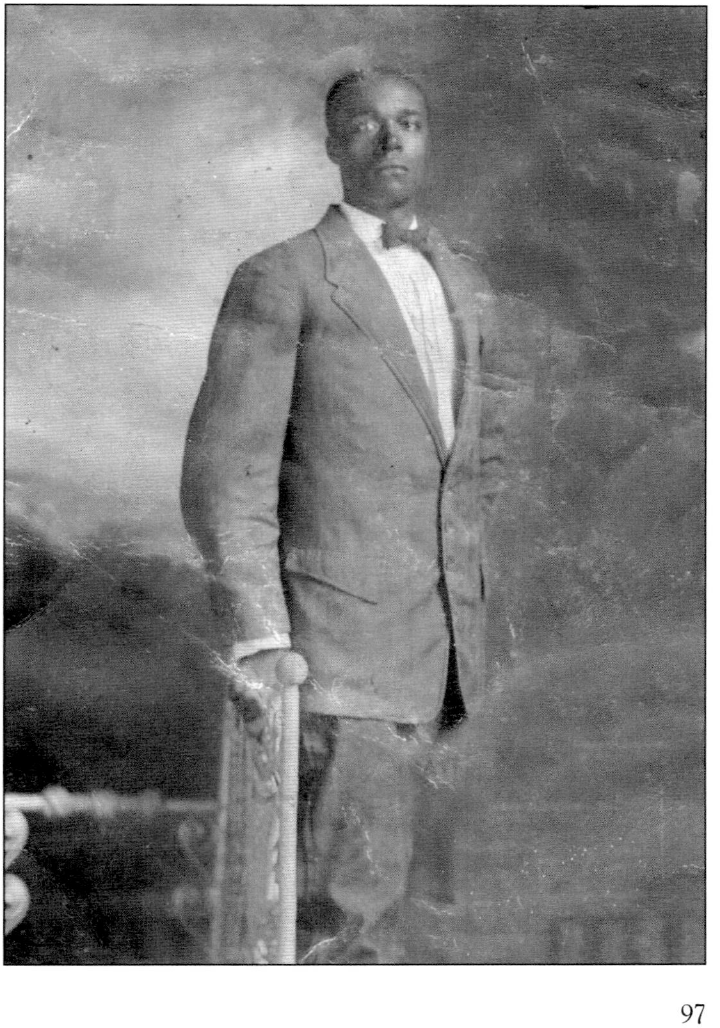

Standing broad-shouldered and upright is Steven Gardner. His parents were Rachel (Vasser) and Tom Gardner. Steven was born on May 6, 1862, and was the second son of Rachel and the first of Tom. Steven, a farmer, married Mary Swinea on January 25, 1885, and to their union was born one child, Stephen Jr.

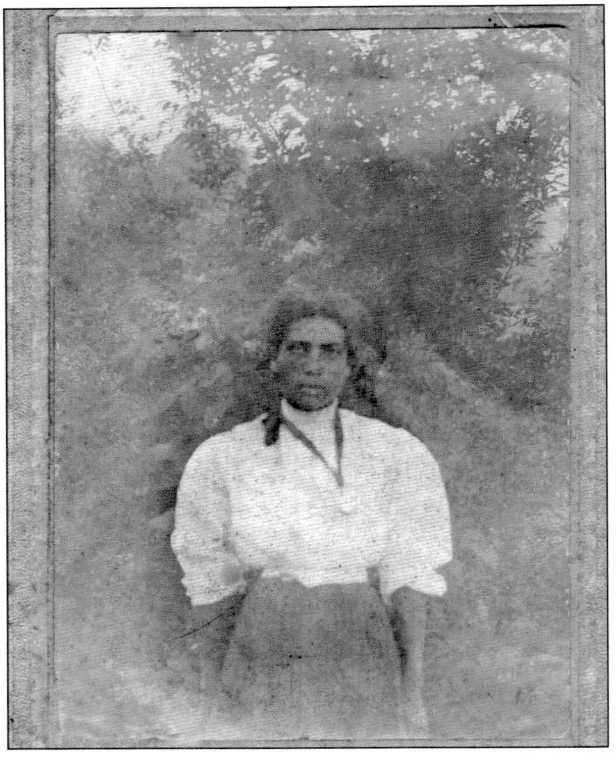

Emma (Holt) Neese was born on May 19, 1884, to George and Amanda (Brown) Holt. She was raised in Popular Hill near the community of Lick Skillet. Emma's siblings included Henrietta Jenkins, John "Jack" and Samuel Jenkins (or Brown), and Lula and Robert Holt. Emma later married William Neese, and to their union came two boys, William Jr. and Robert Dean. Emma died on September 5, 1980. She is buried in the Browns Temple cemetery in the Harms community.

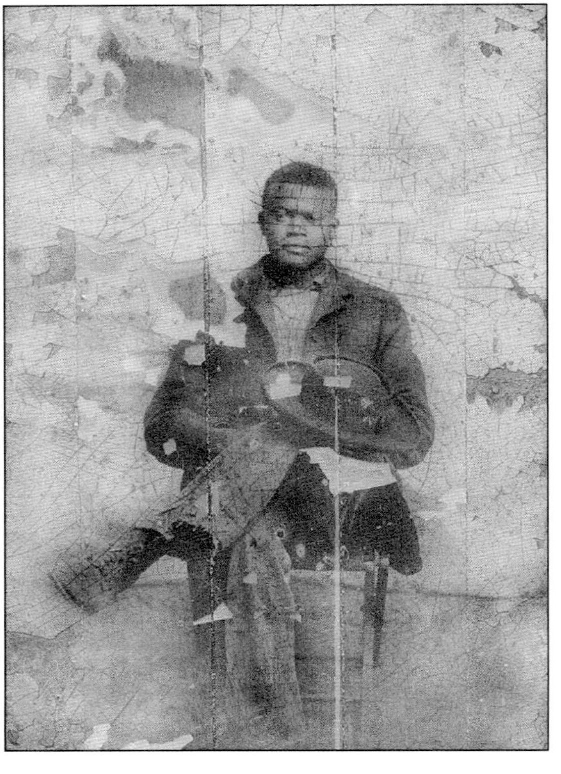

Hezekiah Bridgeforth is seen in an old tintype. Hezekiah was born in the 1880s to Sam and Millie (Gardner) Bridgeforth. He was raised and schooled in the Elkton community. He married Sadie Benson, and at some point, they left Giles and moved to Birmingham, Alabama. Some of their children were Hezekiah Jr., Martin, Henry, and Joel.

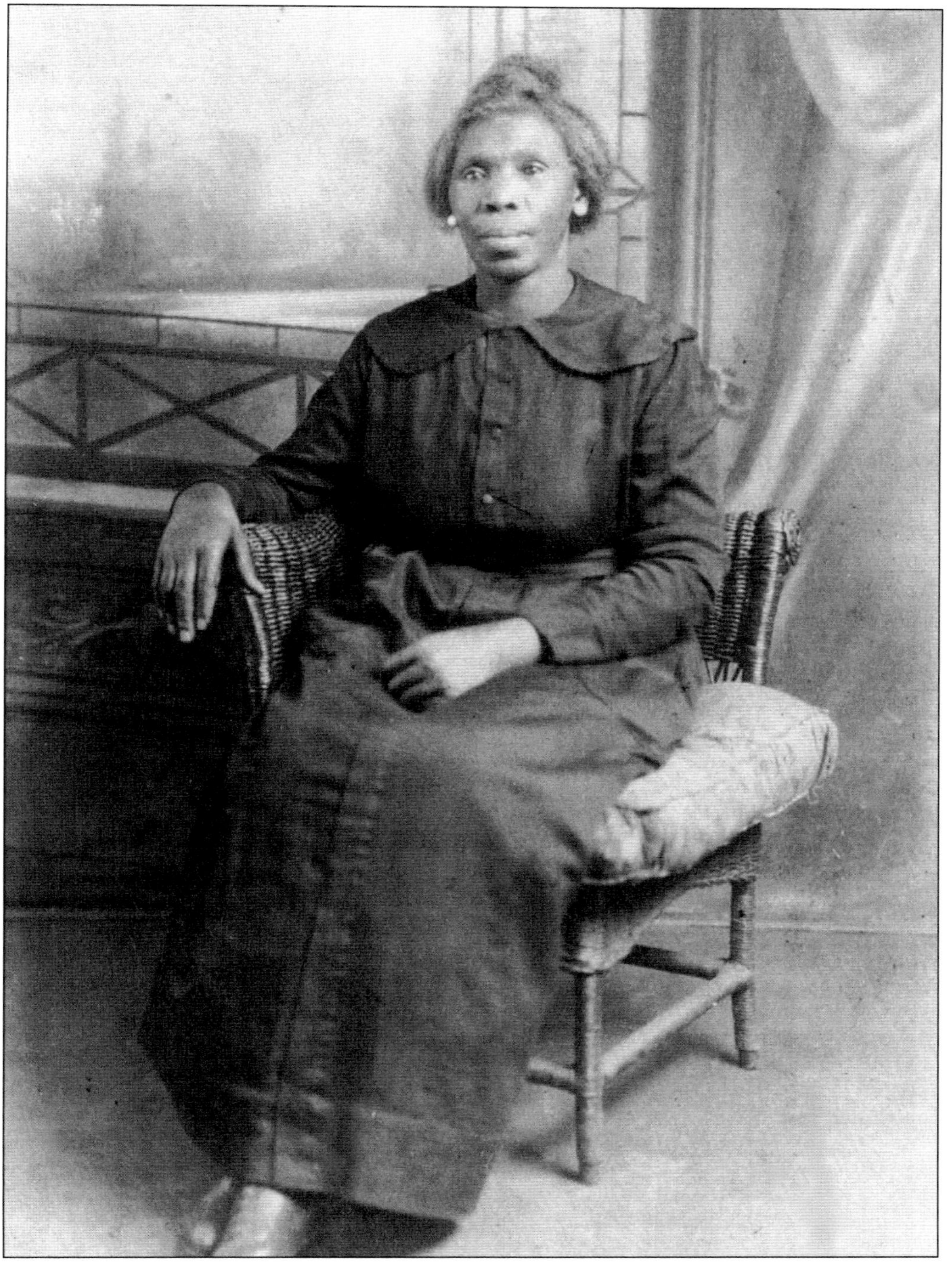

Lizzie (Gardner) Swinney was born in 1863. She was the third child of Thomas and Rachel (Vasser) Gardner. Lizzie married Robert Swinney on March 4, 1882, and from their marriage came five children: Tom, Mitchell, Richard, Melissa, and Ella Lou. Lizzie died on October 12, 1926, at the age of 72 in the community of Bodenham. She is buried in the New Hope cemetery. (Courtesy of Rosa Harding.)

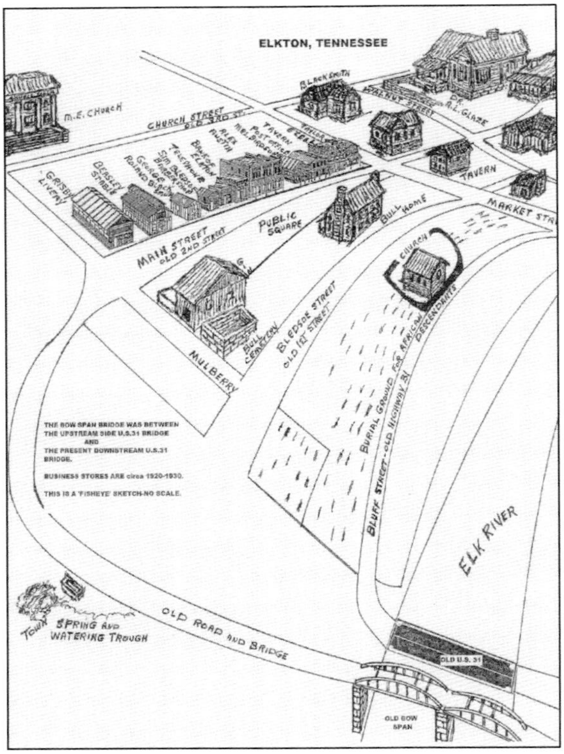

The city of Elkton has changed significantly over the past years. Pictured here is a 1920s composite sketch of the town of Elkton showing houses and businesses. The bridge on this picture was located between the existing two bridges over the Elk River. Also depicted on the right are the burial grounds for African descendants, known today as the Union Hill cemetery. (Courtesy of James Croley Smith.)

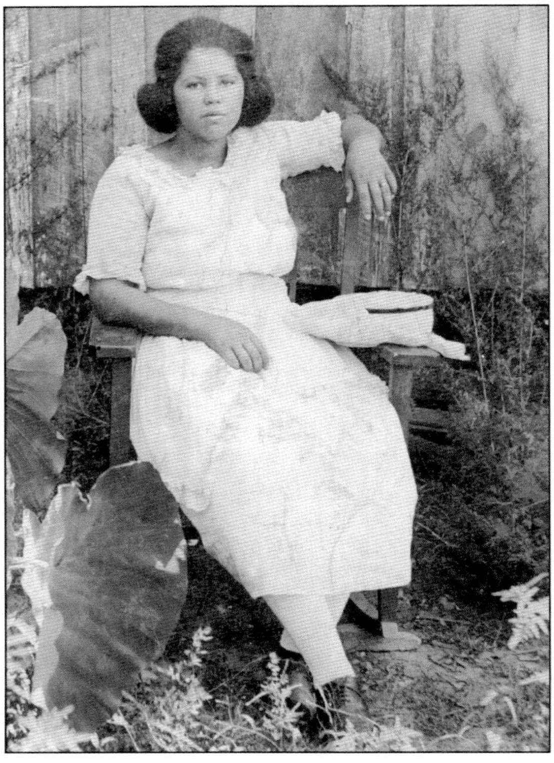

Named after her father, Yancy Swinea was born about 1907 to Yancy and Violet Swinea. On September 19, 1925, Rev. Raymond Gardner married Yancy and Herbert Bledsoe, and to this married couple came two children: Herman and Elizabeth "Lizzie B." Herbert's parents were Herman and Nettie Bledsoe of Elkton.

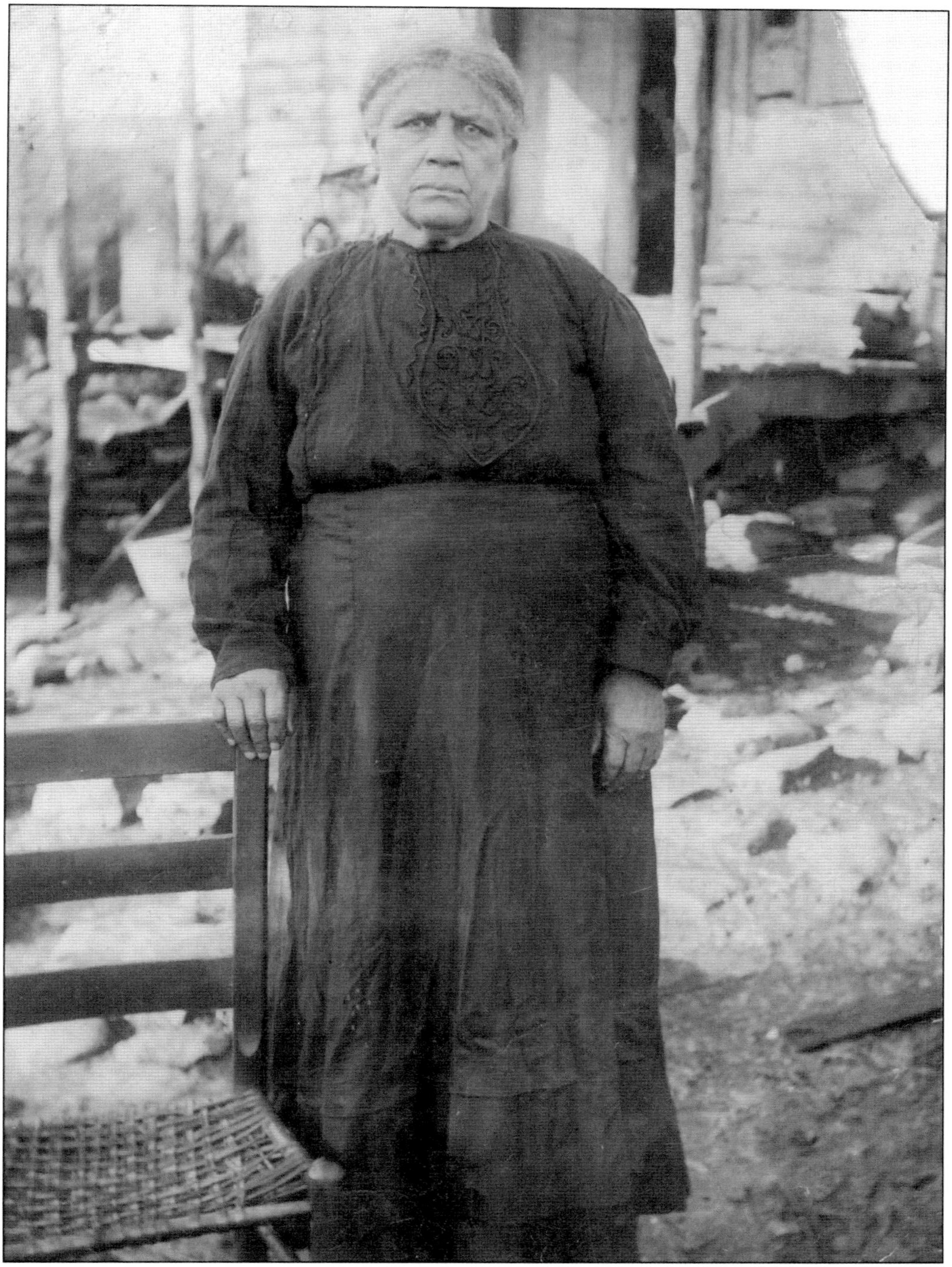

Amanda (Brown) Holt, also known as "Mandy," was born around 1840 and at one time was on the Brown plantation. While enslaved, she had three children, Henrietta Jenkins, Jack, and Samuel Brown (or Jenkins). At some point after being freed, she married George Holt, and together they had three children: Lula, Robert, and Emma.

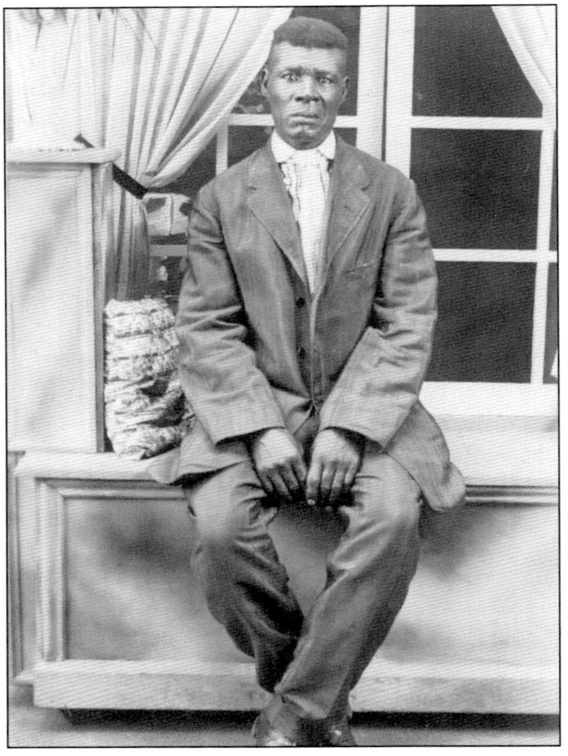

Pictured is Grant Davis, born in August 1873 to Isabella (Pruitt) Davis. He was raised in the Pulaski community of Giles. Grant was person with special needs and spent many years of his childhood in an institution known then as the Giles County Insane Asylum. Grant's siblings included his two brothers, Otis and Tommy. It is worth noting that Grant later moved to Indianapolis, Indiana, and lived a productive life, even outliving all of his family members. (Courtesy of Philena Morgan.)

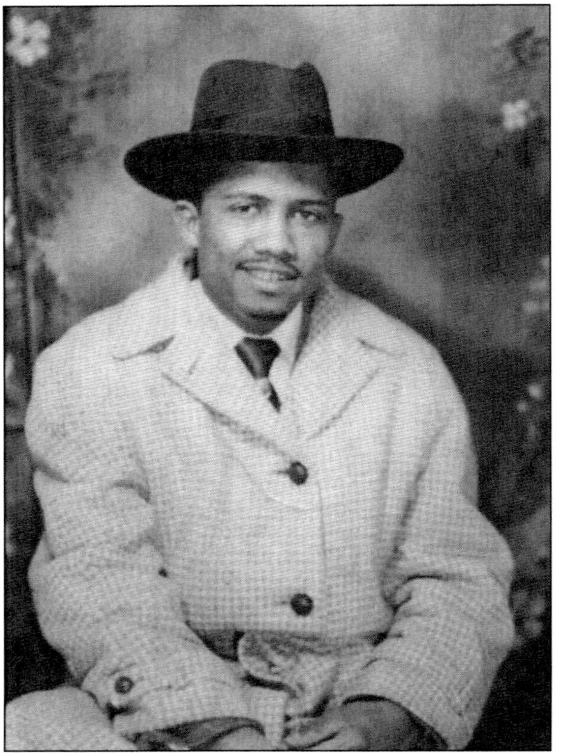

Buford W. Gardner Sr. was born December 18, 1934. He was the son of Walker and Lizzie Mae (Hogan) Gardner of Dixontown in Elkton. He attended Holts Elementary and Bridgeforth High Schools. He married Callie (Mae) Cutts in the 1960s, and to this union came children Rochelle and Buford Jr. Buford later remarried and had two more children, Lawanda and Sean. Buford was the second black county alderman elected in 1984. He served in this position for 12 years. In honor of his dedication to the office and the community, the new bridge over the Elk River in Elkton is named the Buford Gardner Bridge.

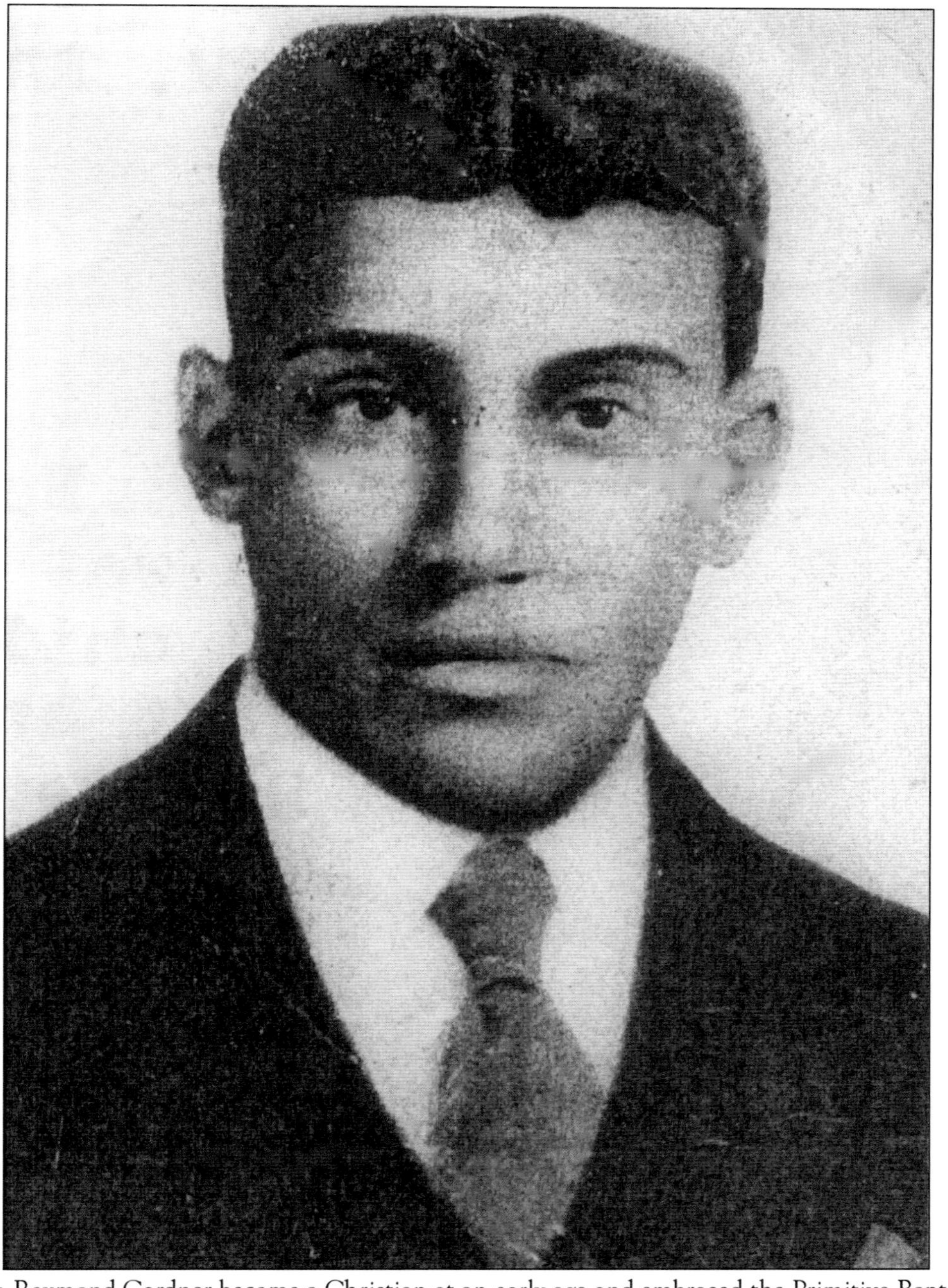

Rev. Raymond Gardner became a Christian at an early age and embraced the Primitive Baptist faith. Raymond began preaching at the age of 24 and was later known by all to be a dynamic preacher. During his ministerial career, he served at St. Elizabeth in Elkton, at New Hope in the Conway community, at Rebecca Church in Pulaski, and at St. Minor Church in Guntersville, Alabama, until his death in 1963. Known as a ready scribe, he served for 26 years as clerk of the Indian Creek Primitive Baptist Association, where he penned the "Abstract of Principles of the Primitive Baptist" in a book entitled *Indian Creek Primitive Baptist Church and Associates Dicipline.* He served as vice moderator from 1937 to 1962.

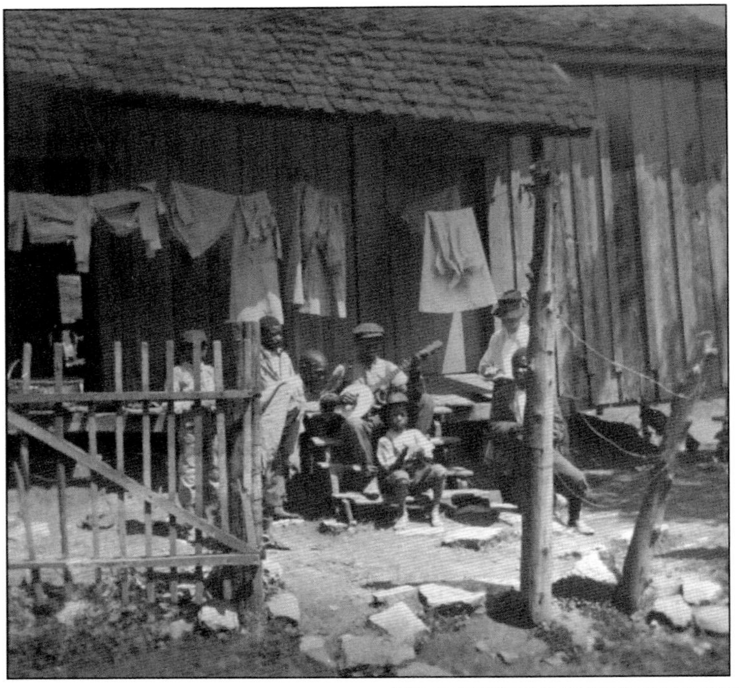

Pictured here is a family in the Giles community spending time together. The kids are all playing and are gathered around the person picking on the banjo. Playing the banjo was one of the few things during slavery that brought joy to many blacks. Stories are told that once the slave master retired for the night, the slaves would kick up their feet and dance to the fiddle and banjo or sometimes to the rhythms beat out by bones, sticks, rocks, or calloused hands and bare feet. (Courtesy of Tennessee Library and Archives.)

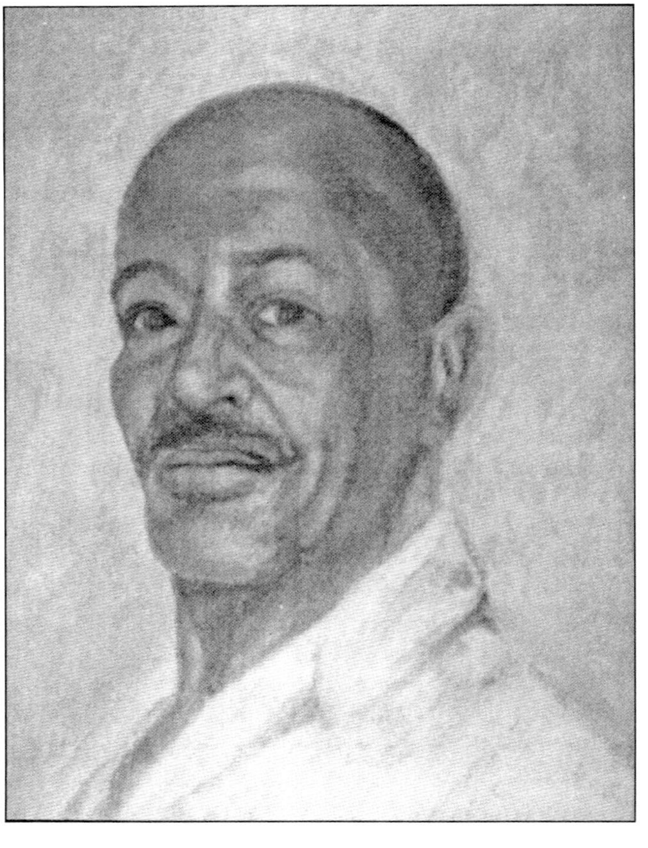

Kelso Vance was the second son of Philmore and Ethel Bailey. Vance, also known as "Hard Rock," was born in November 1912 in Giles County, Tennessee. Kelso lived with his parents in Elkton, and he attended school there until the eighth grade, when his family moved to Logan, West Virginia. In school, Kelso was always known to be a smart boy. In July 1977, Kelso passed away at 65 years of age. (Courtesy of Michiko Bailey.)

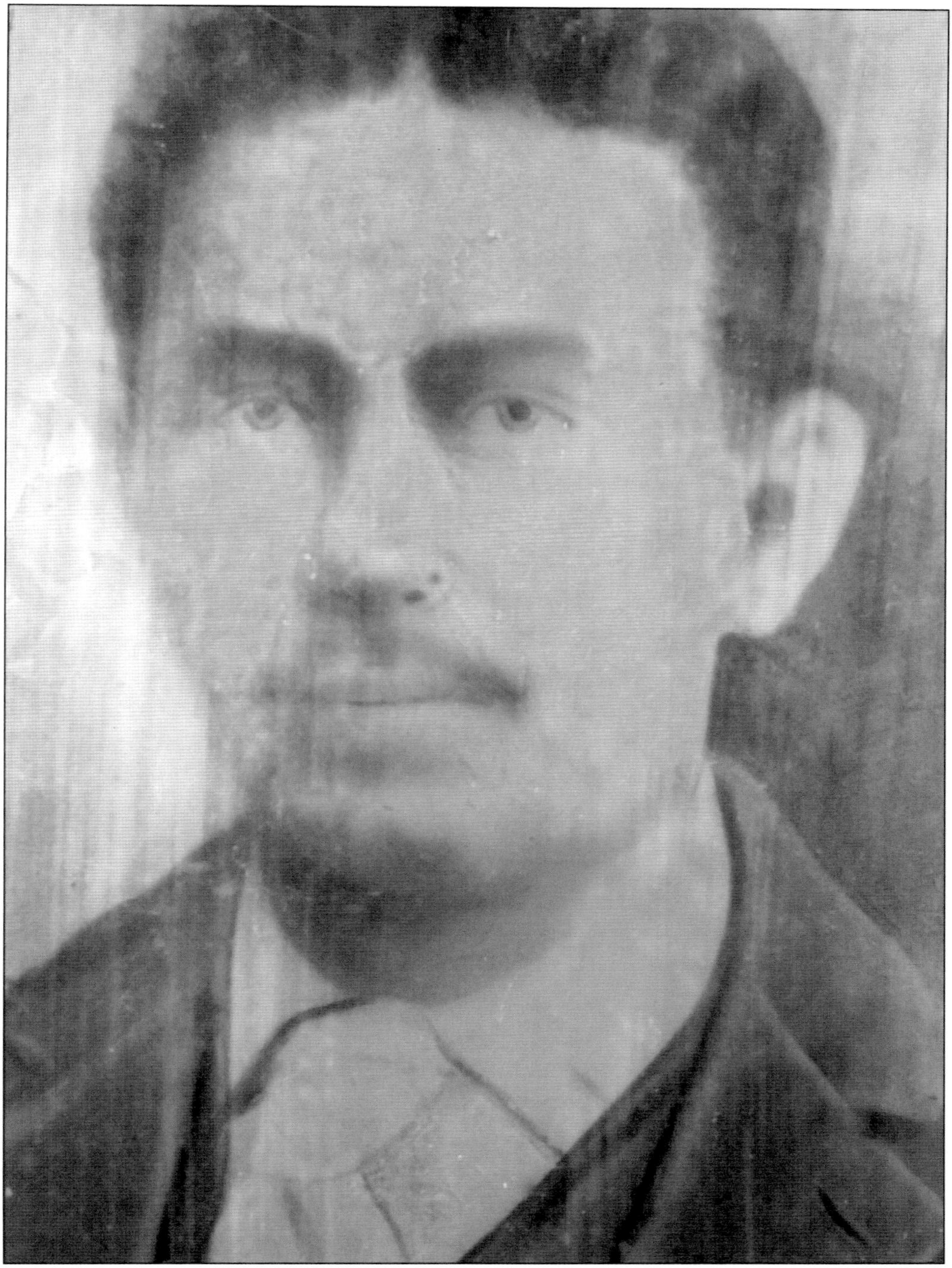

Yancy Swinea was born about 1889 to Howell and Mary (Holloway) Swinea in the Elkton community. Yancy married Violet Scruggs on May 1, 1906. Yancy was a farmer and teacher and taught his wife in elementary school. Violet was a housewife and mother to their 11 children: Yancy (Bledsoe), Bivens, Quabon, David Elizabeth (Lee), Pittsfield, Hestown (Twines), Arthora (Glass), Violet (Bledsoe), Mary (Driver), Howell and Bobbie. (Courtesy of Bob Swinea.)

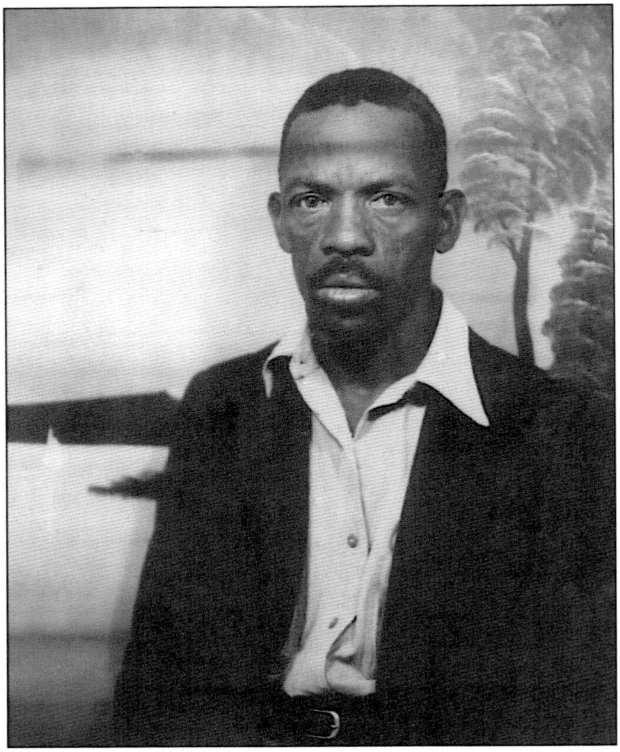

Henry "Lem" Lee Stevenson was born in Elkton about September 4, 1905, to Prince and Georgia (Benson) Stevenson. Lem's hobby and favorite pastime was playing the banjo, which he did quite well. Lem later married Fannie Mae Whitfield, and to their union came two children: Elizabeth and Alonzo. (Courtesy of Emma Bledsoe.)

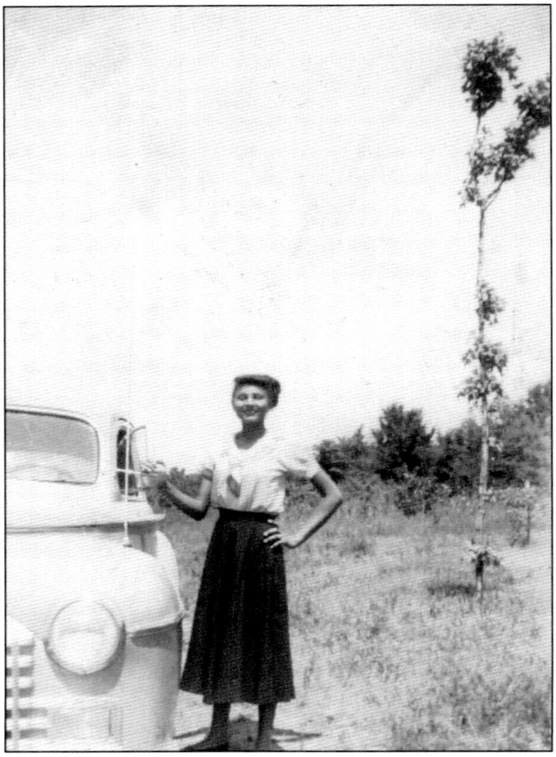

Dorothy Jean (Gardner) Henry is seen standing by the family car. Her parents were John and Alma (McClaurine) Gardner, and the family lived in the Elkton community. Dorothy went to grade school at Holts Elementary and continued her studies at Bridgeforth High School in Pulaski. She later moved to Evanston, Illinois, and started her family with her only daughter, Kathy.

This picture is believed to be of Rachel (Vasser) Gardner. Rachel was born on February 1, 1830, and lived on a plantation in Richmond, Virginia. Before she was 10, she cried as her two older sisters, Mindy and one whose name is undocumented, were sold on a Virginia auction block. Rachel was shipped and sold three times, from Chester, North Carolina; Limestone County, Alabama; and Giles County, Tennessee. Slave owners included Isaac Franklin, Richard Whitehead Vasser, and Richard C. Gardner. When freedom came, Giles is where Rachel and her family decided to call home. Rachel and her first husband, Martin, were blessed with Millie, Ida, Martha, and Matt. After Martin died, she jumped the broomstick with Tom Gardner, and they were blessed with Stephen, Mary, and Lizzie. Rachel died on January 11, 1922, and was buried in the burial grounds for African Americans, the Union Hill cemetery. (Courtesy of Claudette Turner.)

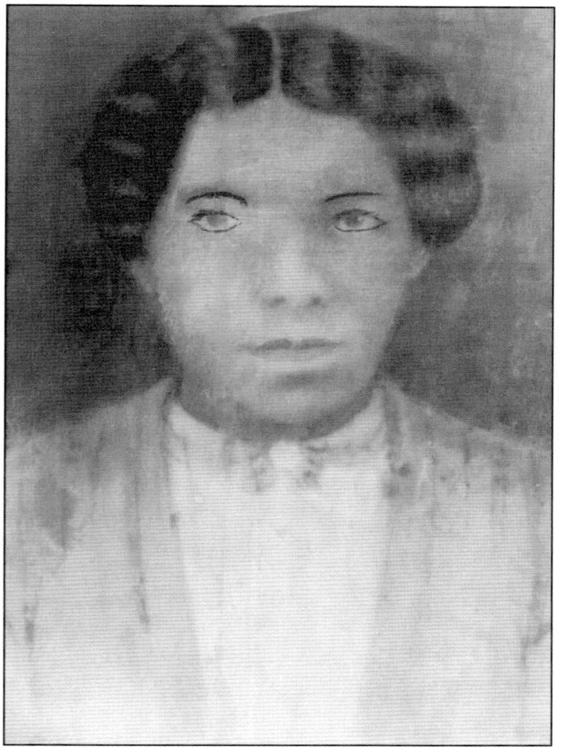

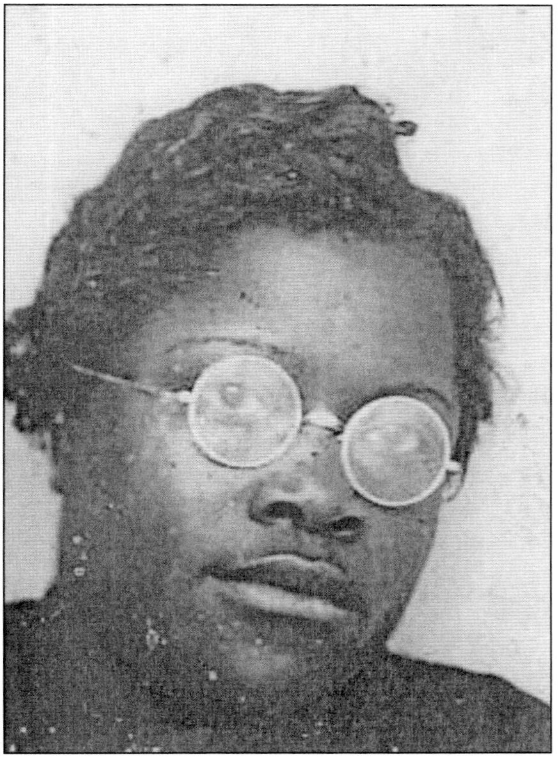

Mary Magdelene "Maggie" Gardner was born in 1921 off Tucker Bend Road in the Conway community of Giles. Her parents were William Ed and Darthula (Vasser) Gardner, and her siblings were Louie and William Gardner. Maggie married Luther L. Brown, and to their union came three children: Martha Ann, William, and Patsy. Maggie was Luther's second wife. Previously, Luther had married Lula Bell Beatty in 1925, and their children were Charity Elizabeth, Geraldine, and George. (Courtesy of William L. Brown Sr.)

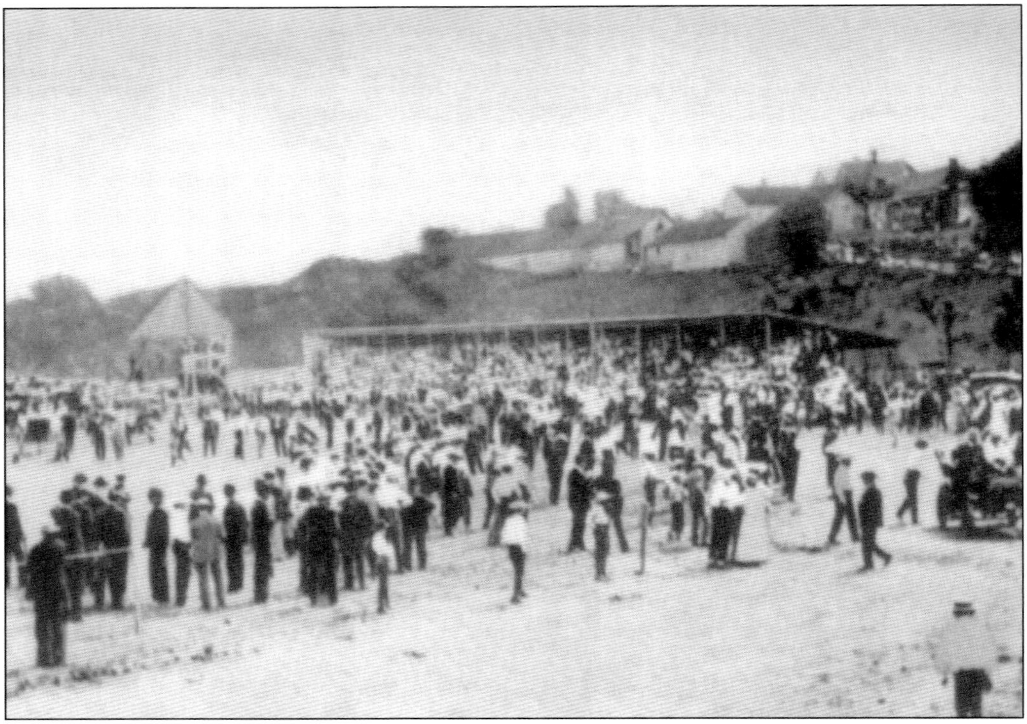

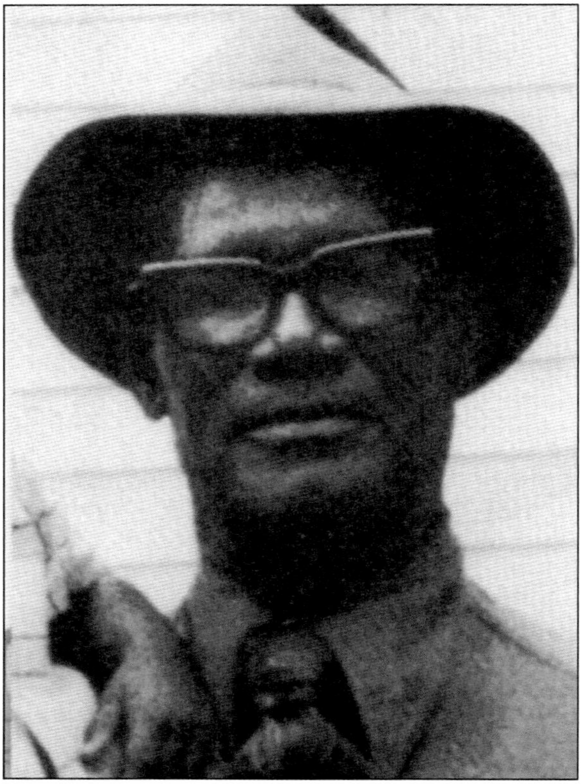

The first Giles County Negro Fair began the week of October 18, 1906, and was pronounced an incredible success. It was largely attended, and there was a grand parade on the second day. The organizers of the first fair were Pres. J. M. Gentry, secretary A. Thomas Hill, and Cliff Brown Marshall. The fair was such a success that it continued for approximately 31 years, until about 1938. (Courtesy of the Giles County Bicentennial Committee.)

L. Z. "Hog" Gardner was the son of Atha and Ether (Bonner) Gardner. He was born on December 21, 1914, in the Elkton community, where he grew up and attended school. On November 20, 1938, he married Novella (Horton) of Prospect, and they had nine children: daughters Mary, Shirley, Patricia, Yolanda, and Kelli and sons Bobby, Ruffin, Lewis, and Harold. Gardner passed away on June 6, 1985, at the age of 70. (Courtesy of the L. Z. Gardner family.)

Pictured in the heart is John Vassar, son of Manville "Man" and Martha (Gardner) Vassar. John was born in June 1891. He was raised and educated in the Elkton community. On August 2, 1907, he married Georgia Driver, the daughter of George and Tennie (Davidson) Driver. His wife died a short time after they married. Georgia's sisters and brothers were William, Lizzie, Myrtle, Harrison, Rogers, Charlie, Lura, and Buford. John and Georgia had no children. John later left Elkton to work in the coal mines in Logan, West Virginia.

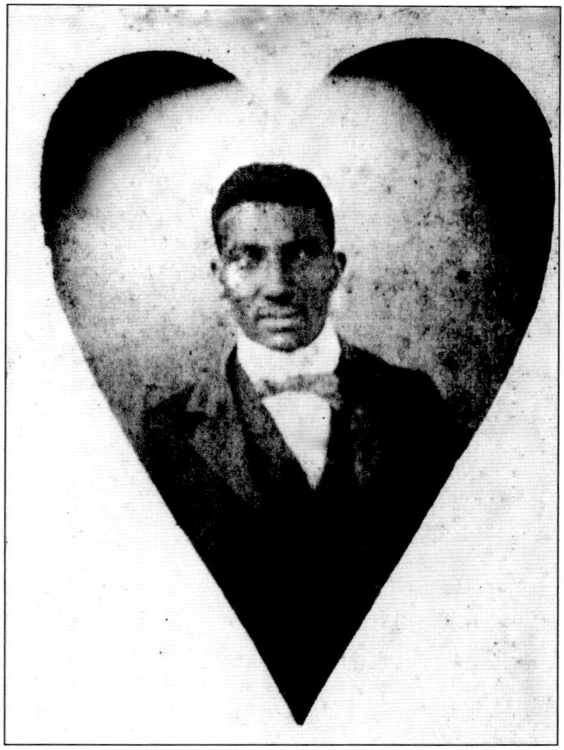

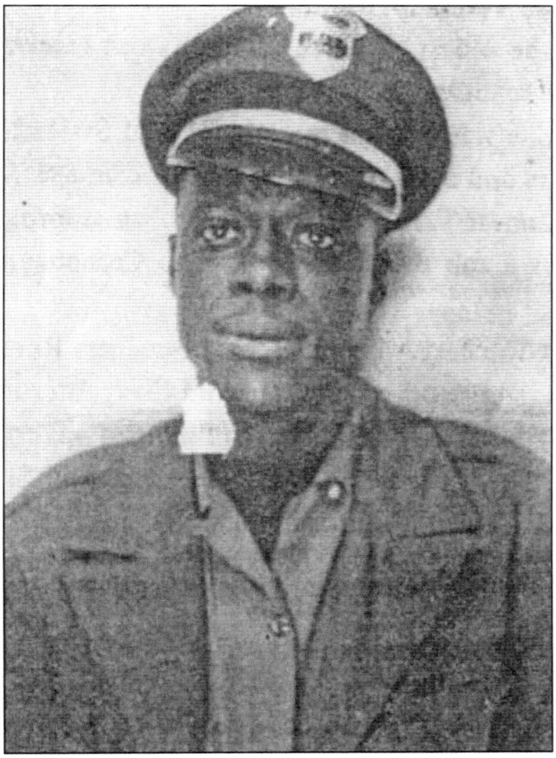

Louie Gardner was born in 1919 to William Ed and Darthula (Vasser) Gardner of Conway. He and his brother William and sister Mary "Maggie" were the grandchildren of Ed and Ella (Sloss) Gardner, great-grandchildren of Spencer and Patience (Gardner) Sloss, and great-great-grandchildren of "Ma" Jane Gardner, once a slave on the Richard C. Gardner plantation in Elkton. Louie, a military man, served in the U.S. Army. After leaving the military, he became a cab driver in Nashville. Louie had no children. (Courtesy of William L. Brown Sr.)

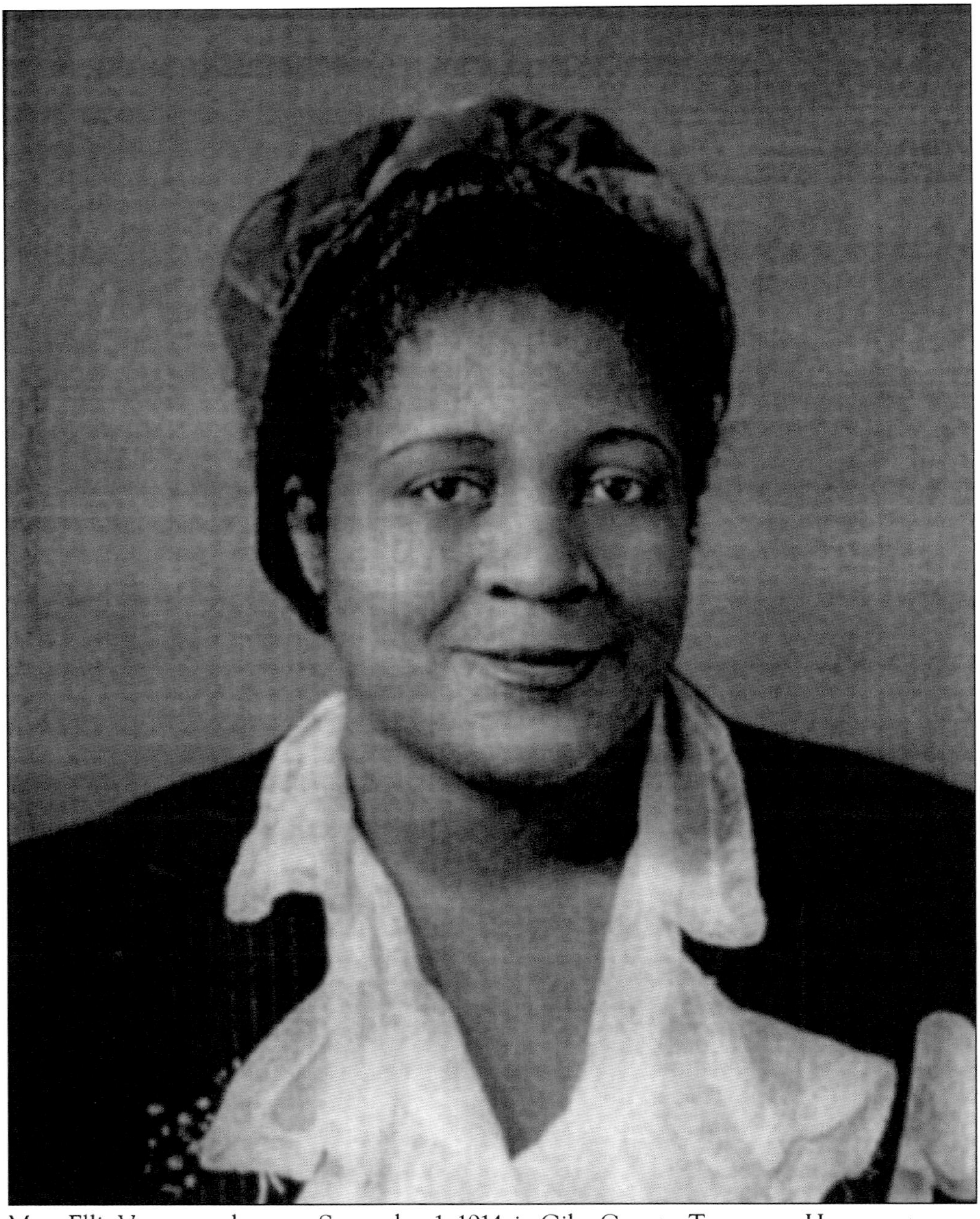

Mary Ellis Vassar was born on September 1, 1914, in Giles County, Tennessee. Her parents were Ellis and Sarah (Holt) Vassar. Other sisters and brothers of Mary Ellis included Shelton, Collier, Percy, Ruth, Louise, James, John, and Xie. On September 18, 1937, Mary married George Hogan. To their union came four children: George Ellis Jr., Albert, James, and Joanne. (Courtesy of the Hogan family.)

Bertha (Blair) Vassar was born about 1908 to Elmer and Dorcas Blair. On December 22, 1914, she married Ervis Vassar of Elkton. To their union came two children: Lillar (Lillie Mae) and Clinnon. In the 1920s, Bertha and Ervis moved to Ohio, but Bertha missed Giles County so much that they moved back in 1930. (Courtesy of John Vassar.)

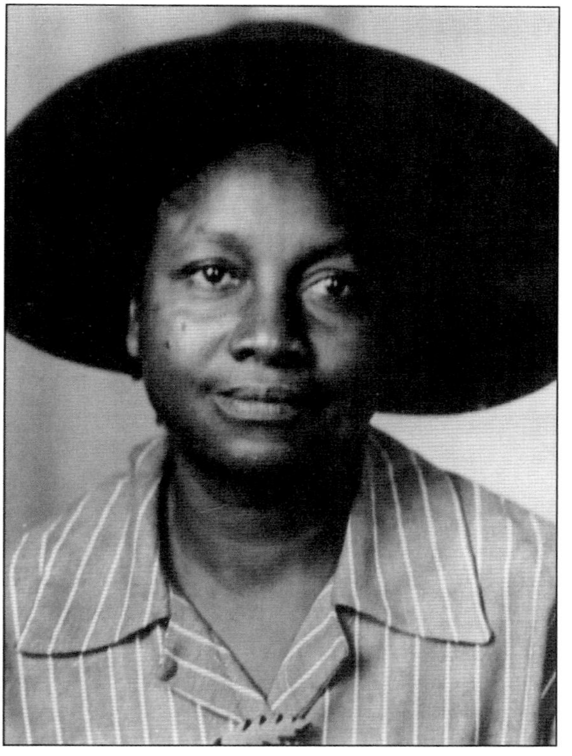

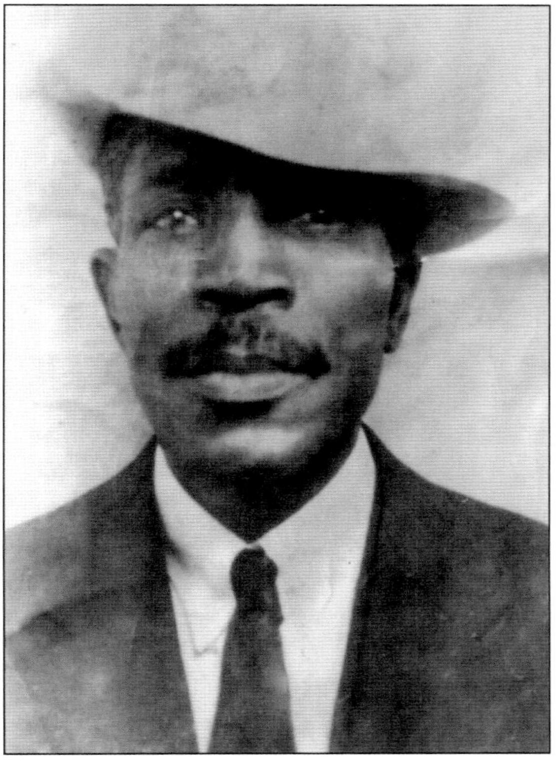

After the death of Mariah (Bailey-Garrison) Brunson's husband, Atwater Garrison, she wed Alfred Brunson. They were married on March 3, 1916, and lived in the Bunker Hill community of Giles. He was a sporty man and a great father to Mariah's children, Flavor, Raymond, Forrest, and Robert. (Courtesy of William McNairy.)

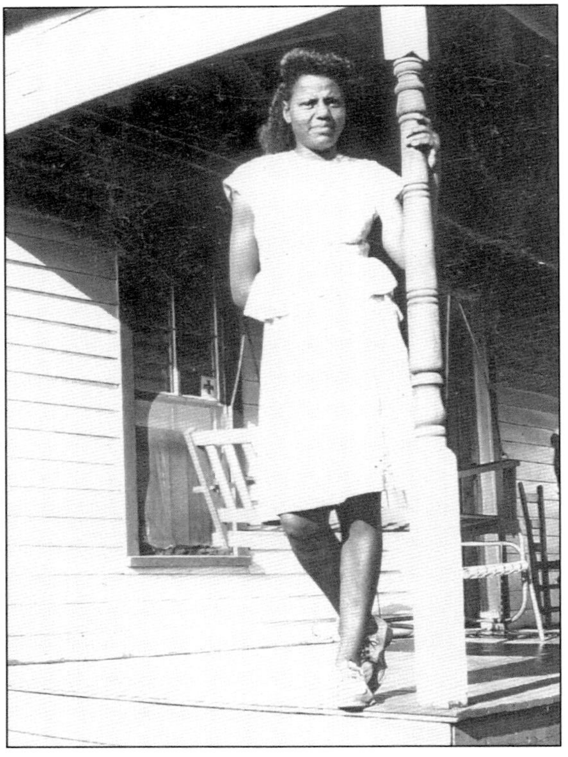

Elizabeth (Gardner) Clack was born on January 24, 1928, to the union of John and Alma (McClaurine) Gardner of Elkton. She attended Holts Elementary in Elkton and Bridgeforth High School in Pulaski. Elizabeth married Albert Lee Clack, and they moved from Pulaski to Detroit, Michigan, in1952. To their marriage came six children: Elmorie, twins Janet and Jeanette, Brenda, and twins Alma and Alvin. (Courtesy of the Clack family.)

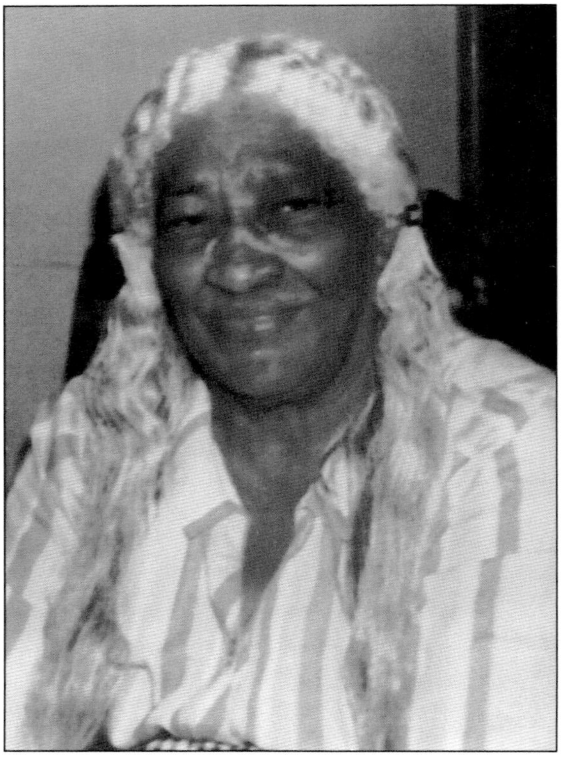

Paralee (Gardner) Coleman was the seventh child of Matt and Henrietta (Jenkins) Gardner. She was born on May 21, 1889, and was educated in the Elkton community. Because of the high cheekbones and long hair, the family always said that she was carrying their Blackfoot Indian heritage. (Courtesy of Thurmond Coleman.)

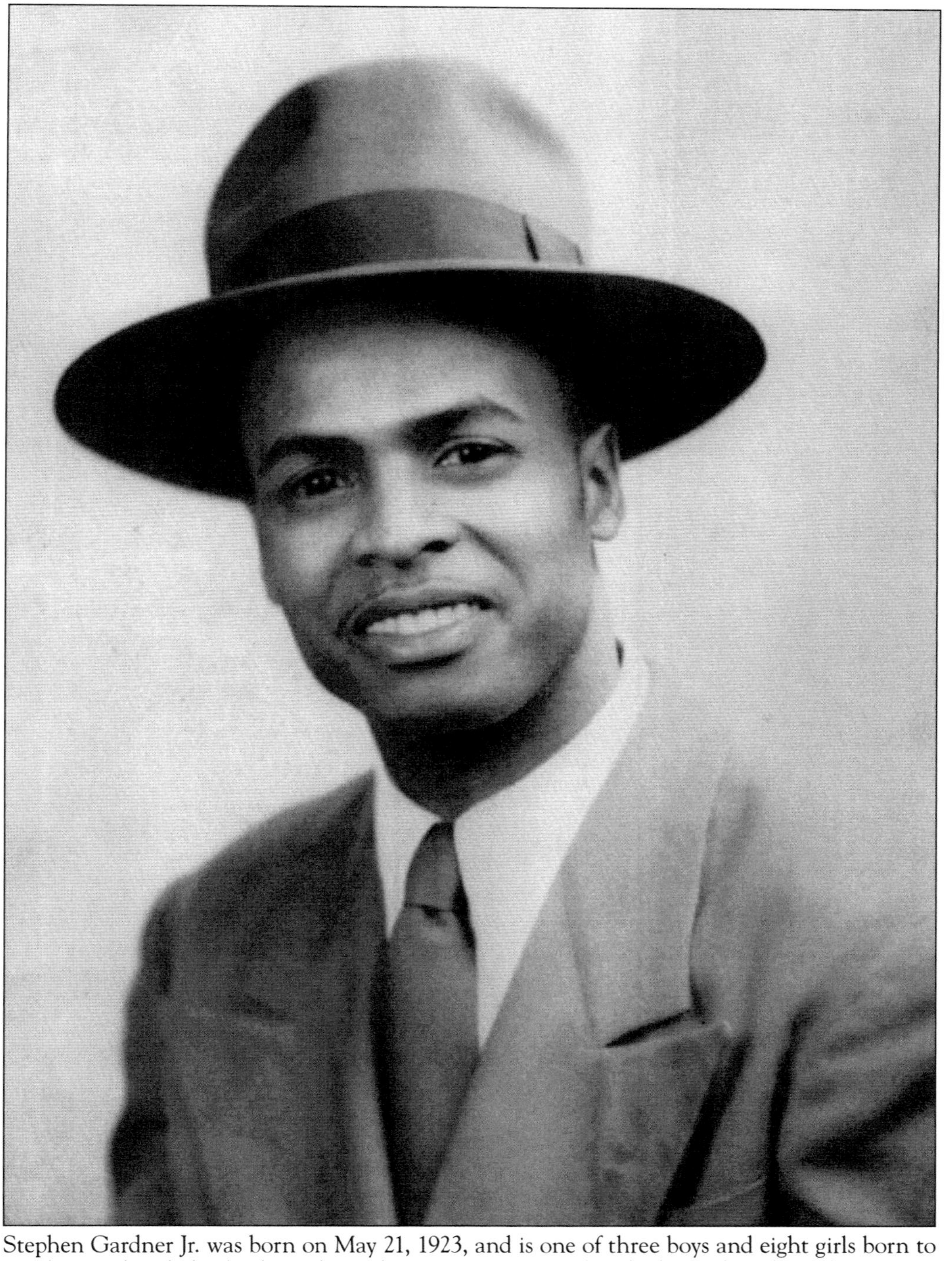

Stephen Gardner Jr. was born on May 21, 1923, and is one of three boys and eight girls born to Stephen and Ophelia (Coleman) Gardner Jr. He was raised and educated in the Giles County school system. Steven later met and married Bennie Mae Lewis of Texas, and they moved to Indianapolis, Indiana. Stephen and Bennie had one son, Stephen Eugene Gardner. Stephen Gardner Jr. passed away on September 19, 1981. (Courtesy of Stephen E. Gardner.)

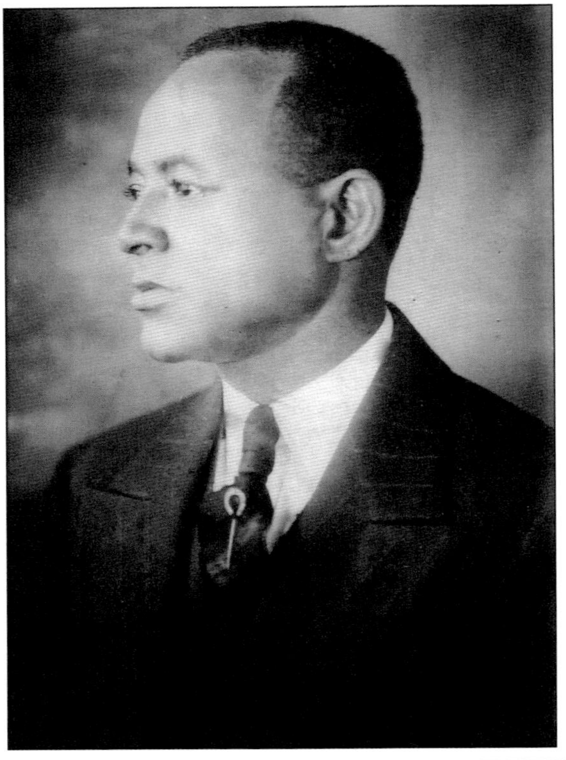

Charles Atwater Garrison was born in December 1885 in Pulaski, Giles County, Tennessee. His mother was Adline, and his father is undocumented. In 1907, he moved with his mother and stepfather, Marshall Abernathy, to Oklahoma. The following year, he returned to Giles and married Mariah Bailey on March 6, 1908. To their union came one daughter, Flavor, and three sons, Raymond, Forrest, and Robert. (Courtesy of William McNairy.)

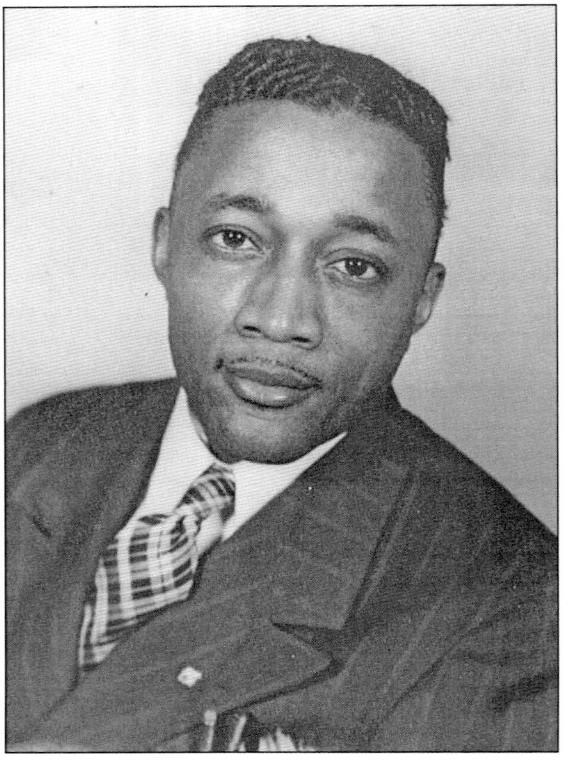

Thaddeus "Thad" Holt was born on February 20, 1910, the first of two children of Lee Holt and Ethel Bridgeforth in Elkton. Upon the death of Lee Holt, Ethel married Lex Driver, and Thad became the eldest of nine children. Thad was educated in Elkton and went on to farm in the community. He married Mattie Reedus, and two children were born to their union: LeeRona and Charles. Thad moved to Indianapolis, Indiana, in search of employment and a better life. After the death of Mattie Holt, Thad married Alzata Sloss, a widow with two children, and to their marriage came two girls: Theresa and Cynthia. (Courtesy of LeeRona McKinney.)

Robert Percy Gardner was the son of John and Lera (Driver) Gardner. He was born on October 14, 1918, and he went to grammar and high schools in Giles County. Soon after school, he left Giles and moved to Cleveland, Ohio, where he met Willie Pearl Thomas. In October 1940, the couple married and were blessed with three boys: Ronald, Robert, and Malcomb. (Courtesy of Malcomb Gardner.)

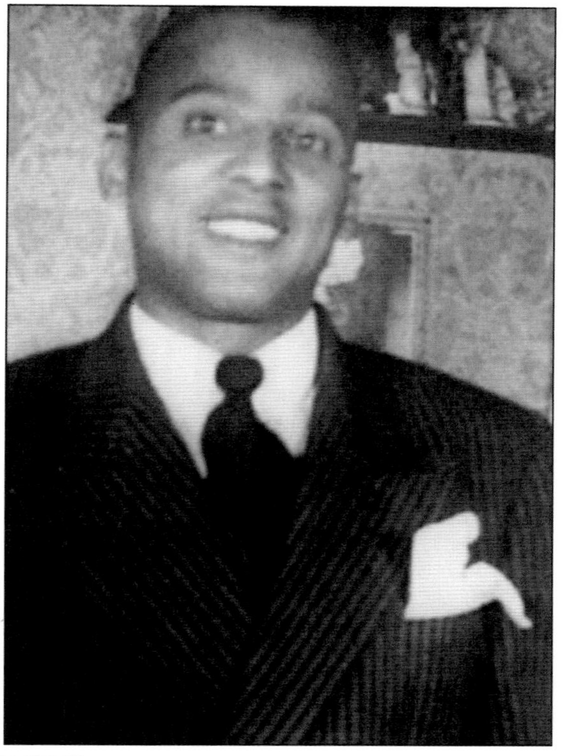

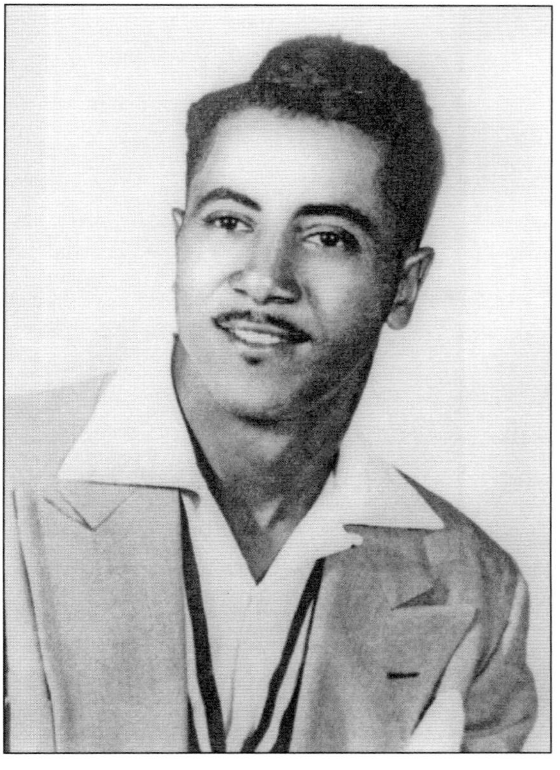

John Robert Gardner was born to Raymond and Frances Gardner on March 2, 1922. He was raised in Elkton and educated in the colored school that his grandfather Matt Gardner financed and helped to build. Later in life, he moved to Canton, Ohio, and married Ethel Johnson, and to their union came nine children: Raymond, Amelia, Tony, Victor, Clyde, Tammy, Wanda, John Jr., and Steven. (Courtesy of Ethel Gardner.)

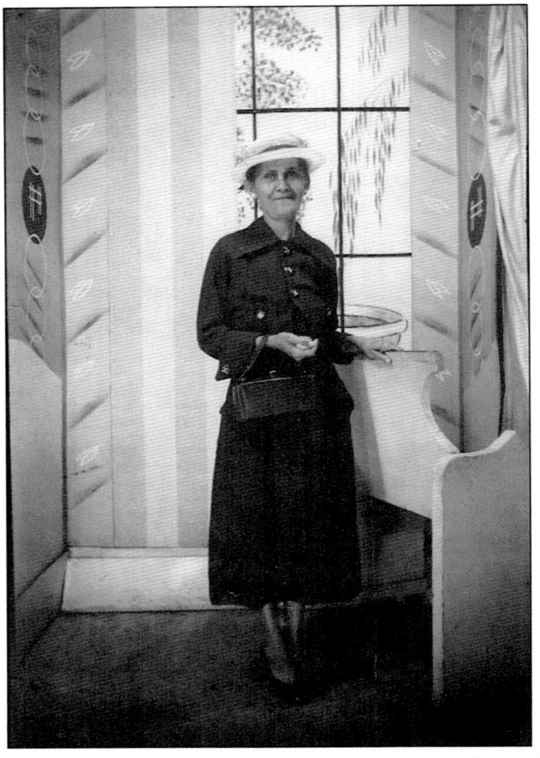

Mattie "Pinkie" Smith was the last daughter of Jones and Mattie (McKinney) Smith. She was born in March 1892. Her mother died in childbirth. She was raised by her older brothers and sisters in Pulaski after her father's death. Pinkie had eight children of her own. (Courtesy of descendants of Mamie Woodson, Alice Kline, and Mattie "Pinkie" Lane, children of Jones and Mattie Smith.)

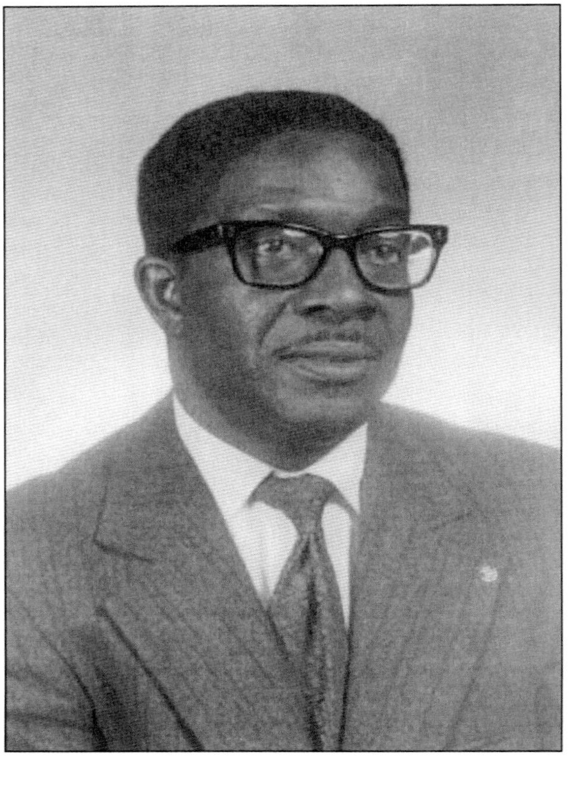

Rev. William Gardner was born in 1923 in Giles County and was one of three children of William Ed and Darthula (Vasser) Gardner of Conway. He was educated in the Giles school system. William's sister and brother were Louie and Mary "Maggie" Gardner. William had one son, John, with his wife, Mary, and was the stepfather of William and Marsha. He later settled in Nashville and became a prominent minister of Mount Cavalry Baptist Church. (Courtesy of William L. Brown Sr.)

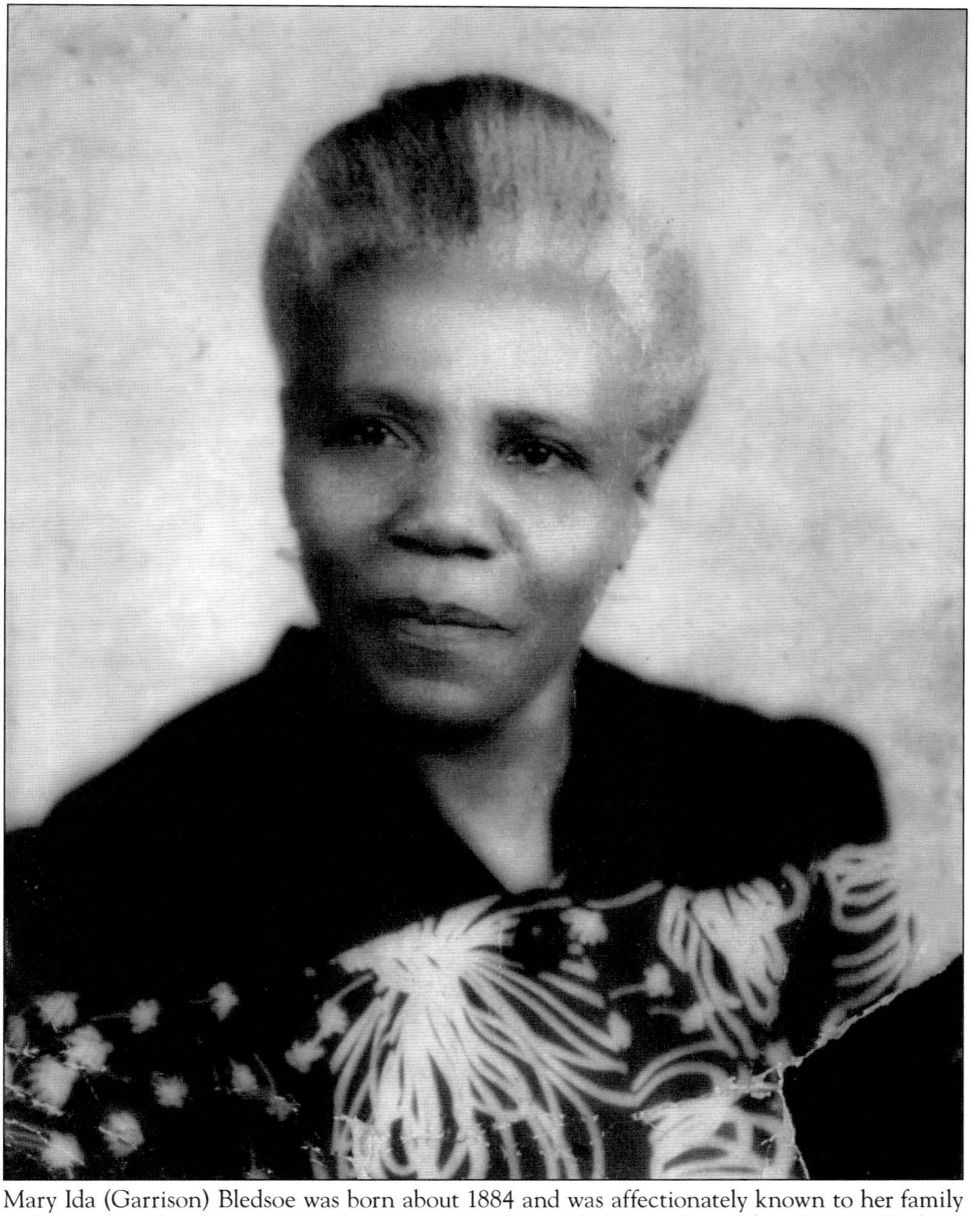

Mary Ida (Garrison) Bledsoe was born about 1884 and was affectionately known to her family and close friends as Mama Mae Ida. Mary married Dee Bledsoe on December 27, 1899. Early in their marriage, they lived and worked as cooks for his former slave owners at the Elkmont Springs Resort. The white resort had a lodge, cabins, health spa, and a dance pavilion for society dances. In front of the resort were seven springs: sulfur, natural spring, limestone, iron, salt, one unidentified, and one that was poisonous. The couple later became farmers—Dee was also a day laborer—and parents of John, Lizzie, Charles, Thomas, and Will. (Courtesy of the Lizzie Bridgeforth family.)

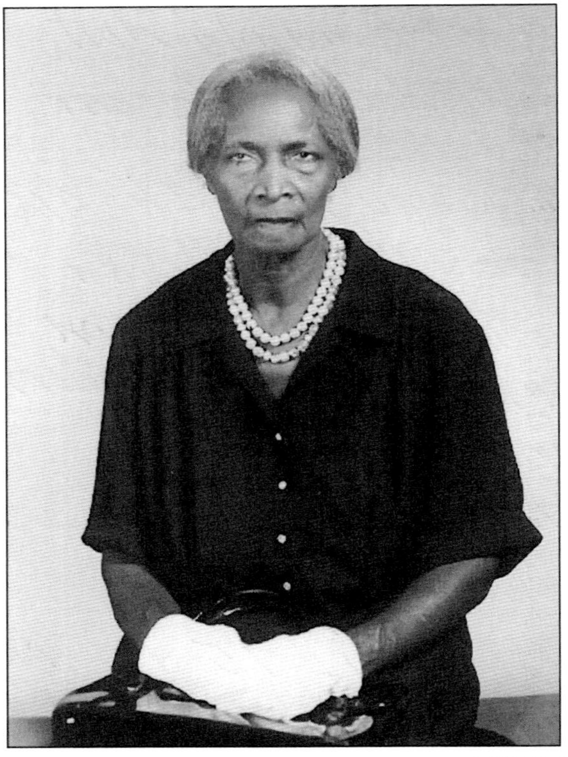

Pictured is Sarah Holt, born in January 1884. She was the daughter of Ralph and Amanda (Abernathy) Holt. Sarah had eight sisters and brothers: Rufus, Frank, William, Martha, Lincoln, Ralph Jr., Florinda, and James. On April 12, 1913, the Reverend Howell Swinea joined Sarah and Ellis Vassar in holy matrimony, and they set up housekeeping in the Conway community. Ellis and Sarah had six children: Mary, Ruth, Louise, James, John, and daughter Xie, who died as an infant. (Courtesy of John Vassar.)

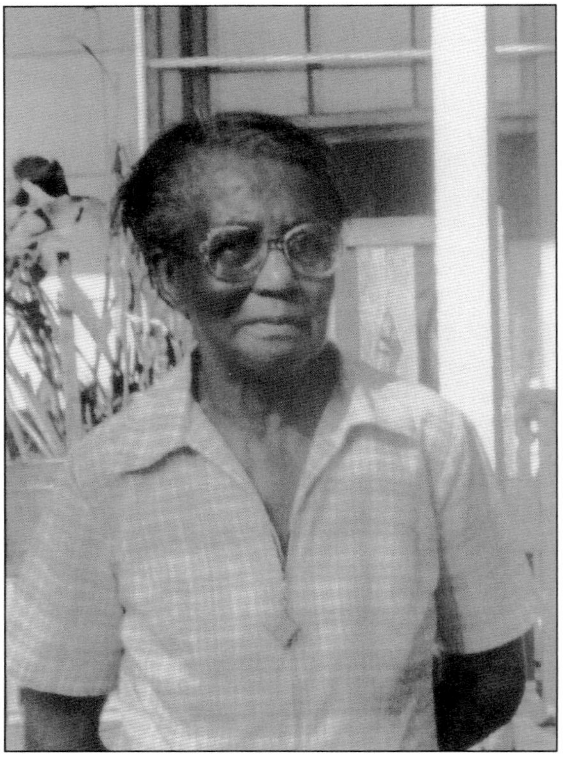

Pictured is Alma (Bridgeforth) Gardner. She was the daughter of Dave and Mattie (Sloss) Bridgeforth. Her sister and brothers are Mable, Vanilear, and Isaiah. On March 15, 1931, at the age of 26, she married John Milton Gardner. To this union came children Floradine, Eugene, and Virginia. (Courtesy of Floradine Wilson.)

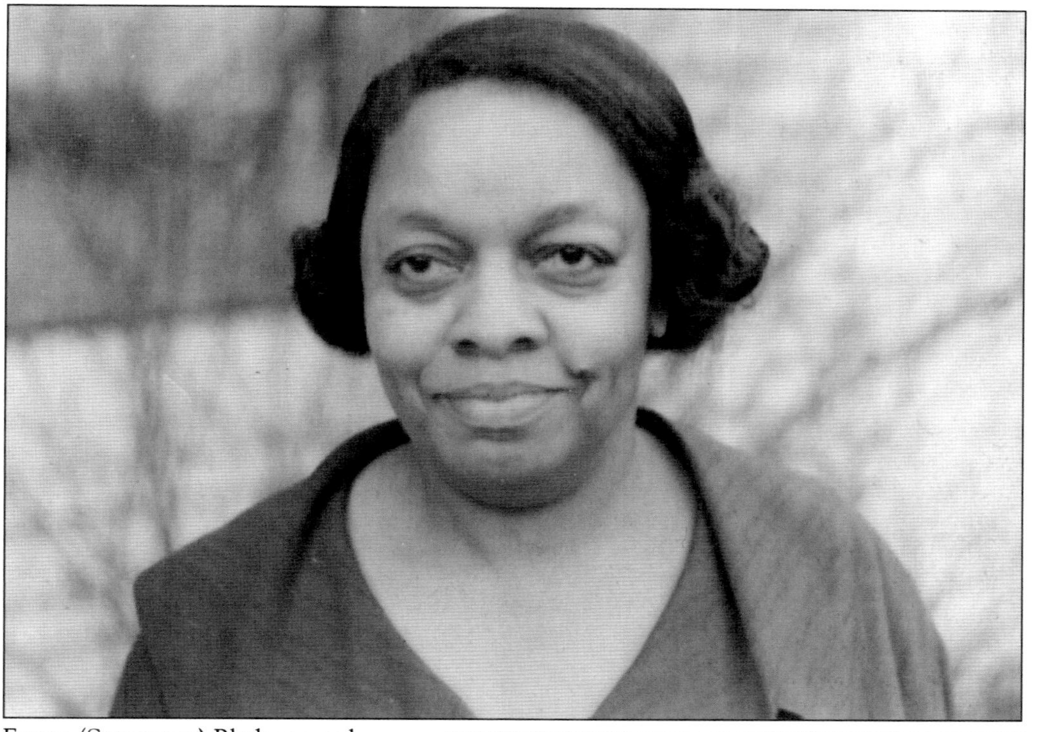

Emma (Stevenson) Bledsoe was born on January 16, 1915, to Prince and Georgia (Benson) Stevenson. Born and educated in Pulaski, she worked on her family farm while a young adult. She later married A. D. Bledsoe and moved to Nashville. Emma and A. D.'s children were Emma Jean, Martha (Kitty), and Robert Louis (Bobby). (Courtesy of Emma Bledsoe.)

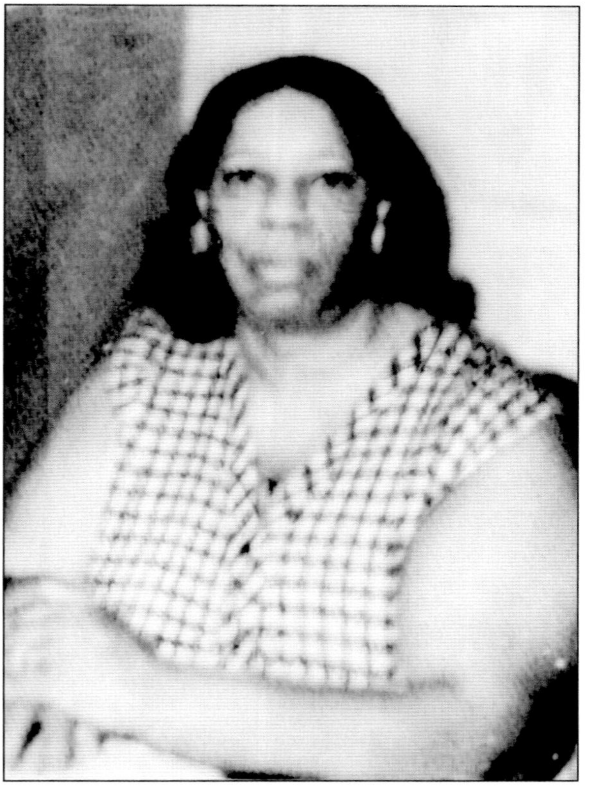

Anna Lee Bledsoe was the daughter of Willie and Susan (Gardner) Eddings. She was raised and educated in the Elkton community. Anna Lee and John Bledsoe married on December 27, 1927. They later moved to Indianapolis, Indiana, seeking better employment for her husband. To their marriage came four children: Clarence, Verona, Myra, and Dorothy.

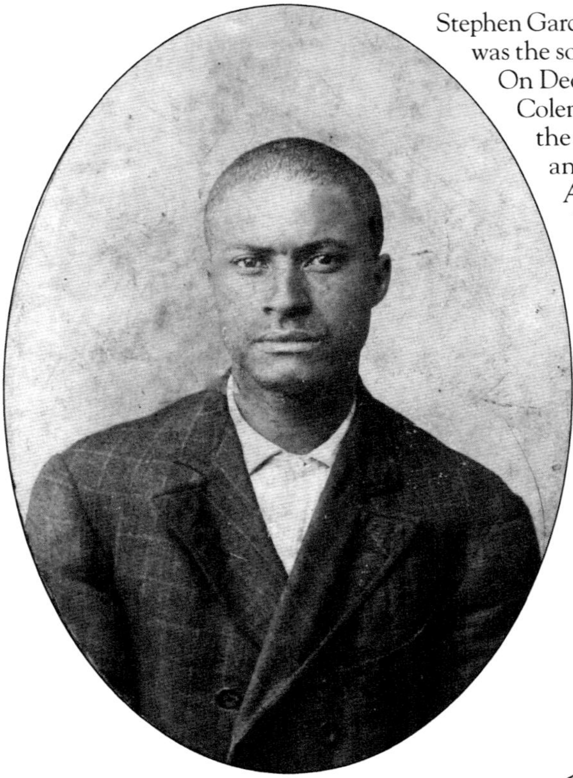

Stephen Gardner Jr. was born on December 12, 1886, and was the son of Stephen and Mary (Swinea) Gardner. On December 25, 1907, Stephen married Ophelia Coleman. Elder Samuel Bridgeforth presided over the wedding ceremony. Stephen was a farmer and father to his and Ophelia's 11 children: Alberta, Amy, Rosetta, Ella Mae, Violet, Luertoria, Louise, Shannon, Napoleon, Alton, and Stephen.

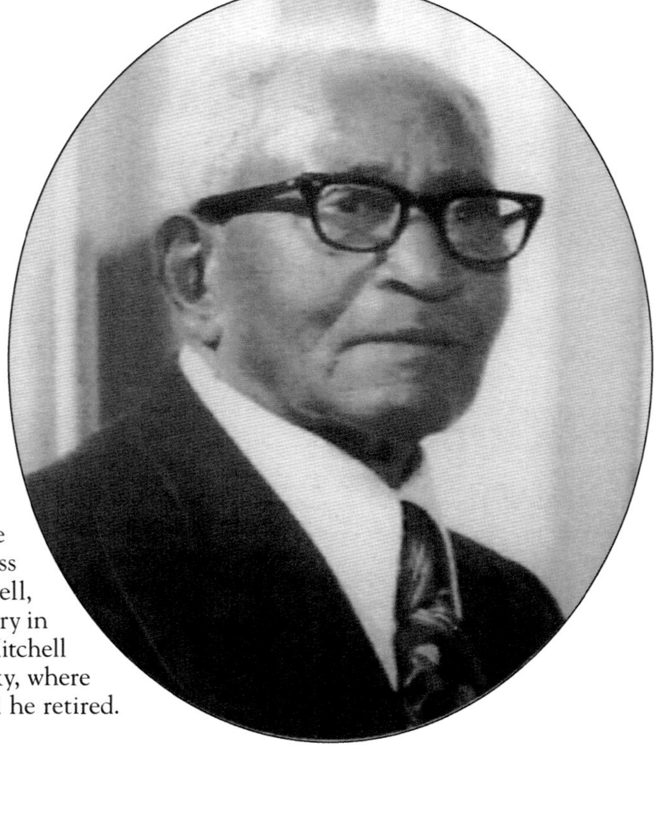

Mitchell Swinney was born June 2, 1893, and was the first child of Robert and Lizzie (Gardner) Swinney. Robert married Josephine Reed December 24, 1911, and they worked and raised their children, James, Robert, Mable, Lucy, Margaret (Sankie), Rosa, and Emma, in Pulaski. The federal government's Work Progress Administration employed Mitchell, and his assignment was a rock quarry in Giles, which was very hard labor. Mitchell later moved to Louisville, Kentucky, where he worked for Sealtest Dairy until he retired. (Courtesy of Emma Price.)

Nine

Artifacts and Remembrance

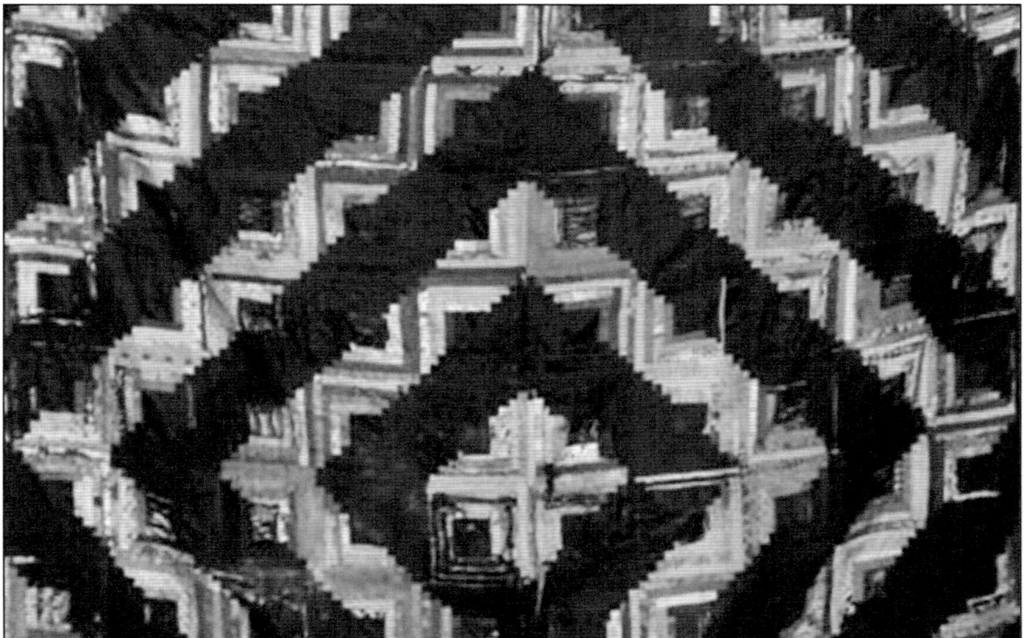

This *c.* 1880 handmade parlor quilt pattern is known as "barn-raising log cabin." It is hand stitched of cotton and silk fabrics. The textile is unique to southern Tennessee and northern Alabama. The artist and designer was Henrietta (Jenkins) Gardner. This quilt is part of a collection of quilts made by Henrietta at the Matt Gardner Homestead Museum in Elkton.

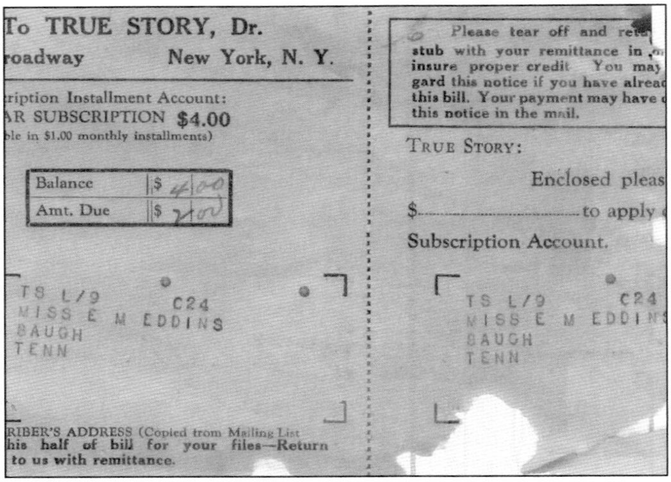

To TRUE STORY, Dr.
roadway New York, N. Y.
ription Installment Account:
AR SUBSCRIPTION $4.00
le in $1.00 monthly installments)

Balance	$ 4.00
Amt. Due	$ 2.00

TS L/9 C24
MISS E M EDDINS
BAUGH
TENN

RIBER'S ADDRESS (Copied from Mailing List
his half of bill for your files—Return
to us with remittance.

Please tear off and ret
stub with your remittance in
insure proper credit You may
gard this notice if you have alread
this bill. Your payment may have
this notice in the mail.

TRUE STORY:
Enclosed pleas
$.............................to apply
Subscription Account.

TS L/9 C24
MISS E M EDDIN
BAUGH
TENN

True Story Magazine started publication in 1919. Today it is the world's largest and best-selling women's romance magazine, and many African American women in the early 20th century enjoyed reading the magazine. Today the discounted price (by 69 percent) for a one-year subscription is $14.95 and $29.95 for two years. The standard in-store price is $3.99 an issue. This invoice for a two-year subscription is for $4.

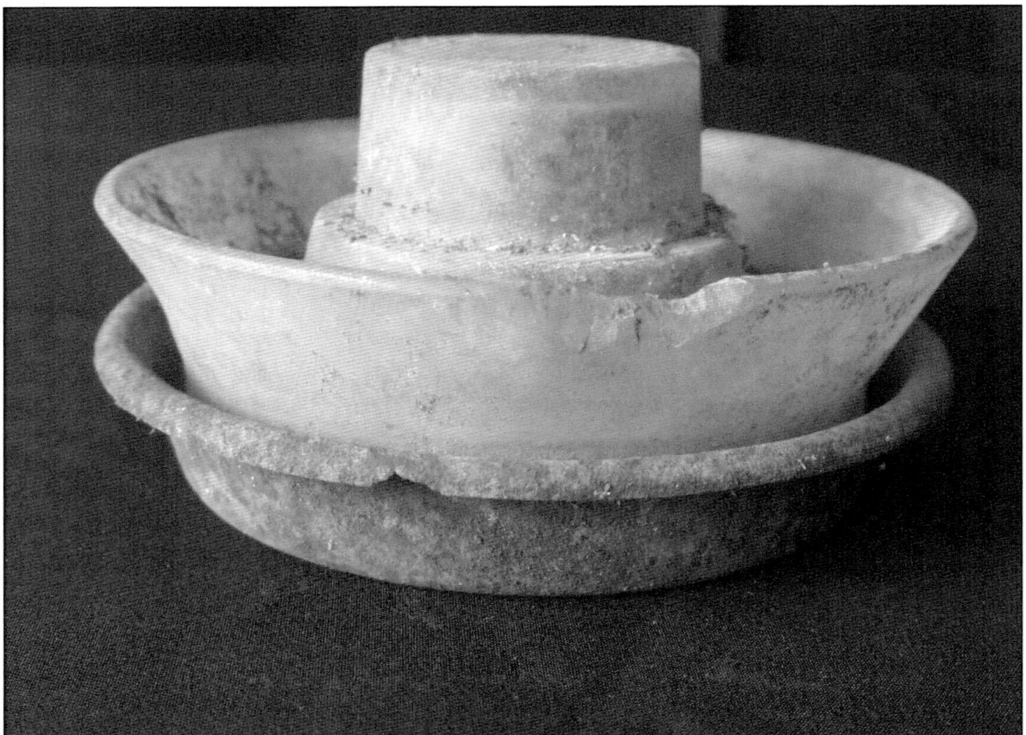

The chicken waterer was an early-1900s farming necessity. Waterers were round tin cans with an attached or molded trough around the bottom edge, with a small hole near the trough. Over this was put any type of masonry jar filled with enough water to slide down to the trough; this is how chickens got their water on many Giles County farms.

Today's medicine cabinet looks a lot different from yesterday's wooden medicine box. Pictured is William W. Lee and Company, Inc., Save the Baby salve for rubbing on children's chests for coughs and colds; J. R. Watkins Laxative Cold pills for cold and fever relief causing mild, temporary diarrhea; and crystal minerals along with multiple droppers, ointments, salve, prescription medicine, and oil of wintergreen from L. E. Moore Drug Company in Lynnville, Tennessee.

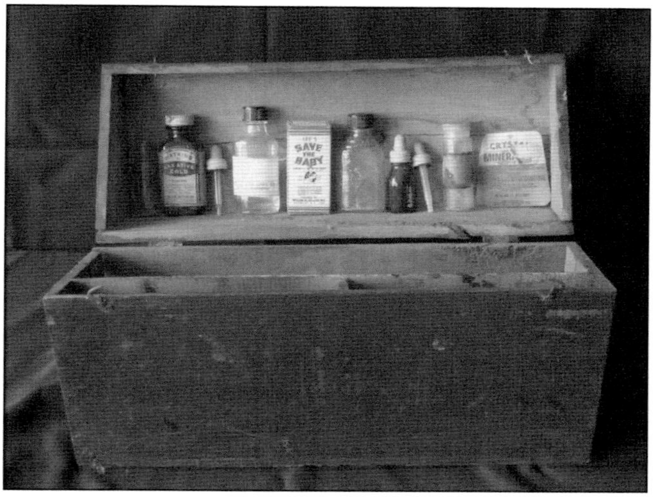

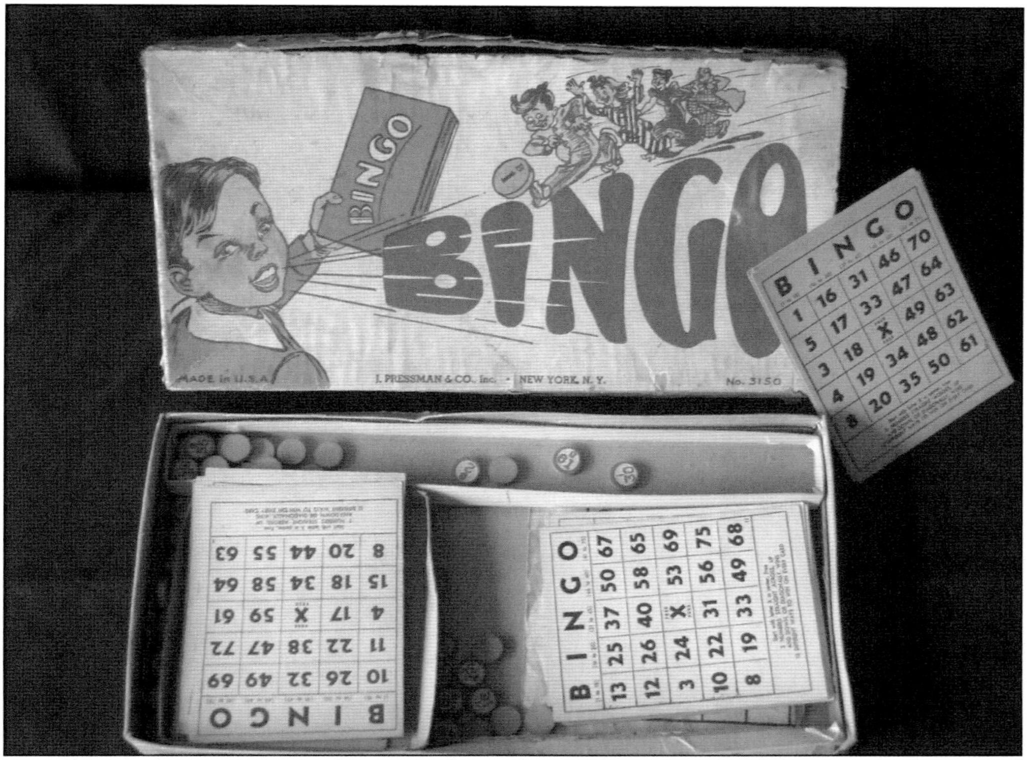

Even though there was not much time for fun and games between school, housework, chores, and running a farm, African Americans occasionally did find family time around the dining-room table to play a game of bingo. This *c.* 1925 J. Pressman and Company, Inc., bingo game belonging to the Gardner family of Elkton was a game favorite.

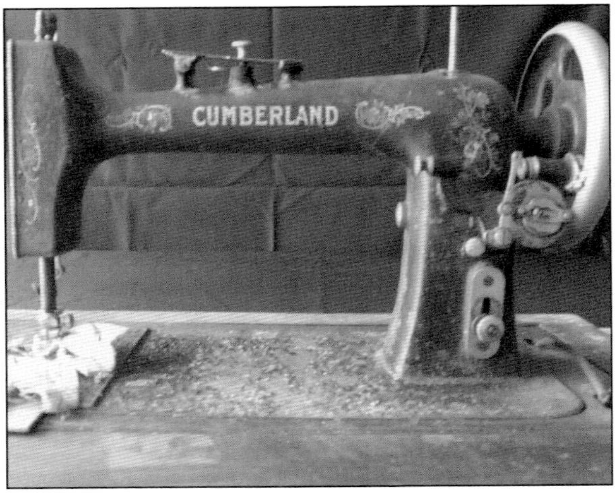

There were more brands of sewing machines around in the late 1880s and early 1900s than just the Singer Company. This early-1900s treadle machine is believed to have been manufactured by New Home Sewing Machine Company and used by Henrietta Gardner to make her family's clothing and several quilts. If they had enough money, dealers of merchandise and catalog orders could have their name or business name put on the sewing machine for advertisement. It is believed that at one time Cumberland was a sewing machine dealership in Tennessee.

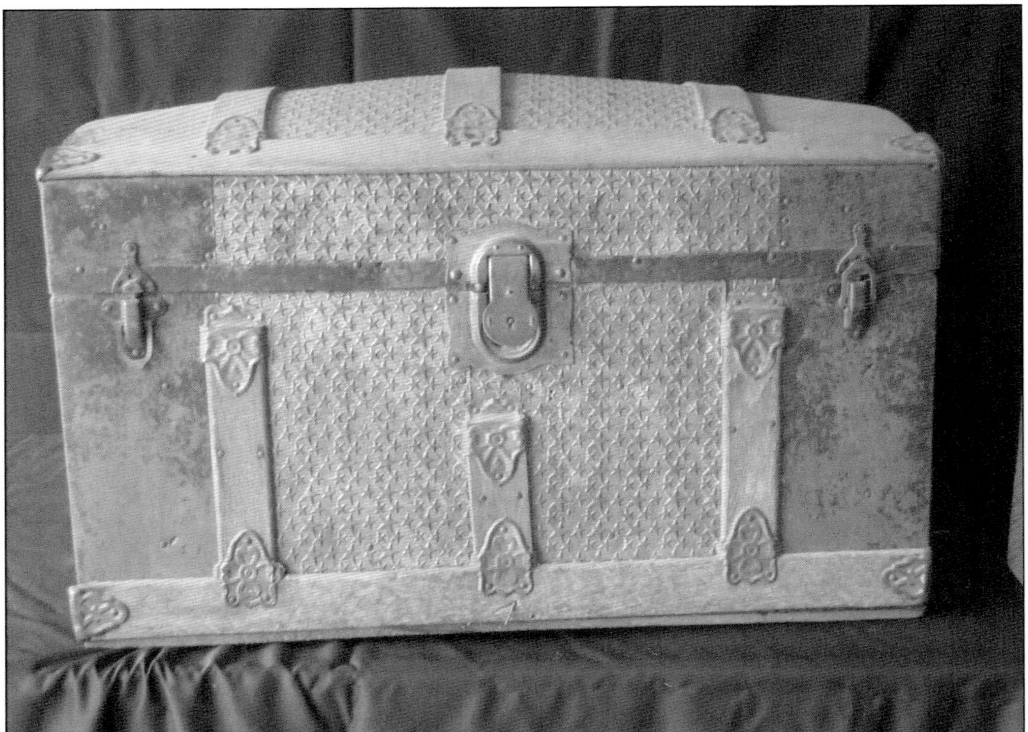

This 1890s stars-embossed metal Camel Back Trunk, one of several belonging to the Gardner family, came in a wide range of sizes and coverings. Early trunk catalogs and advertisements stated that the trunks were of the highest class. These sturdy wooden trunks were also called traveling chests and were standard luggage for carrying clothes and family possessions. It is believed that the round tops were made for those who wanted to try to have their trunks packed on the top in the coaches and baggage cars, so they would not be damaged and would be the first to be unloaded.

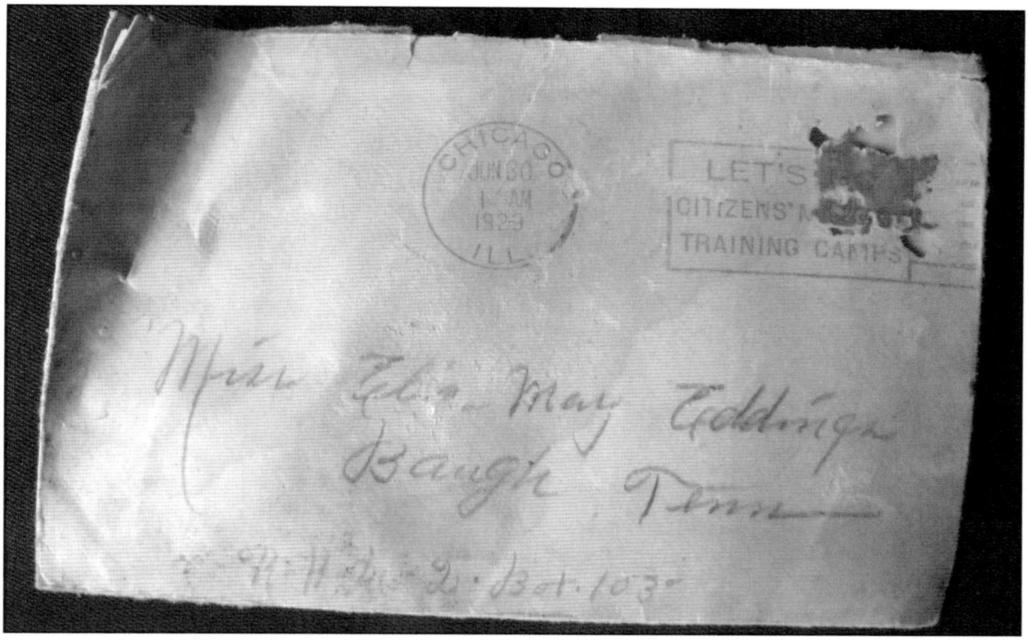

This letter from Chicago, Illinois, is dated June 30, 1929, and is addressed to Ella Mary Eddings in Baugh, Tennessee. Baugh was the name of a prominent family in the Giles community. There used to be a time when people claimed ownership of a community when their families owned a lot of property and businesses in the area. Such is the case with this letter being addressed to Baugh, Tennessee, which is really Elkton.

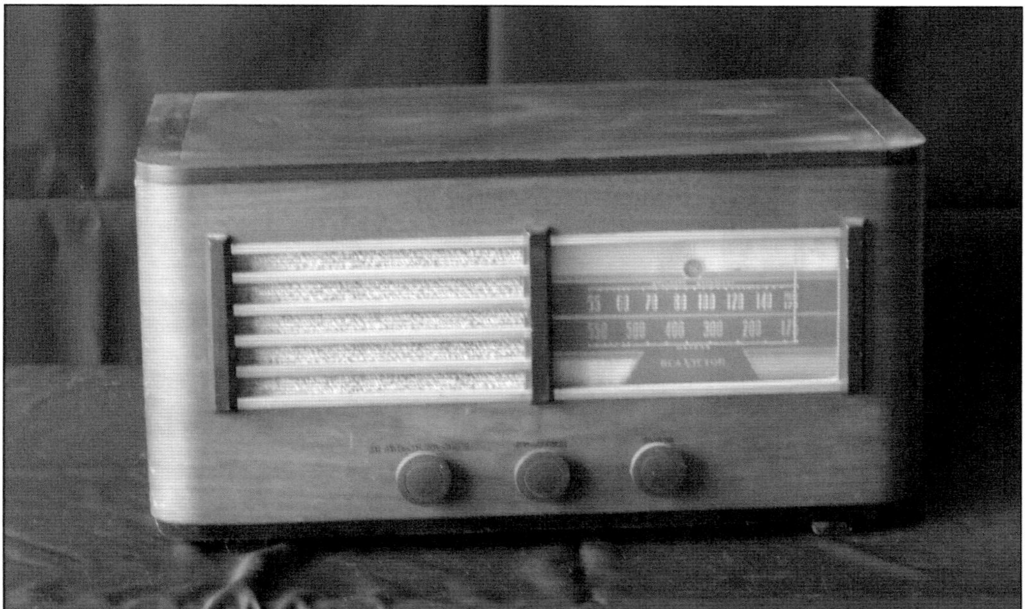

Pictured is a 1940s Victor radio. Before there was television there was the radio. Many black families did not have radios in Giles; radios were not necessities, and they couldn't afford them. They found other ways to entertain themselves.

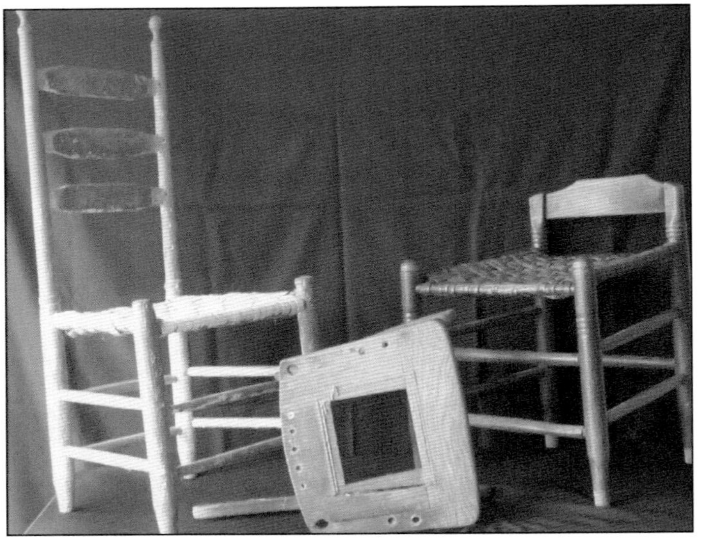

Pictured are three different chairs that an African American family might have had in their home. The high-back weaved chair was used for general sitting and eating at the table. The shorter but sturdy version, the low-back weaved chair, was used for small children or for sitting at a dresser doing hair or applying makeup. Lastly, the potty chair was made from another chair. This child's potty chair was made from a small rocking chair by cutting a square in the seat.

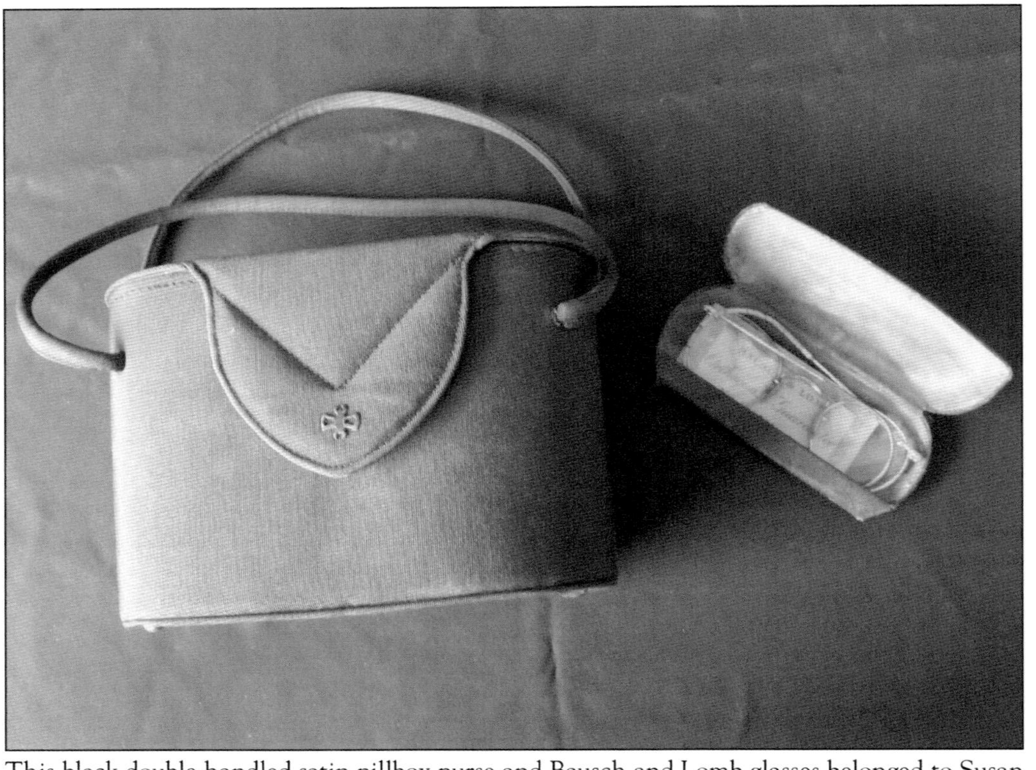

This black double-handled satin pillbox purse and Bausch and Lomb glasses belonged to Susan Eddings, who was said to be a fashionable lady. These *c.* 1925 Bausch and Lomb spectacles are in a leather case and have a certificate of guarantee and authenticity. They were guaranteed to be a superior bifocal in performance with genuine B&L orthogon "D" color-free corrected lenses. Dr. E. H. Murray, an optometrist of Pulaski, prescribed these spectacles for Eddings.

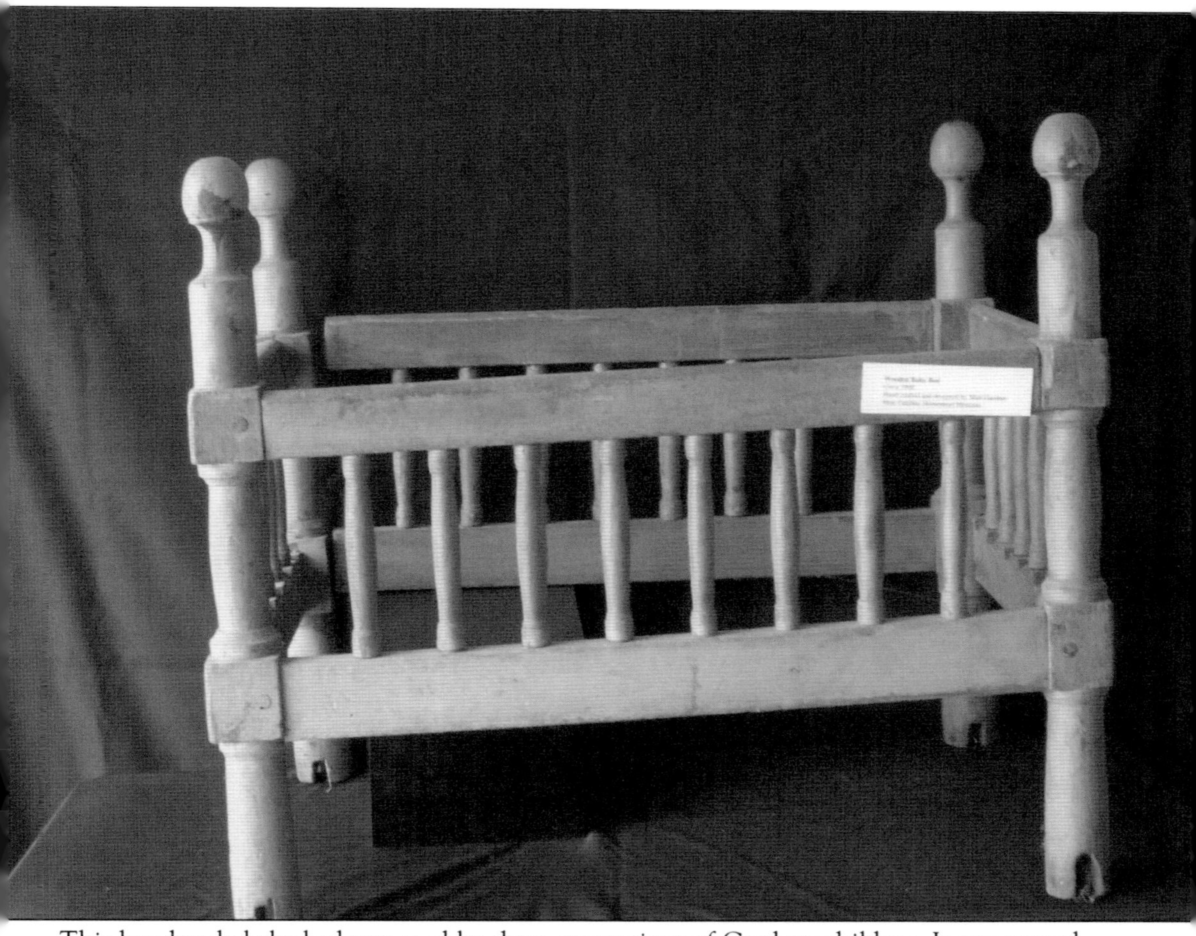

This handmade baby bed was used by three generations of Gardner children. It was carved and crafted by Matt Gardner and used by his children, grandchildren, and some of his great-grandchildren. It is pale green, not pink or blue, so it could be used by all, and it has slats that seem to be made of regular wood pieces.